DECONSTRUCTION, FEMINIST THEOLOGY, AND THE PROBLEM OF DIFFERENCE

Religion and Postmodernism
A series edited by Mark C. Taylor

DECONSTRUCTION,

FEMINIST THEOLOGY,

AND THE PROBLEM

OF DIFFERENCE

Subverting the Race/Gender Divide

Ellen T. Armour

THE UNIVERSITY OF CHICAGO PRESS ~ CHICAGO AND LONDON

Ellen T. Armour is associate professor of religious studies at Rhodes College, Memphis, Tennessee. She is coeditor for theology for *Religious Studies Review*.

Portions of chapters 1, 4, and 6 are reprinted by permission from *Transfigurations*, edited by Susan M. Simonaitis, Susan M. St. Ville, and C. W. Maggie Kim. © 1993 by Augsburg Fortress.

Portions of chapters 2 and 4, appeared in "Crossing the Boundaries between Deconstruction, Feminism, and Religion," by Ellen T. Armour, in *Feminist Interpretations of Jacques Derrida*, edited by Nancy J. Holland (University Park: Pennsylvania State University Press, 1997), 200–209. © 1997 by The Pennsylvania State University. Reprinted with permission.

Portions of chapter 3 appeared as "Questions of Proximity: Woman's Place in Derrida and Irigaray" in *Hypatia* 12, no. 1 (1997): 63–78. © 1997 by *Hypatia*, Inc., Indiana University Press. Reprinted with permission.

Portions of chapter 4 appear in *Reinterpreting the Political*, by Watson and Langsdorf, eds. Excerpted by permission of the State University of New York Press. © 1998 State University of New York. All rights reserved.

Cover illustration: Les Christiansen, *Mixed Signals*, 1997. 15½" × 15½" × 1⅞". Lead, aluminum wire, nails, wood. © Les Christiansen.

The University of Chicago Press, Chicago 60637
The University of Chicago Press, Ltd., London
© 1999 by The University of Chicago
All rights reserved. Published 1999

08 07 06 05 04 03 02 01 00 99   1 2 3 4 5
ISBN: 0-226-02689-2 (cloth)
ISBN: 0-226-02690-6 (paper)

Library of Congress Cataloging-in-Publication Data

Armour, Ellen T., 1959–
    Deconstruction, feminist theology, and the problem of difference : subverting the race/gender divide / Ellen T. Armour.
        p.   cm.—(Religion and postmodernism)
    Includes bibliographical references and index.
    ISBN 0-226-02689-2 (alk. paper)
    ISBN 0-226-02690-6 (pbk. : alk. paper)
    1. Feminist theology. 2. Race—Religious aspects—Christianity. 3. Deconstruction. I. Title II. Series.
    BT83.55.A75 1999
    230'.082—dc21   98-48860
                                                                             CIP

♾ The paper used in this publication meets the minimum requirements of the American National Standard for Information Sciences—Permanence of Paper for Printed Library Materials, ANSI Z39.48-1992.

To my parents
Rollin and Mary Anne Armour

Contents

Acknowledgments

One never writes a book entirely on one's own, I understand. This book is no exception. I owe a debt of gratitude to many people for support of various kinds. My professors at Vanderbilt University, particularly Charles Scott, Sallie McFague, Peter Hodgson, and Edward Farley, helped to launch this project. They provided the freedom and guidance I needed to begin to think through the issues and the texts that the book treats. For their inspiration and training, I will be forever grateful. Hours of conversations with fellow graduate students also shaped this book in many ways. Wendy Farley, in particular, pushed me to clarify my thinking about the relationship between deconstruction and ethics. This project owes much to her passion for intellectual rigor.

My debt to Vanderbilt extends to the Divinity School community as well. Had I gone to school anywhere else, I doubt that I would have written this book. Being at Vanderbilt in the late 1980s when the Divinity School found its historical commitment to racial justice challenged by its African American students was painful for me, as it was for the entire community. However, I learned a great deal from (failed and successful) attempts at coalition building in that context. This project began out of that life-changing experience. I thank my colleagues in these struggles for this, especially Marcia Riggs. It is my hope that this book puts that experience to productive use.

A number of people have read this manuscript in its various stages. Their advice and constructive criticism helped immensely. Amy Hollywood has read more drafts of the chapters herein than should ever be required of any friend. Being able to develop my own thinking in conversation with her has been one of the great pleasures of working on this book. Marcia Riggs' careful and thoughtful response to the book early in its career and again at the end proved invaluable. Comments from Wendy Farley, Mary McClintock Fulkerson, and Vanessa Dickerson were also enormously helpful. The two anonymous readers for the University of Chicago Press helped me strengthen and clarify my argument. I am grateful for their help. I thank Kathryn Wright for reviewing my translations of French texts, and I hereby relieve her of any responsibility for errors that remain.

Two Rhodes College students, Heather Lea and Shaila Mehra, provided invaluable research and editorial support at different points during the writing of this manuscript. I truly cannot imagine making it through this process without their help. My colleagues in the religious studies department have provided support in various ways, not least through developing creative French variations on the names of American snack foods. The weekly gathering of the Sisters of St. Beatrice da Silva (a.k.a., the Grouse Club) provided vital comic relief from the rigors of writing and teaching, for which I am always grateful. Rhodes College contributed to this project's completion through Faculty Development Endowment Grants for the summers of 1995 and 1997.

Alan Thomas, Randy Petilos, and others at the University of Chicago Press also receive my deepest thanks. Their consistent support and expert assistance through the process of review, revision, and now publication have been invaluable. My thanks also to Jacques Derrida, Mark C. Taylor, and Martha Reineke for their support of this project.

I am grateful to Les Christiansen, David McCarthy, and Marina Pacini for permission to use Les's work on the cover of this book. Darlene Loprete and Jack Green provided technical support when I needed it most. For that, I think them.

Last but not least, I thank my family. Barbee Majors agonized over this project almost as much as I did. Her support in bringing it to fruition took many forms, and I am grateful for each of them. Needless to say, not a page would have been written or an idea conceived without the love and support of my parents and two brothers. Academics themselves, my parents modeled for me the pleasures and pains of the academic life. For that and so much besides, I owe them more than I can ever repay. I dedicate this book to them as a gesture of gratitude.

I cannot close without a word to Barbee's mother, Harriet Short Majors. She died long before this project was completed, but I know she would be happy to hear that my "little paper" is finally done.

Ellen T. Armour
Memphis, Tennessee

Introduction

A book by a white feminist interrogating feminist theology and theory on race may seem untimely, at first glance. After all, it has been over ten years since African American feminists and womanists first called attention to feminism's shortcomings in this area.[1] Surely, such a book is no longer necessary. However, a survey of the scene in feminist theory surrounding feminism and race suggests that feminism has yet to come to terms with this legacy; "feminism" is still largely "white feminism." In a recent issue of *Signs*, Kimberly Christensen indicts white feminism for its lack of sustained commitment to antiracist agendas.[2] Recent controversies around Jane Gallop's treatment of race suggest that an ongoing unease with race still plagues white feminism.[3] A new volume on race and psychoanalysis opens with a lengthy description of the interactions and conversations that surrounded the conference that led to the book's publication.[4] The scene described is replete with signs of progress and of lingering tension and misunderstanding, elements all too familiar to black and white women who have struggled to form cross-racial feminist coalitions.

These signposts suggest that far too little has changed in the years since critiques of feminism's shortcomings first registered. Christensen's article offers a well-founded critical analysis of these problems in both activist and academic circles. Because her analysis is so useful, I want to position my project against that background. Christensen notes that white feminists tend to treat racism as a problem of attitude rather than of institutionalized inequities in economic, political, and social power. Instead, white feminists focus on eradicating and uncovering racist attitudes among themselves. This focus follows a pattern that feminists find problematic in some men's dealings with feminism: those under critique substitute self-analysis for genuine engagement with those they claim to support. Christensen urges white feminists to do what feminists ask men to do: decenter ourselves and take our cues from those deemed our others. As a first step, Christensen urges white feminists to read work by women of color in order to understand issues from their perspective.

Christensen is right to urge white feminists to read the work of women of color. My project begins and ends with discussions of work by African American feminist theorists and womanist theologians. However, I do not think that simply reading these texts will be enough to dislodge white feminism's exclusionary and appropriative tendencies. Indeed, Christensen herself provides evidence to that effect when she critiques white women for abstracting black women's writings from their historical contexts. Ann DuCille has recently questioned the commodification of black women's writing in the service of white academics' careers.[5] That white feminism remains subject to such questions and problems—especially despite white feminists' repeated well-intentioned efforts to address them—suggests that what gives rise to white feminism's difficulties with race runs deep.

Like Christensen, I see what I will call "whitefeminism" as itself a reflection of larger cultural forces.[6] Whitefeminism's inability to sustain inquiries into race reflect systemic difficulties that my project seeks to uncover and address. In *Ethics of Eros*, Tina Chanter compares the status of sexual difference in feminism to the status of the question of being in philosophy as analyzed by Martin Heidegger.[7] Like the question of being, feminism simultaneously takes sexual difference for granted and suppresses it. And yet, Chanter writes, "There is a sense in which sexual difference forms the silent center of feminist theory, which is left unthought as such, but which nevertheless acts as a pivot round which feminist categories are constructed" (230). This book aims to show that racial difference occupies a similar place within whitefeminist thought. Race constitutes an unexamined, unthematized, unthought ground of whitefeminist theory and theology. Whitefeminist theologians and theorists often acknowledge the importance of race but fail to sustain attention to its effects. Strategies developed to deal more productively with race go astray and lose sight of their original targets. As I will argue, whitefeminist theology and theory remain subject to a divide between race and gender.[8] For the work of African American feminist theorists and womanist theologians to affect whitefeminism more profoundly, the roots of this divide must be uncovered and the divide subverted.

This analogy between racial difference and the question of being is also useful in setting up the approach to the problem my project will take. Moving toward asking the question of being required that Heidegger first clear the ground that had given rise to its obfuscation in the first place.[9] Similarly, I will argue that enabling white feminism to think racial difference requires uncovering and clearing the ground that has nurtured the divide between race and gender. The resources and strategies that I find most helpful in this undertaking have roots in Heidegger's work, as well. In what follows, I draw primarily on the work of two figures associated with "deconstruction," Jacques Derrida and Luce Irigaray, for assistance in clearing the ground.[10] Like Heidegger's *destruktion* (destructuring), Derridean *deconstruction* interrogates and disrupts the systemic conditions that stand in the way of what remains to be thought.[11] Deconstruction might best be described as a set of strategies for intervening in particular contexts. I will argue that these interventions are not neutral, though they occasion neutralizing effects. They intervene in order to disrupt strategies of mastery by eliciting a play of differences that is already "there," although submerged, in the context in question. These interventions open these contexts up for those whom they define as their "others." To get "outside" these contexts—or, more accurately, to inhabit them in a different way—is a complex and difficult task, but both Derrida and Irigaray open the door to that possibility.

The strategies used by Derrida and Irigaray involve what Derrida calls double reading and writing. Double reading sifts through the western philosophical tradition and its contexts in search of strategies of mastery *and* signs of resistance to that mastery.[12] Insofar as double reading uncovers what is already occurring, it reveals a double writing at work in this tradition and its contexts. Double reading and writing also describe the approach I will take toward reading Derrida and Irigaray. I will read their work both for their own submission to mastery and for resistances to it; for signs of their work's inscription by the divide between race and woman and resistance to it.

To my theological readers, turning to deconstruction for resources in furthering a feminist project may seem patently absurd. As I will note in chapter 2, Derrida's work has only recently begun to shake its association with nihilism in theological circles, an association that dates from the early 1980s. Recent positive discussions of deconstruction's proximity to negative theology are largely responsible for this shift.[13] However, those familiar with these conversations may still be skeptical about positive connections between Derrida's work and *feminist* theology. As positive as they are about his work, little in these discussions to date offers any hint that feminist theology might find an ally in Derrida. Irigaray's work is less familiar to theological readers and remains subject to stereotyped readings as well. As I will note in chapter 4, early discussions of her work in Anglo-American scholarship read her as a biological essentialist. That is, they read her as grounding a new femininity in bodily experiences that appear to transcend historical or social context. While this view has largely been discredited by Irigarayan scholarship over the past fifteen years, whitefeminist theologians may be unaware of this development. Paula Cooey's *Religious Imagination and the Body* (1994), the most recent monograph in whitefeminist theology that discusses Irigaray's work, cites Irigaray as a primary example of biological essentialism.[14] Thus, putting resources drawn from these two thinkers to work in this project will require that I clear ground around them, as well.

Readers familiar with continental philosophy and feminist theory may, on the other hand, lose patience with this essay, insofar as it seems to revisit what is to them well-traveled ground. If Irigaray has been successfully defended against charges of biological essentialism, what remains to be said about that issue? Similarly, my opening chapter on Derrida focuses on the now infamous Derrideanism, "There is nothing outside the text." As I shall note, a number of Derridean scholars have defended Derrida against charges of nihilism grounded in misconstruals of this phrase. If others have mounted such defenses successfully, why raise these questions again? If my aim were simply to give an account of Derrida's work, Irigaray's work, or their relation to each other, then such impatience would be justified. However, this project's aim does not ultimately lie in those directions. I return to these well-traveled territories because they are essential to clearing the ground around whitefeminism's inability to sustain attention to race. I will argue that whitefeminist theory and theology take their bearings on race and woman from these figures' places within a larger system, what Derrida calls "the text" outside of which "there is nothing." In putting forward a reading of Irigaray that counters essentialist readings, I align myself with the winning side in a relatively dated debate. However, laying out such a reading is crucial to my project for two reasons. Whitefeminist theory and theology have both identified essentialism as a serious impediment to thinking racial difference. If I want to draw on Irigaray's work in order to enable whitefeminism to think about race, then I must take on this issue in her work. Moreover, traveling through the question of essentialism opens access to the resources that I will argue Irigaray offers my project.

Though this project revisits some familiar terrain, it approaches this terrain from a distinctive angle formed by the figures of "woman," "God," and "race."[15] This approach highlights particular features in that terrain and links them in what I hope are distinctive ways. Approaching Derrida's work through this triad of figures also offers a new perspective on the relationship between deconstruction and feminist theology, and between deconstruction and ethics. In taking up a reading of Irigaray through issues of race, I test the common claim that Irigaray's work could fund a feminism that attends productively to differences between women.[16] Exploring Derrida's and Irigaray's work through this trajectory also takes me to less familiar territory. Derrida's work on race has received little attention from his feminist readers, nor has its connection to his work on sexual difference been explored. Much of Irigaray's more recent work takes up theological issues and themes; an aspect of her work that has received little attention among her Anglophone readers, to date. Through following race and woman through terrain marked by religious tropes and themes, I also aim to highlight feminist philosophical theology's importance to feminist theory.

In closing, a word about the title and the ultimate aim of this project. The title calls attention to "the problem of difference," but the subtitle mentions only one axis of difference, the divide between race and woman. Critiques of feminism from postcolonial studies, gay and lesbian studies/queer theory, and so on, show that feminism's difficulty in dealing with differences between women extends beyond whitefeminism's difficulties with race.[17] Whether enabling whitefeminism to sustain inquiries into race will open feminism to other differences remains to be seen. I am wary of monolithic treatments of "difference" as though any one difference were substitutable for another. As the first chapter in this essay will show, approaching race through difference in general has had little effect on whitefeminism's white solipsism. Indeed, Ann DuCille, Evelynn Hammonds, and Evelyn Higginbotham have criticized whitefeminism for citing race as the "ultimate trope of difference" while often bypassing any serious inquiry into its effects.[18] Though I cannot back up this claim here, I suspect that each axis of difference (race, sexuality, class, etc.) follows a specific itinerary through particular fields of force that constitute and sustain it. While these axes, their itineraries, and their histories intertwine with one another, they are not reducible to one another. A full account of the history of what has counted (and has not) as "feminist" would involve following these various strands and their comings and goings. In taking up the question of race within whitefeminism, I isolate a particular nexus of difference—and one that has proven particularly resistant to intervention—in order that its workings might become more visible. It is my hope that this project moves one step closer toward feminism's (im)possible vision of a platform from which oppressions women face can be contested in their variety.

1

What "Woman"? The Problem of Race in Whitefeminist Theology and Theory

One of the principal issues facing whitefeminist theology and theory today involves coming to terms with the diversity of issues and perspectives that need to be and are addressed in the name of "woman."[1] Critiques raised of feminist theology by women of color argue that feminist theology speaks from and to the concerns of white women. Womanist scholars like Delores Williams criticize the assumptions behind the descriptions of women's experience in whitefeminist theology. Womanists argue that what whitefeminists name "women's experience" reflects white middle-class women's experience (with white males and white-male-dominated institutions) but not that of women of color and/or of lower classes.[2] The signs of the limitation that they identify emerge from the feminist tendency to read racism as a subset of patriarchy. Whether patriarchy is defined as direct male dominance over women *or* as a socioeconomic pyramidical system of graded dominations with white men at the top and lower-class women of color at the bottom, Williams argues that focusing on patriarchy (1) fails to name accurately the distinctiveness of *racist* oppression experienced by women of color and their families at the hands of white-controlled American institutions; (2) threatens to obscure the benefits that white women and their families receive at the hands of these same institutions; and (3) threatens to obscure racism as it is perpetuated—intentionally or unintentionally—by white women, including white feminists.[3]

These criticisms come as something of a shock to whitefeminist theologians. Most would say that their intentions with regard to inclusiveness have been good. This response itself points to a significant problem. Womanist critiques and responses to them suggest that whitefeminist theologians have assumed that all women share a common female identity. Feminist theologians tend to align women together as victims of oppression (which differs only in degree depending on race/class/sexual orientation) and all men as perpetrators of oppression. If women are all, at bottom, the same and if the oppression they suffer differs only in quantity (depending on race and/or class and/or sexual orientation), then women share a common enemy/oppressor: patriarchy. Yet, as womanist theologian Jacquelyn Grant reminds whitefeminist theologians, black women see white women as "more oppressors than victims" because of the history of relations between white and black women—a history that is too often repeated in current relationships (Grant, 191). This is nowhere more evident than in the differences in accounts of the racism of the nineteenth-century suffragette movement in the work of white and black feminist scholars. Whitefeminists will, on occasion, acknowledge this history, but they tend to explain it as a symptom of white women's victimization by patriarchy.[4] African American feminists, on the other hand, without exception call it what it is. Jacquelyn Grant argues that this reluctance to face up to our history renders whitefeminists' call for sisterhood either a "cruel joke, or . . . the conciliatory rhetoric of an advantaged class and race" (196).

To their credit, whitefeminist theologians have listened to these criticisms and have taken important steps to attempt to correct them. These corrections also occur around the concept of "women's experience." Many whitefeminist theologians, faced with the truth of this claim, take the step of acknowledging the limitations of their perspective and explicitly deny that they speak for all women.[5] Indeed the frequency with which this claim opens whitefeminist theologians' work suggests it has become de rigueur in whitefeminist theology. This is a laudable first step—especially when one uses one's social location as some whitefeminist theologians do.[6] However, womanists point out the limitations of this strategy. Emilie Townes argues that white women also experience racism, but from the side of the oppressor rather than the oppressed.[7] Therefore, simply backing away from the claim to speak universally is not sufficient. White women also need to investigate ways in which they are implicated in racism.[8]

This criticism raised of feminist theology provides the impetus for the first step of my argument. By following the trajectory of race and class through the writings of two centrifugal feminist thea/ologians,[9] Mary Daly and Rosemary Ruether, I will investigate the ways in which their work perpetuates problematic ways of dealing with the difference of race. My investigation will show that both thea/ologians' texts are governed by the discursive structure of an essential woman. This discursive structure, I will argue, blinds them to the full effects of racial difference on their work and on the women for whom they intend to speak.

Whitefeminist Theology and the Problem of Essentialism:
Mary Daly

Mary Daly is arguably one of the most creative and powerful voices in feminist thea/ology today. The feminist critique of patriarchal Christianity has never found a more eloquent voice than Daly's in her groundbreaking works *Beyond God the Father* and *The Church and the Second Sex*.[10] In *Gyn/Ecology* and *Pure Lust*, Daly's passionate desire to eliminate the pain women suffer and to envision new possibilities for their lives funds an unhesitating critique of whatever she sees that hinders, represses, or oppresses women.[11] However, disturbing difficulties emerge when one examines her recent work in light of criticisms of feminist thinking raised by womanist scholars. In *Gyn/Ecology* and *Pure Lust*, Daly targets worldwide patriarchy in some of its most horrible manifestations. In *Gyn/Ecology*, she undertakes powerful critical examinations of the structures of patriarchal thinking that make Chinese footbinding, Hindu suttee, African genital mutilation, and the practice of American gynecology possible. She refuses to be distracted by charges of racism or imperialism, arguing that, below these realities lies "the oppression of women that knows no ethnic, national, or religious bounds" (111). The charge of racism does come from African American feminist poet Audre Lorde. Daly's response to Lorde exhibits tensions and resistances that are much more problematic than productive. In "An Open Letter to Mary Daly,"[12] Lorde praises Daly for her creativity and courage and obvious love for women, yet criticizes the locus granted to women of color in *Gyn/Ecology*. Nonwestern women, she argues, appear only as victims and predators in this text. Nowhere do they appear as examples of love, goodness or of the divine or human power to resist oppression. This dismissal of nonwestern women obliterates the distinctiveness of racist oppression and continues what Lorde and other womanist writers argue is the historical relationship of white women and women of color.

Though never explicitly named, this exchange (and others like it), leaves traces in Daly's next book, *Pure Lust*. On the one hand, Daly seems to have listened to criticisms like Lorde's and has attempted to broaden the scope of her analysis of women's oppression to include their experiences of racism and poverty. In the introduction to the book, Daly names racism as one of the "man-made racetracks" (*PL*, 5) of phallocratism and insists that, as such, it should be a target of confrontation by "Lusty" women. Daly makes repeated references in this book to the multiple problems faced by women of color and poor women. She also uses novels by Toni Morrison and Alice Walker to illustrate the kind of female bonding she wants to promote. However, racism and classism, which are subsets of misogynism in Daly's scheme, triple the *amount* of oppression faced by women. Nowhere does Daly address racism or classism as *distinctive* oppressions. As Jacquelyn Grant argues, neither racism nor black women have "lives of their own" in Daly's work (Grant, 169–70).

As for relations between white women and women of color, Daly places at least a share of the responsibility for white women's racism in their laps (especially those of their slaveholder ancestors). However, she attributes white women's perpetuation of racism to patriarchy. Patriarchy has so separated white women from their true Selves (which would, by implication, be loving and nonoppressive) she argues, that they act in accordance with patriarchal values rather than their truest values. Daly uses the same strategy to protect feminism from womanist critiques. In the "Foreground to the First Realm" (see *PL*, 67–72), Daly condemns "women who have chosen to name themselves feminists and/or lesbians" who "irrational[ly] conver[t] terms such as *racist, classist,* and *elitist* into labels that function to hinder rather than foster the Movement/Race of women" (*PL*, 67; author's emphasis). Daly even goes so far as to use the term "horizontal violence" to name these articulations of complaints by women of color against feminists. She writes, "Instead of Naming the *active perpetrators* of the social evils they claim to oppose, they choose the cowardly device of scapegoating women" (*PL*, 68).[13] This anonymous "they" who accuse other feminists of racism are letting themselves be used as tools of patriarchy and failing to place blame where it finally belongs: in the hands of the fathers. Audre Lorde (along with any others who might have joined her in criticizing Daly) has truly been dismissed from *this* text, and, in fact, from feminism itself.[14] Although Daly says later in *Pure Lust* that women should be held accountable for their conscious racism, her discussions of the dynamics of relationships between women across boundaries of culture or religion (Jew and Arab, Northern Ireland and the South, e.g.) always blame any divisions caused by one or the other camp's racist rhetoric on patriarchy's use of these women as tools. Thus, I would argue, women who knowingly or unknowingly perpetuate racism are, in the final analysis, excused by Daly.

Daly's interpretation fails to take seriously the complexities of the legacy of the intertwining of race and gender issues. The history of the women's suffrage movement, if nothing else, shows that one can be both a feminist and a racist. When, for example, Susan B. Anthony argues for women's suffrage on the grounds that granting the vote to black men "dethroned fifteen million white women . . . and cast them under the heel of the lowest orders of manhood,"[15] she is just as culpable for her racist ideology as any man. Paula Giddings's *When and Where I Enter*, for example, provides compelling evidence that second wave whitefeminists have done the same thing. Dismissing African American feminists' criticisms of white women's complicity with racism as effects of patriarchy impedes attempts to work across racial boundaries.

The stage for this *aporia* in Daly's work is set by the structure of essentialism that operates unquestioned and even celebrated around the figure of woman in her work. I am not referring here to what many have criticized as a biological essentialism in which women are by nature good and men by nature evil.[16] I read Daly's categories as applying to men *in their concrete social incarnations within patriarchy* rather than *in esse*. Under patriarchy, men are the agents of its evil in ways women are not.[17] Whether they are redeemable is a moot point for Daly. Her concerns are exclusively with arousing the Spark of divine goodness in women. Daly wants to promote female self-identity, unity with the power of Be-ing, and the final cause. She calls women forward to claim their true Selves and their true position in the cosmos. Though situated within a fabric woven from words used to hurt women now reclaimed by Daly, this call is cast largely in the discourse traditional to western philosophy.[18] Human being (in this case, female human being) is aligned with Be-ing itself, with a telos as its essence—as what it truly and most fundamentally is.[19] Moreover, what "woman" most truly and fundamentally is, according to Daly, turns out to be the free, autonomous and whole human being familiar to us from the western tradition (see, e.g., 3, 87, in *PL*). For all its powerful radicality, Daly's Spinning, Sparking Crone remains bound by the construct of a free, self-constituting, whole liberal-woman whose essential sameness binds her to herself and others like her in an unproblematic and undisturbed unity.[20]

The Problem of Essentialism in Feminist Theology: Rosemary Ruether

When one follows the intersecting paths of race, class, and gender analysis through the feminist theological writings of Rosemary Ruether in light of the critiques raised by womanist scholars, one finds issues of racism and classism interwoven with gender oppression throughout her work. Of her feminist writings, *New Woman/New Earth* gives the most fulsome account of the interplay among these oppressions. She traces the history of the development of women from prehistoric times to the industrial revolution, arguing that, as economic life increased in complexity, women were moved farther and farther away from control over the means of production. Our locations within the capitalist economic system have hardly been symmetrical, according to her analysis. For example, the pedestal on which perched the Victorian ideal of womanhood rested on the backs of women of the lower classes who worked in sweatshops and as domestic servants, thereby freeing the upper-class woman for her role as ornament. The similar position accorded to slave owners' wives in the Old South depended upon slave women's enforced domestic and sexual servitude. Ruether also attends to the speckled history of relations between white and black women since the days of the abolition movement and recognizes that this legacy shapes their interactions in the present. However, she places the blame for this situation not on white women's racism *primarily*, but on patriarchy's strategy of divide and conquer.[21]

In the first chapter of her next book, *Sexism and God-Talk*, Ruether lays out the method, sources, and norms that will govern this more systematic incarnation of feminist theology.[22] She names "women's experience" (*S&GT*, 13) as the norm governing her claims. The differences between women, which were so much a part of her analysis in *New Woman/New Earth*, mark this text, as well. She writes, "Feminist theology makes explicit what was overlooked in male advocacy of the poor and oppressed, that liberation must start with the oppressed of the oppressed; namely, women of the oppressed" (*S&GT*, 32). This articulates both a critique and an embrace of other theologies of liberation. Ruether also goes on to acknowledge that, like men of oppressed groups, women of dominant classes also will find *their* blind spots challenged by those whom *they* oppress. Thus, she recognizes that women's experience may vary depending on one's socioeconomic location.

Race and class concerns also figure prominently in her third book, *Women-Church*.[23] The collection of powerful and eloquent rituals that Ruether offers as resources in the second half of the book include several which intertwine racism, classism, sexism, and homophobia.[24] In the narrative description of the women-church movement that comprises the first half of the book, Ruether describes briefly and appreciatively the impact made on the Chicago women-church conference by the diversity in culture and class of its attendees. However, when she does finally speak in detail of ways in which diversity threatens divisiveness in communities struggling for liberation, blame for that divisiveness is accorded differently to male theologians of liberation and to feminists. Male liberation theologians are held directly accountable for their hostility to women's issues (see *WC*, 54–55). Similar problems within women's groups are described quite differently, if not glossed over altogether. Ruether recognizes that race and class differences erect barriers between women, but the blame for this divisiveness is, as it was in *New Woman/New Earth*, diverted from the shoulders of possibly hostile or ignorant feminists to the broader shoulders of patriarchy. In fact, what proves divisive enough in African American and Third World theological communities to be termed an "explosion within an explosion" (Mercy Oduyoye), hardly makes a ripple on the smooth surface of feminist theology.[25] I am not disputing Ruether's contention that our society's value system is in some sense to blame for racist/classist attitudes among white middle-class women. I am suggesting that it does not seem equitable to place the blame on society *only* for white women's racism, but not men of color's sexism. In the same vein, is it fair to hold male liberation theologians accountable for their failure to recognize the validity of women's issues but to grant a kind of general amnesty to white middle-class women for their failure to take seriously issues of race and class?

Ruether is to be applauded for maintaining the interconnectedness of race, class, and gender oppressions in her analysis. However, could it be that something in Ruether's texts shapes the trajectory according to which they interact in her texts? Are Ruether's texts, despite explicit intentions to the contrary, structured by an essential woman? Does this explain why racism and classism simply triple the *quantity* of oppression on lower-class women and women of color in Ruether's analysis? Is this why, in Ruether's texts, patriarchy takes the role of the "father" of oppression whose children, racism and classism, serve to further subject and subdivide women, the objects of his attention?

Like Daly's writings, Ruether's texts are also marked by traditional concepts of human subjectivity even as she calls these same structures into question. Throughout these three texts, Ruether employs a critical typology of feminist thinking. The first type, liberal feminism, argues that women are just as _____ (fill in the blank) as men (i.e., women share the same essential humanity); women should, therefore have access to the same opportunities and benefits that men have in our society. The second type, romantic feminism, accepts and celebrates society's definition of woman as aligned with nature, emotion, and so on, and argues that what needs to change is society's valuation of these attributes. Often, romantic feminists' dissatisfaction with society leads them to adopt separatist strategies. Ruether is critical of both types of feminism. Romantic feminism's separatist path ghettoizes women's concerns and effects little or no change in the system of male privilege. In *Women-Church*, Ruether roundly criticizes the philosophical tradition of liberal humanism on which liberal feminism is modeled because it has "devised a variety of ways of keeping gender, class, and racial hierarchy intact, despite its claims of establishing universal human rights" (*WC*, 52). Liberal feminism at least tacitly approves of the structures that support male privilege and often settles for token individual achievements rather than systemic change.

Ruether's constructive positions attempt to find a way between liberalism and romanticism. However, liberal-woman continues to mark the boundaries of these positions. In *Sexism and God-Talk*, the romantic/liberal typology figures most prominently in the chapter on anthropology. A liberal feminist anthropology defines woman as equal to man (who is associated with society's "goods": intelligence, spirit, culture). A romantic feminist anthropology defines woman (aligned with emotion and nature) as good. Ruether suggests a different equation wherein the subsets of both man and woman come together to form "good" *and* to equal human being. While her definition of woman/human being could be said to incorporate the best of *both* liberal and romantic feminism, the philosophical structure underpinning her constructive position is very much a free, self-constituting, whole and essential human subject. The attributes that Ruether brings together to constitute human being make up a smorgasbord from which individual men and women choose what is most appropriate for themselves. In its female incarnation, Ruether's ideal human being is liberal-woman.

The discursive structures of liberal-woman and her enemy, patriarchy, inscribe both the rituals and the narrative portion of *Women-Church* in such a way as to submerge differences of race and class. Let me cite two quotations from the narrative section: "Although undoubtedly Third World women have to *contextualize feminism* in terms of their own situation, greater communication between women of the two worlds would undoubtedly reveal they have many issues in common" (*WC*, 55; emphasis added). The encounters of cultures and classes at the women-church conference confirms this expectation: "Communication between women across the divisions of class and race drawn by patriarchy is not insurmountable if women of resources reach across the divisions and provide the means while, at the same time, really allowing the space for disenfranchised women to define their own experience" (WC, 68). The boundaries between women are, as in Daly's work, the responsibility of patriarchy. Crossing the boundaries requires action on the part of "women of resources" who "reach" and "allow space" (what do the disenfranchised do, by contrast?). Once the boundaries are crossed, space is made, and the ground of unity appears—"feminism" that, even when contextualized, remains common to all women.

I am not suggesting that women from different social backgrounds cannot find common ground. We do indeed *forge* such ground but Ruether's rhetoric here suggests it exists independently and that its name is "feminism."[26] I am also not arguing that the women of the women-church gatherings should have taken different roles (i.e., women of resources should have done something other than providing the means or allowing the space and the "disenfranchised women" should not have "define[d] their own experience"). I am moving those questions aside to push to an underlying problem. These assignations show that the way power is allocated between those who have resources and those who are disenfranchised occurs in and through discursive patterns as well as economic and political structures.

The same structures of patriarchy as "father" of oppressions and liberal-woman inscribe the goals of women-church praxis for both the individual and the community. The communitarian goal of women-church is to bring into existence true church; namely, "a community that seeks to overcome patriarchy as the root expression of oppressive relations between men and women, between generations, between those who are powerful and those who are weak" (WC, 64). Patriarchy is the fundamental problem under which other oppressions are subsumed. The purpose of coming to terms with ways in which patriarchy has affected women's psyches is to "come out to a firm ground of autonomous humanity as a female who can continually resist and refuse the snares of patriarchy without confusing this with the humanity of males. . . . [We must] be able to affirm the humanity of males behind the masks of patriarchy" (WC, 60). Clearly, this ideal woman resembles the liberal philosophical ideal of essential human being both in her autonomy and in her ability to see truly to the true male hidden behind the masks of patriarchy.[27]

I noted earlier that several of the rituals intertwine critiques of or confessions of participation in gender, race, and class oppression. Is it merely accidental that, in Ruether's rite of reconciliation, the repentance of horizontal violences against lower-class women of color is included under the heading "Rite of Mind-Cleansing from the Pollution of Sexism" (*WC*, 133)? What about Ruether's suggestion that "U.S. Americans and Latin Americans" may want to commemorate the martyrdom of Archbishop Romero and others on December 6 while "other nationalities" may want to focus on South Africa (*WC*, 117)?

I want to make it clear that I am not criticizing either Ruether's or Daly's intentions as authors of these texts. The attention they both give to issues of diversity suggests that they intended to write feminist thea/ologies that addressed the multiplicity of concerns facing women. Nor am I suggesting that feminist theology's problem lies in its cooptation by male theory or theories of liberal humanism.[28] My questioning is directed toward what courses below authorial intentions, good or bad; I suspect the workings of a con/text beneath their texts, so to speak. The traditional discursive structure of liberal-woman inscribes/prescribes/proscribes both thinkers' writing about women in such a way as to preclude the full acknowledgment of the substantial differences among women. To the degree that such differences occur in both thea/ologian's works, they seem to all too easily resolve and dissolve into an untroubled unity of "women."[29]

One would think that a turn to feminist theory would be helpful to feminist theology at this point because feminist theorists of many stripes have been preoccupied recently with eradicating notions of women's essential sameness.[30] However, an examination of these discussions that expects to find evidence of sustained discussion of the difference race makes to gender will be disappointed. That the divide between race and gender still persists after attempts to eradicate essentialism have run their course suggests that an inquiry into the roots of this divide must lie at a deeper level.

Feminist Theory and The Problem of Essentialism

The drive to unearth and eradicate the assumption that women share an essence that transcends socioeconomic location, historical location, and other variables became arguably *the* central issue in feminist theory in the 1980s. What came to be known as "the problem of essentialism" took its mark from, among other things, critiques of feminist theory's failure to deal with race. In the early 1980s, African American feminist writers such as bell hooks and Angela Davis wrote landmark texts that exposed whitefeminism's blindness to the difference race makes to what it means to be a woman.[31] Like their counterparts among womanist theologians and ethicists, hooks and Davis charged feminist theorists with missing the effects of substantial differences in historical experience between black women and white women. They provided ample evidence that these differences suggested that being a woman meant significantly different things for white women and black women. The history of slavery showed that black women and white women were subjected to very different kinds of social control. While plantation mistresses were construed as the frail flower of Southern womenhood and denied sexuality, slave women were construed as sexually voracious. This construal justified their sexual exploitation by white men. The difference in status and stereotype also affected the role of motherhood. While the plantation mistress gave birth to children who could inherit property, slave women gave birth to children who *were* property. While the plantation mistress might lose her children to childhood diseases, the slave woman's children were at the mercy of the master as well. Since her children belonged to him, he could sell them at any point. As long as he owned them he could subject them to whatever treatment he deemed appropriate. When it became illegal to import slaves, plantation owners turned to their female slaves as sources for new slaves. Sexual exploitation combined with economic self-interest as slave women were turned into breeders—by force and with impunity. During Reconstruction and Jim Crow, antimiscegenation laws aimed to prohibit black men from having sex with white women; they did nothing to prevent white men from having sex with black women. Lynch mobs justified their violence on the grounds of protecting white women from the threat of black sexual predators.

Perhaps even more damning, hooks and Davis also exposed solidarity among women across racial lines as a rarely realized romantic idea. Davis and hooks provided strong evidence that plantation mistresses not only passively witnessed but actively perpetrated cruelties on slave women. Their analysis of the first wave of feminism exhibited its frequent elevation of race and class interests above the interests of women in general. White suffragists resorted to racist rhetoric when it suited their purposes and only grudgingly allowed black women to participate in public meetings.

Davis and hooks argued that this history continues to effect black and white women to this day. Subsequent work by African American feminists has further substantiated, developed, and nuanced this claim. In *When and Where I Enter*, the historian Paula Giddings describes the vicissitudes of racial relations and strategies in the first wave of feminism *and* shows that the second wave of feminism was not much better. Patricia Hill Collins's *Black Feminist Thought* offers compelling evidence that, as a result of this history, the stereotypes faced by black women and white women are very different.[32] Black women confront the stereotypes of mammy, matriarch, and whore—concepts with clear roots in the history of slavery—while white women confront the stereotypes rooted in slavery's historical counterpart, the cult of true womanhood.[33] The persistent effects of these stereotypes are clearly legible in current events. Essays by Valerie Smith and Patricia Williams offer compelling evidence that cultural accounts of interracial rape vary dramatically with the race of the perpetrator and the victim.[34] The most striking contrast appears when the press's response to and portrayal of the so-called Central Park jogger (white victim, black perpetrators) analyzed by Smith is compared to the alleged rape of Tawana Brawley (black victim, white perpetrators) analyzed by Williams. In the first case, the press portrayed the black alleged perpetrators as animals and protected the white victim's anonymity as it asserted and reasserted her virtue. By contrast (and long before the grand jury had reached its findings), press coverage of Brawley's case quickly came to bear the marks of stereotypes of black women. Brawley's name was made public as soon as suspicions about whether the rape had actually occurred came to light. Her alleged perpetrators turned into the innocent victims, in contrast to Brawley, a "wild black girl who loves to lie, who is no innocent (in New York TV newscasters, inadvertently but repeatedly, referred to her as the 'defendant') and whose wiles are the downfall of innocent, jaded, desperate white men; this whore-lette, the symbolic consort of rapacious, saber-rattling buffoonish black men asserting their manhood."[35] The ultimate resolution of the criminal case (and the recently resolved civil suit) does not substantiate Brawley's original allegations and may obscure the effects of racism that Smith and Williams are describing. The outcome of Brawley's case does not explain (or justify) recourse to racist stereotypes. That such stereotypes came into play well before the facts had been sorted out underscores Smith's (and Williams's) analysis.

Whitefeminist theorists quickly acknowledged the validity of the critiques from African American feminists. Their attempts to theorize woman more adequately focused primarily on unearthing and eradicating essentialism, which they saw as the underlying barrier to acknowledgement of diversity. As Teresa de Lauretis points out in "Upping the Anti," conscious or unconscious essentialism became the cardinal sin of feminist theory.[36] A central tenet of American feminist theory, the distinction between sex and gender, channeled this attempt at self-policing for diversity. According to this paradigm, "woman" was a composite of two layers: "sex" (biological/anatomical female-ness) and "gender" (cultural definitions of "femininity"). The paradigm assumed that sex was the same for all women across historical/cultural locations while gender varied. Feminist theorists were critical of those who drew too tight a connection between the two. Accounts of a distinctive female subjectivity grounded in "sex" were rejected in favor of those that resided in "gender."

This paradigm determined the course that eradicating the problem of essentialism would take in whitefeminist theory. Early on in these debates, biological essentialism named only one of a number of sites where a problematic assumption of sameness might reside. In, for example, "*Am I That Name?*" Denise Riley marshaled evidence about what it meant to be a woman in different historical epochs in an effort to warn feminists against assuming that *gender* was the same across time and place. Biological essentialism was criticized primarily for its tendency to support biological reductionism. Emphasizing women's connectedness with nature, for example, played right into the hands of those who would use that connection to keep women in their traditional places. As the debate wore on, however, biological essentialism came to stand for essentialism in toto. Because sameness was understood to be grounded at the biological level, the critique of essentialism became focused on unearthing and eradicating any vestiges of biological essentialism in whitefeminist thought. Whitefeminists came to assume that avoiding biological essentialism would ensure avoidance of assumptions of an overarching sameness.

The focus on eradicating essentialism did little to ensure that whitefeminists paid serious attention to the difference race makes for gender, much less for sex. Asserting a concept of woman understood as socially constructed tacitly left room for the assertion of other versions of woman, but it gave whitefeminist theorists an alibi for *not* dealing with those women in their own work. Whitefeminist theorists regularly refused to claim universal status for the figure of woman in their texts, but paid little more than token attention to texts by women of color. Race appeared in the requisite list of variables that produce differing women, but the specifics of race as a factor in black women's lives, much less in white women's lives, rarely registered.[37]

The high point of the critique of essentialism and race came at the end of the decade with the publication of Elizabeth Spelman's *Inessential Woman.* Unlike any whitefeminist theorist before or since, Spelman made race the centerpiece of her critique of essentialism, with very fruitful results. Spelman moved beyond simply acknowledging the cri-

tiques that women of color had been making of whitefeminism; she
sought out the various points where, as she put it, "white privilege has
to lodge in order to do its work" (*IW*, 75). Spelman argued that, in
whitefeminist theory, race and class are often predicated only of black
women or of lower-class women. Middle-class white women, by contrast, are raceless and classless—"women" who need no other identifying label. This approach toward intersecting oppressions ignores the
role of race and class privilege in shaping what it means to be a white
woman. She argues that this arises, in part, from whitefeminist assumptions that the experience of white middle-class women exhibits
gender oppression in its purest form (since it is, presumably, the only
form of oppression they face). This mistaken sense that gender has been
successfully separated from race (and class) perpetuates white privilege's heretofore invisible inscription.

Spelman goes on to identify symptoms of white supremacy in feminist theory that recall those that womanist scholars find in feminist
theology. She argues that whitefeminist theorists, like whitefeminist
theologians, tend to use "women" and "men" as monolithic terms and
name the enemy of women as patriarchy. Feminist rhetoric assumes
that, under the conditions of patriarchy, all women as women are
deemed inferior to all men as men. Such an assumption ignores the
fact that, for example, black men are not considered superior to white
women in our culture.[38] This conception also makes it impossible for
feminist theorists to acknowledge white women as active oppressors
or men of color as victims of oppression.

Feminist theorists also tend to posit gender oppression as both the
root and the model of all other forms of oppression. Comparisons
drawn between, for example, "women" and "slaves" render slave
women invisible.[39] Like their colleagues in feminist theology, feminist
theorists also tend to see race and class oppressions as increasing the
quantity of oppression but not its quality. Whitefeminists assume that
feminism, as the site of resistance to gender oppression, includes African American women in its constituency. Whitefeminist theorists
rarely note specific features that distinguish the oppression women of
color experience from that experienced by white women.[40]

Spelman's far-ranging exposé of the problems attending whitefeminism's attempt to thematize racial difference reveals that gender can
be just as essentialist as sex.[41] Spelman's account suggests that the outline of feminism and of the woman for whom it speaks has been drawn.
African American women add color to the outline but do not change

its shape. Differences of race and class are largely construed as social constructions layered on top of sex and running parallel to gender. Thus, "woman" constitutes one of at least two facets of, for example, a black woman's identity, but what it means to be a woman remains the same regardless of one's race or class.

A survey of whitefeminist theorists' bibliographies suggests that Spelman's text has been widely read (or at least widely cited) but a survey of those same whitefeminist texts suggest that Spelman's insights have made little significant impact on whitefeminism's concrete dealings with race.[42] Spelman directs her critique at Simone de Beauvoir, Nancy Chodorow's early work, Betty Friedan, and Shulamith Firestone. Yet other whitefeminist theorists who presumably know better after reading Spelman use the same conceptual vocabulary that Spelman criticizes so forcefully. "Man" and "woman" are deployed as monolithic terms; race is specified only of men and women of color. While racism, imperialism, heterosexism, and other "isms" get mentioned in the usual litany of problems women face, none of these issues receive anything close to the degree of intense analysis that sexism receives.

If critiques of essentialism did not end in an embrace of Spelman's suggested reforms, what career *did* they take? As the 1980s came to a close, attempts to ferret out biological essentialism seemed to be running their course. A number of feminist theorists began to call the whole project into question. A survey of the so-called cultural feminists (Mary Daly and the like) and the charges leveled against them led Teresa de Lauretis to argue that charges of biological essentialism were largely red herrings. She claimed that essentialism had become the trendy weapon that whitefeminists used in the ongoing game of "I'm more theoretically sophisticated than thou." In her judgment, feminist theorists stretched one another's claims to inordinate degrees to make charges of essentialism stick.[43] Other feminist theorists advocated relinquishing the project of eradicating essentialism on political grounds. "Taking the risk of essentialism" is necessary, they argued, because feminist politics requires a single concept of woman as its organizational center.[44] Many cited subaltern feminist theorist Gayatri Chakravorty Spivak as authorizing this move, to Spivak's dismay. She has strongly criticized the career taken by this offhand remark.[45] Within feminist theory, she argues, taking the risk of essentialism functions most often as an alibi for not attending to differences between women. Other whitefeminist theorists rejected taking the risk of essentialism in favor of its opposite; refusing the very project of normatively defining woman.[46] In Spivak's view, this strategy only homogenized differences, effectively preventing them from challenging white hegemony.

What began as a desire to open feminism to women's diversity made minimal progress in the area of racial difference through the 1980s. Where feminist writers paid attention to the historical differences between white women and black women, something conspired to prevent that attention from seriously disrupting woman's inscription in sameness. In whitefeminist theology, an unrecognized essence of woman was primarily to blame. Attacks on essentialism within whitefeminist theory, however, also failed to make space for full recognition of the difference race makes to gender. The decade of antiessentialism may have secured feminist theory's woman's residence at the level of social construction, but her racial diversity remained at best a logical possibility. Whitefeminist theorists went on with their work as though race did not *really* matter to it. Whitefeminist theorists failed to inquire after whiteness as a racial mark or even acknowledge that their own theoretical woman might carry its imprint. Whitefeminist theory's woman passed through the critique of essentialism with her masquerade of racial neutrality virtually intact.

The occurrence of these failures calls for careful analysis. Whitefeminist theorists and theologians can and should be held accountable for willful disregard of the importance of race to feminist analysis. However, whitefeminism's tendency to lose track of race cannot be explained as simple willful disregard. So much of its dealings with race seem to be shaped by something that lies outside the intentions of whitefeminist authors. Clearly whitefeminist theorists, like whitefeminist theologians, want to escape the hold of sameness over their subject. Teresa de Lauretis's defense of radical feminist theorists like Daly cleared them of biological essentialism, but my analysis of Daly uncovered a *discursive* essential woman governing Daly's dealings with difference. Spivak's critique of essentialism's last gasp also suggests that the barriers to overcoming the race/gender divide lie deeper than the problem of essentialism. Whitefeminist theory has left debates over essentialism behind, but the problems outlined here continue to plague this field, as I argue in the next section of this chapter.[47]

Theorizing and Theologizing in Essentialism's Wake

As whitefeminist theory and theology face the end of yet another decade (and a millennium), the sex/gender distinction is nearing its point of exhaustion. Full analysis of the factors involved in bringing the sex/gender paradigm to this point is beyond the scope of this inquiry, but its detractors invoke sex/gender's failure to ground sustained attention to women's diversity as a sign of its imminent collapse.[48] Whitefeminist critics of the sex/gender paradigm argue that the focus on gender tends to play into the hands of perpetuating the assumption of sameness. Some find the sex/gender paradigm problematic because it fails to break with liberal humanism with all its attendant problems (mind/body split, nature/culture split, etc.), including its essentialism.[49] Its critics hope that attacking sex/gender will get closer to the root of whitefeminism's resistance to difference. My analysis suggests cautious optimism at this point. Insofar as the sex/gender paradigm shaped the trajectory of debates over essentialism, its exhaustion offers another opportunity for whitefeminist theory to become more open to women's diversity. At the same time, whitefeminists' failure to follow up on the opportunity represented by critiques of essentialism sounds a note of warning.

As the sex/gender distinction comes to a close, whitefeminist theorists and theologians are turning toward two sites for feminist investigation: toward the deployment of a concept of woman founded in difference and multiplicity and toward theorizing the body. Whitefeminist theorists working at both sites intend to overcome both the vestiges of liberal humanism and feminism's indifference to difference. Drucilla Cornell and Rosi Braidotti are at the forefront of the first strategy. Both begin with the recognition that each woman is the product of the interaction of a number of cultural subjecting forces. Feminist theory should, therefore, reconceive its subject to fit this reality. Conceiving of women as the products of multiple forces—and as differing from each other as a result—would enable feminist theory to move beyond merely acknowledging the diversity of its constituency to constructing feminism on the basis of that diversity. In *Patterns of Dissonance* and *The Nomadic Subject,* Braidotti attempts to formulate concepts of woman that make room for diversity.[50] The only mention race receives from Braidotti in *Patterns* comes in a brief discussion of Lorde's criticism of Daly. Braidotti blames Daly's blindness to race on Daly's nostalgic feminist and philosophical tendencies. She seems confident that better philosophies will help feminists avoid the problems Daly faces. Indeed, no one could accuse Braidotti of presenting women of color as "token torturers" because no woman of color appears anywhere else in her work. *Sexual* difference's claim to center stage—and apparent racial neutrality—goes unchallenged. The following passage from an earlier article by Braidotti exhibits the dangers of thinking only through sexual difference:

> The affirmation of the *differences within* [each one of us] joins up with the assertion of a collective recognition of the *differences between* all of us and the male subject as well as the *differences* which exist *among* us female subjects [author's emphasis]. *The recognition of the sameness of our gender, all other differences taken into account, is a sufficient and necessary condition to make explicit a bond among women that is more than the ethics of solidarity and altogether other than the sharing of common interests* [emphasis added].[51]

It is difficult to see how anyone who had *really* taken serious account of "all other differences" could assert with any degree of confidence that gender is the source of any kind of sameness. This logic acts as though individual women are composed of "differences" such as race that are attributes added to a "woman" all women share in common. African American feminists (and Spelman) have established this paradigm's inadequacy for accurately describing the interaction between race and woman, for black as well as white women. In leaving the difference between "all of us and the male subject" in place, Braidotti also ignores the impact of racial inequities on the relative value and power of majority and minority women and men.

In her more recent book, *The Nomadic Subject*, Braidotti argues for a new feminist politics based in "temporary and mobile coalitions" (105). This kind of politics requires a new form of subjectivity—which she calls the nomadic subject—that is constituted by multiple differences. Braidotti clearly intends this concept of feminist subjectivity to ground articulations of the various forces that go into the construction of women in all their diversity. However, examining it through the issue of race calls its adequacy as such a ground into question. First of all, the nomadic subject's diversity is so abstract that any difference, other than being a woman, would appear to be as important as any other. For example, Braidotti offers no guidance in helping me weight the relative importance to my subjectivity of my being born in Switzerland and growing up white in the American South in the 1960s and 1970s. Nor does her concept of subjectivity suggest a way to theorize the interactions among these biographical facts. Furthermore, since nothing in Braidotti's theory would compel me to include either factor in an analysis of my own subjectivity, it offers no access to forces whose work might be invisible to me. Thus, its deployment within whitefeminist thought is not likely to render whiteness visible, much less call whitefeminists to analyze it. Given feminism's history, I cannot share

Braidotti's confidence that a nomadic vision of sexual difference can "provid[e] shifting locations for multiple female feminist embodied voices" (172). That Braidotti fails to attend to any difference other than gender, and that her treatment of gender fails to recognize it as always already racially marked, only confirms my skepticism.

In *Beyond Accommodation*, Drucilla Cornell refuses to posit an essence of woman, proposing instead to write feminine specificity in all its variety.[52] To her credit, she asserts in her next book that "we cannot even begin to understand gender unless we understand how gender is 'colored' and how 'color' is in turn engendered, in the psychosexual dynamics of desire" (*Transformations*, 131). This insight, however, is only partially realized in *Transformations* and what follows it. Cornell highlights the effects of race (and sexual orientation) but primarily when what she is analyzing bears on African American women (or on lesbians). Cornell's longest discussion of race occurs in the final essay in *Transformations*, "What Takes Place in the Dark" (170–94; see, esp., 187–94). Cornell acknowledges here that *all* women are always already raced, at least within American culture. She also sees white and black women as dialectically related; that is, each is defined sexually in opposition to the other. White women are the unattainable pure prize; black women are sexually available. She draws this analysis out of a very troubling autobiographical incident that occurred in the early 1970s when she was a labor organizer. The incident ends with Cornell and her fellow organizers devoting considerable study to the intersection of race and gender. This is clearly a powerful incident in Cornell's life, but it is significant to the problem I am describing that, despite this baptism by fire, the theme of race does not receive substantial attention in her own work until twenty years later. It takes yet another apparently powerful experience—learning in the company of an anthropologist on race—to bring Cornell's attention back to the specifics of race. To her credit, the lesson she draws from these experiences about race's inextricability from gender is vital. Indeed, it is key to the conclusions I reach in chapter 6, below. However, her subsequent work has largely failed to follow through on this insight. Whiteness slips back into invisibility in Cornell's most recent book, *The Imaginary Domain*. Here, Cornell again devotes several pages to issues of race—but this time, only with regard to African American women.[53] Race returns to its standard place as an attribute of "other" women.

Whitefeminist theologians who work with whitefeminist theory have offered their own constructive proposals for theologizing and theorizing in essentialism's wake. To their credit, these theologians incorporate the work of women from diverse locations into their scholarship to a far greater degree than do whitefeminist theorists. Sharon Welch's *A Feminist Ethic of Risk* (1990) and Wendy Farley's *Eros for the Other* (1996) both take their mark on this issue from concerns about the enervating effects of antiessentialism on feminism. Both acknowledge critiques of whitefeminism's exclusionary tendencies as legitimate. Their own work attempts to right that wrong in the resources they use and in the theoretical perspective they articulate. Welch develops a platform that aims to empower women to work together in coalitions across lines of race and class.

Following the lead of the African American literary scholar Barbara Christian and the womanist ethicist Katie Cannon, Welch finds in this literary tradition strategies and resources for pursuing political change in the face of seemingly insurmountable odds. Access to these resources also involves acknowledging the critiques of whitefeminism's implication in racism as articulated in these texts. While focused on experience, Welch also makes an important move away from a focus on individuals to what makes collective struggle in the face of divisive differences like race possible. The ethic of risk Welch develops does not aim to erase differences; Welch insists that perspectives will always be partial. In response, she urges feminists to seek solidarity in the form of coalitions across racial and other lines. While I applaud Welch for refusing to withdraw in the face of the challenge of diversity, I worry about moving too quickly into coalition building. For such efforts to succeed, the roots of white solipsism must be uncovered and its silent and invisible governance disrupted. Otherwise, feminism will remain captive to white solipsism's ability to absorb and deflect challenges to its mastery. Indeed, Welch's own work may be vulnerable to critique from African American feminists for the use she makes of African American women's fiction. Deborah McDowell and Valerie Smith both argue that certain schemas mark whitefeminism's dealings with African American feminist literature. McDowell identifies a tendency among whitefeminists to situate African American feminist work on the "practice/politics" side of the theory/practice divide.[54] Valerie Smith argues that counting African American feminist writing as "material" and "historical" reproduces the figure of black women as appropriable bodies.[55] In these instances, Smith writes, black women "are employed, if not sacrificed to humanize their white superordinates, to teach them something about the content of their own subject positions" (46). To be fair, Welch's careful and thorough reading of African American women's texts surpasses their treatment in the hands of those

McDowell criticizes (Jane Gallop and Toril Moi). And yet the marks of these schemas are nonetheless present. Welch primarily draws political lessons from African American feminist fiction; she turns to predominately white male philosophers for theoretical tools. Similarly, while the political lessons she draws are clearly and appropriately contextualized within the historical context that gave rise to them, aiming those lessons toward a white audience repeats the gesture Smith describes.

Wendy Farley argues that neither essentialism nor antiessentialism is capable of adequately theorizing women in their unity and diversity. Through a reconstruction of the history of *eidos* in western culture, Farley argues against reducing the relationship of essence to existence to an opposition between static sameness and random pluralism. She argues that, properly understood and deployed, *eidos* renders unity in and through difference. "Woman," in other words, means "woman" only with reference to particular women in all their diversity. She develops this argument in and through sympathetic readings of a large variety of women's texts, from *I, Rigoberta Menchu* to work by African American feminist theorists. Farley is to be commended for working the *eidos* of woman in such a productive way. She is also to be commended for the quality and quantity of her attention to texts by women from a variety of contexts. However, both Farley and Welch pass too quickly through the fractures in feminism around the issue of race. While I agree with Farley that neither essentialism nor antiessentialism is capable of handling women's diversity, the ground this essay will uncover will suggest that woman cannot yet function as Farley would like, at least within whitefeminist contexts. The figure of woman does not include racial difference recognized and valued as such. Rather, woman seems to be defined in and through exclusion of racial difference. Conscious desire for domination cannot account for this problem, thus its roots must be located and unearthed elsewhere.

Mary McClintock Fulkerson, in *Changing the Subject* (1994; hereafter, *CS*), attempts to develop an account of religious subjectivity that avoids essentialism and can ground women's diversity. Fulkerson takes a distinctive and productive approach to theorizing the subject of feminist theology in light of the critique of essentialism. She identifies two symptoms of feminist theology's difficulties with diversity. Like others, she is convinced by feminist theology's critics that its woman is predominately white, middle class, and heterosexual. Her work primarily addresses the other symptom of feminist theology's narrow construal of its subject: its inability to account for women who share feminist theologians' affiliation with Christianity, but not their affinity with feminism. Two root problems within feminist theology contribute to these difficulties, according to Fulkerson. Like Sheila Davaney, Fulkerson views the category of women's experience as problematic because of its invitation to universalist claims. Like me, Fulkerson sees feminist theology's woman as bound to and by the liberal humanist subject.

Like Braidotti, Fulkerson argues that feminist theology needs a theory that allows for multiple subject positions and a "respect for difference." She writes, "The point is not to lose the subject 'woman,' but to change the subject in the sense that the complex production of multiple identities becomes basic to our thinking" (CS, 7). Fulkerson goes on to develop a complex theory of woman as constituted by the nexus of various discourses that affect women's subjectivities in diverse ways. She puts this theory to work in analyzing three different subject positions: feminist theologians, Presbyterian laywomen, and Pentecostal women. Fulkerson's work is truly innovative in its ability to articulate these three very different subject positions in sympathetic and distinctive ways. She goes beyond Braidotti in providing a theoretical construct that can weight different aspects of subjectivity in different ways. However, her construct of subjectivity, like Braidotti's nomadic subject, fails to sustain any inquiries into race. Fulkerson includes race, like class and gender, in the social relations that shape and produce women. She has quite a bit to say about class and gender, but race as a factor in the production of these subjectivities is never analyzed. This is particularly troubling given Fulkerson's aim, which is to develop a theoretical position that can take account of the difference between feminist and nonfeminist women. This is not to say that race leaves no marks on her text; quite the contrary. Surely, race *privilege* must play a role in white Pentecostal and Presbyterian women's lack of identification with feminism even as race *oppression* plays a role in black women's lack of identification with feminism.

Race also leaves traces in Fulkerson's analysis of feminist theology. Fulkerson rightly criticizes "academic (mostly Euro-American) feminist theology" (CS, 17) for aiming for inclusion. Such a goal "merely support[s] appreciation of varieties of women—those women, that is, who can afford the trip to the table" (16). However, Fulkerson stops short of inquiring after the role that white privilege pays in academic feminist theologians' limitations. At the same time, "mostly Euro-American" appears to identify "academic feminist theology" with whitefeminist theology, effectively excluding womanist theology from the field. To be fair, the nomenclature she adopts is intended to contextualize academic (white)feminist theology in complex ways ("academic" vs. lay-oriented theology, Euro-American vs. theology from other sites). Womanist theologians are far less vulnerable to the charge Fulkerson levels at academic feminist theology. Womanist scholars often explicitly aim their work at both academic and lay audiences.[56] Thus, Fulkerson could be read as implicitly acknowledging a distinction between womanist and feminist theology. On the other hand, one is left wondering whether womanist theology counts as "academic." At best, the "mostly" in "mostly Euro-American" leaves open the possibility that *some* American theologian of non-European descent might count as academic. Undoubtedly, these exclusionary effects of her nomenclature run counter to Fulkerson's intentions, but that they occur speaks to whitefeminist theology's need to think through race's effects on its discourse.

Race's impact is particularly legible in Fulkerson's chapter on Presbyterian women. Fulkerson argues that this subject position arises out of a discursive nexus shaped by the canonical discourses of Presbyterianism and secular culture's ideas about gender, race, and class. She identifies the secular ideal of gender at work in this context as the cult of domesticity. This gendered ideal values women as homemakers who create a haven for their families. Fulkerson acknowledges at the outset that race and class affected women's access to this ideal. She also analyses the role economic factors play in the production of this ideal, but race's role in its production is not discussed. To Fulkerson's credit, she acknowledges that fully accounting for Presbyterian women's subjectivity would require analyzing a number of other factors, including race. In fact, race appears as a shadowy subtext throughout Fulkerson's analysis of Presbyterian women's subjectivity. Fulkerson notes that Presbyterian mission literature directed toward laywomen encouraged them toward acts of charity toward the "other." In these publications' photographs, "women's bodies . . . are often mixed with the 'other,' the native, the foreigner, the object of mission" (*CS,* 221).

Fulkerson argues that the cult of domesticity shaped Presbyterian laywomen's sense of subjectivity and identity. During the Civil Rights era, mission literature asked women to consider how their maids or yardmen (presumably of a different race) might perceive them. They are asked to attend to what their own faces register when someone of another race comes into their presence. Symptoms of the divide between race and gender—and its instability—register in Fulkerson's text. On the one hand, the passage I have just quoted divides woman from the (raced) "other, the native, the foreigner, the object of mission." Whether this division is Fulkerson's or that of the photographic ar-

chives (perhaps none of the "others" depicted are women) matters little. The fact that race's role in producing such an elision—a role as
substantial as that of gender—goes unanalyzed is significant. Given
that race's effects on the subjects of Fulkerson's analysis are so legible,
what enables the analysis of race to be postponed indefinitely?

The turn toward theorizing the body offers another route that whitefeminists have taken toward overcoming liberal humanism's legacy.
In *Ethics of Eros,* Tina Chanter holds out the hope that the turn toward
the body might enjoin whitefeminism to take race on as a necessary
point of analysis; after all, race seems to be at least as indelibly marked
on the body as sex. While a survey of whitefeminist theorists' work on
the body shows signs of progress at that site, it also suggests that *simply*
turning to the body will not ensure that a whitefeminist theorist will
subject race to any kind of analysis. Elizabeth Grosz, for example,
opens *Volatile Bodies* with the acknowledgement that "of course" bodies
are raced as well as sexed, but her analysis proceeds without any attention to the racing of bodies. Moira Gatens's *Imaginary Bodies* provides
a route to thinking race as a body difference intertwined with sexual
difference. Gatens insists that the body is itself historically constituted
by different forces in different times and places. This awareness opens
up the possibility of attending to the impact of the history of race on
what it means to be embodied as a white or black woman in the United
States, for example, though realizing that potential lies in the future.[57]

Whitefeminist theologian Paula Cooey's account of embodied subjectivity in *Religious Imagination and the Body* (1994; hereafter *RI*) holds
out the promise of attending to differences between women, but race
is elided here, as well. Following Elaine Scarry, Cooey turns to the
suffering body as the site of the making and unmaking of the self.
Cooey examines the role of religious symbolism and gender in this
process through readings of Argentinian Alicia Partnoy's accounts of
her experiences of torture, Frida Kahlo's art, and Toni Morrison's fiction. Cooey's choice of examples speaks to her desire to theorize and
theologize on behalf of a variety of women. The template that she constructs to read these women's work theorizes gender, religion, and the
body individually and in relation to each other. The other factors affect-
ing these women's subjectivities and contexts (ethnicity, class, race),
though marked in each case, go untheorized, effectively subordinating
them to categories of selfhood and gender.

The effects of Cooey's template are visible in her reading of Toni
Morrison's fiction. Cooey acknowledges Morrison's fiction as articulating both the effects of and resistance to white racism. However, race

figures only as a factor that increases these characters' experiences of oppression; Cooey fails to recognize that race might qualitatively influence the very dynamics she analyzes. Cooey's introduction to her discussion of Morrison's fiction is telling. She acknowledges that, because of white racism, "conventional subjectivity . . . as this is construed in substantialist terms, is not always available" (*RI,* 71) to African American women. Yet race slips from Cooey's view when she turns to read Morrison's characters' relationship to subjectivity: "[Such] characters as Sula Peace . . . and Pilate Dead . . . represent strikingly contrasting views of *women's* subjectivity as reflected through *female* sensuality" (*RI,* 71; emphasis added). Cooey's reading of Morrison's characters stays true to this trajectory, with problematic results. For example, Cooey notes that Sula's community views her birthmark as a mark of Satan or Cain. She writes, "This connection between birthmark and evil resembles the Western church's eventual identification of women, through Eve's nude body, with sin and death" (*RI,* 73). Cooey completely bypasses the more immediate connection here between the mark of Cain and traditions of Christian racism, where this mark has functioned as a sign of racial and ethnic subordination. To be fair, Cooey's reading is in line with what she identifies as her project: reading the female body as a site of self construction and destruction in and through religious symbols. However, in leaving race out of her analysis, Cooey seriously truncates her own project. This particular intersection of religious symbolism and the female body cannot be properly read without attending to race.[58]

I want to be clear here. As was the case with my readings of Daly and Ruether, I am not criticizing any of these whitefeminist theologians and theorists' intentions. Like Daly and Ruether, all of them want to deal in more productive ways with differences between women. Their projects make some progress toward this aim, but their dealings (or lack thereof) with race call those projects up short. Race's ability to elude analysis is all the more remarkable in those cases where it leaves more pronounced marks on whitefeminists' texts. What enables race to slip so easily through whitefeminist theoretical and theological nets—especially those nets designed in response to the history of race's elision?

From the Trouble with Gender to Bodies that Matter: Judith Butler

The fullest realization of the promise that whitefeminism's turn to a multiple feminist subject or to the body will yield more substantial attention to race occurs in Judith Butler's work. However, her work also marks the limit of the success of these strategies, to date. Butler's *Gender Trouble* undoubtedly played an instrumental role in bringing the dominance of sex/gender to an end. Butler opens this masterful book with an insightful analysis of the trouble with gender. In the opening chapter, Butler names gender's inability to ground more adequate discussions of race as one of its afflictions. Like Spelman, Butler sees the outlines of whitefeminism's woman as too firmly fixed. Butler questions whitefeminism's assumption that making woman inclusive involves completing the picture by simply coloring between the lines (15). Feminism's failure to configure rightly the relationship between sex and gender lies at the root of feminism's inability to deal with differences between women, Butler asserts. Feminist theory has tended to treat the sexual binary as a clearly marked and immutable fact (one is biologically either male or female). Gender has been viewed, in turn, as an interpretation rising out of the immutable binary of sex. Butler challenges both of these suppositions. Anatomical and genetic variability calls into question the naturalness of the binary sex division. Butler argues that the sexual binary reflects not careful attention to nature but the interests of a heterosexist and phallocentric culture. A heterosexual economy founded upon phallocentrism requires two genders/sexes to function. Rather than reading gender off of sex, she argues, our culture reads sex *through* gender or gender *into* sex. Gender is a matter of repeated performance of cultural norms, not an expression of inherent nature, whether one is a "real" woman or a drag queen.

Gender Trouble carries feminism a significant distance beyond the impasses of essentialism, at least on the grounds of the relationship of gender, sex, and sexuality. By showing that gender/sex are products of normative heterosexuality (rather than vice versa), Butler renders legible their double-sided effects on woman as sexual being. If woman is defined in and through heterosexuality, then the connection between "lesbian" and "woman" needs to be rethought. But what about race? Racial difference launched Butler's inquiry into the trouble with gender, but it quietly and quickly slips out of view once the inquiry is underway. *Gender Trouble* leaves uninterrogated race's place in relationship to the sexual economy. Butler's woman continues to masquerade as racially neutral.

While race eludes Butler's view in *Gender Trouble*, it figures much more prominently in her next book, *Bodies that Matter*.[59] This book collects essays that reflect Butler's more recent thinking about the issues raised in *Gender Trouble*, especially in light of the earlier book's critics.

Through several of the essays in *Bodies*, Butler responds to a misreading of her understanding of subjectivity and its relationship to gender. According to some of *Gender Trouble*'s critics, Butler's claim about the performativity of gender rests upon the concept of the liberal humanist subject. These critics read Butler as arguing that the liberal humanist subject gets up in the morning, opens his or her closet, and decides what gender to put on that day. According to this reading, Butler's reconfiguration of sex/gender turns it into an ethereal, even optional attribute of subjectivity—surely not a rendering that feminism would welcome. If, as Butler's critics assert, underneath the performance of gender lies the traditional humanist subject whose identity rests on something neutral to its body and its gender, feminism's subject has been effectively neutered.

"Phantasmatic Identification and the Assumption of Sex" (*Bodies*, 93–119) constitutes a direct response to this misreading. In this essay, Butler clarifies her position on subjectivity. First of all, she argues that identifications are multiple and contestatory; that is, they are "incorporations" of negotiations with multiple "vectors of power" that include sex, gender, race, class, sexuality, and so on. To claim that these identifications are performative (rather than substantive) means first that identifications are a matter of what one *does* and *thus* becomes rather than what one *is* (and *therefore* does). In addition, Butler argues that identifications "unsettle the 'I'; they are the sedimentation of the 'we' in the constitution of any 'I,' the structuring presence of alterity in the very formulation of the 'I' " (*Bodies*, 105). One does not set one's own terms for identifications. One negotiates one's coming-to-be a subject in and through cultural norms regarding gender, sex, race, class, and sexuality. These norms are the products of the disguised violences of liberal humanism which pushes off the threat of challenges to its hegemonic rule through "the multiplication of culturally specific identities" (*Bodies*, 118). Thus, Butler's concept of subjectivity cuts into the very foundation of the liberal humanist concept of the subject as a self-contained "I."[60]

In *Bodies that Matter*, Butler's readings of the documentary film *Paris Is Burning* and Nella Larsen's novel, *Passing*, develop this theoretical position on subjectivity's source and status. Race figures centrally within subjectivity's nexus. *Paris is Burning*, by filmmaker Jennie Livingston, documents the phenomenon of drag balls among the down-and-out of New York City's underclass. Drag balls involve competitions between various "houses" composed of groups of men of color, some of whom are gay, some of whom are transvestites, some of whom are transsexuals, and all of whom are poor and appear to be living on the economy's edge. The drag competitions involve not just gender masquerade, but frequently class or race masquerade as well. Competitors take on the personae of businessmen, fashion models, college students, and military officers with often uncanny accuracy. Competitors are judged according to a standard of "realness"; that is, how perfectly they embody the personae they mimic. The success of some of these imaginary transformations is astonishing. The performances documented in the film call into question any sharp distinction between the "copy" and the "real thing." Thus, the movie bolsters Butler's claim in *Gender Trouble* about the performativity of gender. Drag performances are not related to what they imitate "as copy is to original, but, rather, as copy is to copy" (*Gender Trouble*, 31). That is, real models—military officers and businessmen—are constituted by performativity, too. One's identifications *are* truly what one *is* but not naturally or immediately. That is, one does not create oneself ex nihilo. One negotiates with the various vectors of power inscribed in culture. Identifications reside on the border between consciousness and unconsciousness, nature and culture, body and mind.

The fact that the subjects of *Paris Is Burning* exhibit the interplay of race, sex/gender, sexuality, and class leads Butler to consider seriously the ways these "vectors of power" relate to each other. *Gender Trouble* challenged the separation between sex and gender. In *Bodies,* Butler goes on to challenge the assumption that *race* can be separated from gender. Butler's analysis of the way the drag performances documented in the film rework race and gender goes beyond what Spelman called additive analysis [(white) woman + black (man) = black woman]. The drag performances appropriate gender as "the vehicle for the phantasmatic transformation of that nexus of race and class" (*Bodies,* 130). That the performers are able to do so suggests that "the order of sexual difference is not prior to that of race or class in the constitution of the subject; indeed, that the symbolic is also and at once a racializing set of norms, and that the norms of realness by which the subject is produced are racially informed conceptions of 'sex' " (130).

Butler's discussion of Nella Larsen's novel *Passing* in "Passing, Queering: Nella Larsen's Psychoanalytic Challenge" also features substantive attention to race. *Passing* narrates the story of Clare, an African American woman whose skin is light enough that she is able to pass as white. The novel's dramatic tension centers around the fact that Clare's husband, Bellew, a white man, is also a bigot. Butler reads Bellew through another claim made in "Phantasmatic Identification." There,

Butler argued that coming to be who-one-is involves not just "in-corpo-rating" one particular set of cultural norms for sex/gender/race and so on; rather, Butler argues, one constitutes one's identity in opposition to what one rejects. In that essay, she offers sexual identifications as examples. The heterosexual identificatory position constitutes itself on the basis of what it rejects (homosexuality). To sustain its position, But-ler argues, the heterosexual subject requires the ongoing existence of what it rejects. Bellew exhibits this dynamic in terms of a mix of race, sexuality, and gender. His self-identity rests on the distinction between "white" and "black" articulated through his heterosexuality. Bellew-as-bigot consciously expresses repulsion at the thought of black flesh, even while Bellew-as-heterosexual-subject simultaneously embodies a certain fascination with and attraction to black female flesh. Butler finds the psychoanalytic category of disavowal (the unconscious re-fusal of knowledge) useful for articulating Larsen's portrayal of Bellew. Bellew's attraction to Clare is grounded in his disavowed knowledge that she is a mulatto—a borderline case. The fact that he affectionately refers to her as "Nig," comments frequently on her complexion, and sometimes jokingly threatens to send her back to Africa exhibits a sub-conscious awareness of her race. However, when confronted with the reality of her African heritage, he rejects her in a dramatic scene that ends with Clare falling out of the window to her death. The novel's dramatic action revolves around Bellew coming to the point of being unable to disavow this knowledge any longer. Once again, the forces of race, gender, and sexuality come into play. His suspicions that Clare might be unfaithful to him serve as the lever that pries the lid off of his subconscious motivations, according to Butler.

Butler acknowledges here in concrete terms that race makes a differ-ence to what it means to be a woman. She sees that *Passing* trades on the different configurations of race, sexuality and gender with which one negotiates in the process of becoming either a black or a white woman. Her acknowledgement of the significance of these insights for whitefeminism constitutes the most important aspect of her analysis. Butler comes to recognize that many of feminism's assumptions—as-sumptions she acknowledges sharing in the past—are put in serious question once race is really allowed on the scene. Butler concludes that "it is no longer possible to make sexual difference prior to racial differ-ence or, for that matter, to make them into fully separable axes of social regulation and power" (*Bodies*, 182). She criticizes feminist theory for failing to see that sexual difference is, in fact, always already racially marked (181). The sexual economy is "centrally sustained by racial anxiety and sexualized rituals of racial purification"; likewise, prohibitions against miscegenation rest upon the cultural constructions of "heterosexuality, sexual fidelity, and monogamy" (184). Thus, like Cornell, Butler argues that sex, race, gender, class, and sexuality are mutually "imbricated" in one another—for white women as well as for black women. She recognizes that whitefeminism's failure to deal adequately with race voids its claim to have really understood gender, so deeply is gender entwined with race.

This situation also has important ramifications for rethinking feminism's subject, in Butler's view. She argues that simply proliferating multiple positions within the current hegemony will not truly affect change. Rather, she suggests that feminist analysis needs "to interrogate the exclusionary moves through which 'positions' are themselves invariably assumed" (*Bodies*, 112). She reminds her readers that these exclusionary moves are not made once and for all at the inception of identification and then "left behind in a forgotten past," but must be "leveled and buried again and again" (114). These exclusionary moves constitute the "compulsive repudiation by which the subject incessantly sustains his/her boundary" (114).

These are certainly significant advances. Butler's analysis of race's relationship to gender has moved far beyond additive analysis. Her theoretical position lays the groundwork for attending to whiteness itself as a racial category, but Butler stops just short of fully carrying that out. Spelman argues that race comes into whitefeminism's view only when it is confronted with racial otherness. This is as true of Butler's account as it was of the feminist theorists and theologians I analyzed earlier. Race enters Butler's analysis through the African American men in Livingston's film and through the African American characters in Larsen's novel. Whiteness as a racial mark comes into view fleetingly against the screen of blackness, as it did in Cornell's work, but in essays where blackness is not at issue, whiteness is never raised—despite Butler's assertion that it is impossible to deal with gender apart from race.[61]

I have argued that the course for whitefeminism's dealings with race seems to be set by things beyond whitefeminists' immediate control. Butler's dealings with race in the essays in *Bodies that Matter* exhibit this dynamic, but from a different angle. It is hard to know whether race would have gotten the sustained attention Butler gives it were it not for a happy confluence of circumstances. A conference on "Psychoanalysis in African American Contexts" at the University of California, Santa Cruz, provided the occasion for Butler's writing of "Passing,

Queering." Critics' questions about Butler's claims for drag's potentially disruptive effect on the connection between sex and gender provided the occasion for Butler to revisit drag. Dealing with gay male
drag would not, in and of itself, call forth an analysis of the mutual
imbrication of sex, race, gender, and sexuality, but the fortuitous existence of Livingston's documentary does because of the race of its subjects. This is not to take credit away from Butler; certainly she chose
to take on these projects. The interest she exhibits in *Gender Trouble* in
disturbing assumptions about women's sameness and the theoretical
positions she developed there certainly prepared her to put these occa-
sions to exceptional use. On the other hand, the attention devoted to
race in *Bodies that Matter* is not simply the product of Butler's authorial
intention.

To her credit, Butler follows where her guides take her—to the brink,
even, of calling feminism as a project into question given the separation
of race from gender that has constituted it. She realizes that whitefeminism's inattention to race renders its claim to understanding gender
null and void. She admits her own complicity in these failures by acknowledging that she has "problematically prioritized gender as the
identificatory site of political mobilization at the expense of race or
sexuality or class or geopolitical positioning/displacement" (*Bodies*,
116). However, she steps back from that brink in her introduction.
She rightly resists demands that she cover *everything* on the grounds
that to claim to do so constitutes theoretical imperialism. Yet it is troubling to see Butler put race into an amalgamated category like "everything" so soon after acknowledging its importance to thinking woman.
It is particularly disappointing to see Butler take that route given the
potential in her work for theorizing race and woman together. Butler's
remark here reads to me like a disavowal of the conclusions that follow
logically from the position she has articulated in and through "Phantasmatic Identification" and "Passing, Queering."

In "Phantasmatic Identification" Butler argued that identifications
rest on the exclusion of other positions. Sustaining a sexual identity,
for example, paradoxically requires the ongoing existence of what one
has rejected in order for the exclusionary gesture to be repeated. "Passing, Queering" used this scheme to articulate the nexus of race, heterosexuality, and gender represented by Bellew. Reading whitefeminism's
history on race through this template of inclusion/exclusion gives this
scheme a particular potency. My analysis of whitefeminist theology
and whitefeminist theory unveils a long history to whitefeminism's
failure to attend to the difference race makes for gender. It suggests

that this failure is not on the order of an error of fact or a lack of knowledge; if it were, then surely whitefeminism would have passed beyond
the race/gender divide by now. Whitefeminism exhibits a kind of
Freudian kettle logic with regard to race; it explicitly announces its
intention to speak on behalf of (all) women, even as it admits its inability to do so. It admits its failure to be inclusive in the past even as it
ignores its ongoing shortcomings. It tries again and again to find more
successful strategies for inclusion, yet each new strategy loses its way
and goes astray. It would seem that whitefeminism's inability to sustain productive dealings with race goes to the very heart of the feminist
project. Could it be the case that whitefeminism's woman is constructed in and through the exclusion of "other" women? If so, the
history of whitefeminist theology and theory can be read as a series of
recurrent gestures of inclusion/exclusion. Exclusionary moves are not
made once and for all at the inception of identification and then, to
quote Butler again, "left behind in a forgotten past"; rather, they are
"leveled and buried again and again" (*Bodies*, 114). If whitefeminism's
dealings with race are symptomatic of the "compulsive repudiation by
which the subject incessantly sustains his/her boundary" (114), then
clearly whitefeminist analysis needs "to interrogate the exclusionary
moves through which 'positions' are themselves invariably assumed"
(112). It is no wonder that whitefeminism has so far failed to take on
such a project, no wonder that Butler steps back from the brink. The
race/gender divide constitutes a faultline that seems to open onto an
abyss that threatens to swallow feminism. It is certainly tempting to
step back from the abyss and retreat to familiar ground. Paradoxically,
however, to do so would be to abandon feminism to the abyss by sur-
rendering feminism's explicit desire to work on behalf of all women.
The paradox goes even further. Insofar as whitefeminism deviates from
its foundation in such an explicit desire, then its own founding principles call it into the abyss.

Conclusion/Opening

I began by exploring the problems in whitefeminist theology's dealings
with race. My analysis uncovered an essential liberal humanist subject
at work in whitefeminist texts, which closed them off to womens' diversity. I turned next to discussions of the problem of essentialism in
whitefeminist theory, but found that those discussions had yet to make
substantial progress toward overcoming the divide between race and
gender; in fact, the divide reinstated itself at every turn. I concluded

this section by suggesting that feminism has been constructed by and through the exclusion of "other" women. Symptoms of this register at several levels of whitefeminist analysis. While whitefeminists acknowledge differences between women as important, they rarely attend to the specific marks of difference. The issue of race fades in and out of view in whitefeminist texts. The occasional visit of a woman of color invokes some analysis of race, but whitefeminist thought abandons the issue when women of color exit the scene. Race, when discussed at all, is predicated of women of color but not of white women.

My analysis of whitefeminist theology showed that simply attending to race cannot correct this problem as long as an essential woman governs whitefeminist thinking. Analysis of whitefeminist theory, however, showed that subjecting essentialism to strong critique did little to increase whitefeminists' attention to race either. Finding and deploying a new concept of woman—one that is rooted in difference rather than sameness, one that consciously breaks with the liberal humanist subject—also proved insufficiently helpful. White solipsism's persistence in whitefeminist thought cannot be blamed simply on essentializing tendencies, no matter how pernicious those may be. This suggests that the roots of whitefeminism's white solipsism lie at yet a deeper level.

Analyses from African American feminists, especially coupled with Elizabeth Spelman's exposure of the various ways whitefeminists perpetuate the erasure of race, suggest that race significantly affects gender. As Butler comes to acknowledge, whitefeminism's analysis of gender has been seriously truncated by its failure to attend to race. Indeed, what goes on under the name of "feminist" is called into question on its own terms. My analysis suggests that it has been constituted by its exclusion of race. What is it going to take for the difference of race to register profoundly in whitefeminist thinking? Can this founding and foundational exclusionary gesture and its repetitions be overcome? What has produced this double erasure of race—of black women from whitefeminist analysis and of whiteness as a racial mark in need of analysis? Several interlocking layers of questions need to be asked.

First, the account I have given of whitefeminism raises questions about the relationship between authors and texts, texts and contexts, that need to be addressed. I have argued that discussions of race in whitefeminist texts in theology and theory exhibit a persistent pattern that lies largely outside the control of whitefeminist authors. What is the source of this persistent pattern? If it comes from outside whitefeminist texts, how does it come to be inside them? Can whitefeminism break this persistent pattern? If so, how? Spelman analyzes the various ways that whitefeminism perpetuates essentialism, but my analysis suggests that essentialism is not the sole root of whitefeminism's exclusionary tendencies. What enables whiteness to masquerade as neutrality? What prevents it from emerging clearly as a *necessary* point of interrogation? Where it *does* emerge, what stands in the way of sustained analysis of its effects? Is this exclusion of race unique to whitefeminism or do its roots lie elsewhere? Spelman's project of unearthing white privilege needs to be carried farther and deeper into the context that surrounds whitefeminism.

While essentialism does not appear to be the sole root of the problem, the symptoms that appear in its vicinity highlight subjectivity as an important arena of inquiry. Shifting woman's residence from culture to nature or from sex to gender has little effect on the larger context that shapes whitefeminism's dealings with race. Thus, it would appear that this context must reside below distinctions between nature/culture and sex/gender as well as self/other. This larger context also seems able to absorb shifts from a liberal humanist concept of subjectivity to pluralist concepts of subjectivity without breaching the divide between race and gender. What is subjectivity's place within this context? What relationship to race as well as to woman does this context prescribe for subjectivity? Uncovering deeper roots to the perpetuation of an unacknowledged white hegemony in whitefeminism is a worthy goal, but preparing the ground for more fruitful dealings with women's diversity requires the subversion of the divide between race and gender that circumscribes whitefeminism. What strategies can accomplish this subversion?

To answer these questions and to achieve these aims, this project will mine the work of two thinkers associated with deconstruction, Jacques Derrida and Luce Irigaray. Following the trajectories of woman and race through their work will take this project through each of these interconnected questions. Turning to deconstruction in support of feminist aims—particularly those of feminist theology—may seem, on the face of it, either oxymoronic or just plain moronic. Deconstruction's status in whitefeminist, African American feminist, and theological circles is hardly uncontested. Readers whose knowledge of deconstruction comes through deconstruction's critics will worry that I am proposing a cure that could be worse than the disease—perhaps a cure that may prove fatal to feminism.

On the other hand, readers who know these thinkers' impact on whitefeminist theory and African American feminist theory may be thinking that whatever assistance they offered would have already appeared. Braidotti, Cornell, and Butler all work out of a context informed by Irigaray and Derrida, yet they have not succeeded in breaking out of white hegemony. Evelyn Brooks Higginbotham argues that the influx of poststructuralism into feminist theory has only provided increasingly sophisticated ways to talk about white women's experience.[62] In a recent collection of essays, bell hooks argues that, for all its talk about a politics of otherness and difference, postmodernist feminism continues to perpetuate a cultural hegemony and a commodification of black culture.[63] Deconstruction has gotten mixed reviews from African American feminist scholars. Barbara Christian, Deborah McDowell, and Valerie Smith are all somewhat suspicious of the privileged place deconstruction occupies in what Christian calls "the race for theory" within African American literary studies.[64] Smith and McDowell both see some value in deconstruction, if properly situated historically and materially. However, deconstruction's employment by male scholars in the service of separating black feminist scholarship from "theory" worries both of them.[65]

On the other hand, while Irigaray has yet to receive substantial attention from feminist theologians, turning to her work with the aim of promoting women's diversity may not register as particularly revolutionary to those well acquainted with feminist theory's recent past. As Kelly Oliver notes, the turn to the so-called French feminists played an integral role in whitefeminism's response to critiques of its exclusionary tendencies.[66] The French feminists' appearance on the American scene coincided with the high tide of critiques of American feminism's white solipsism. When Irigaray's work first crossed the Atlantic, she became embroiled in the debate over essentialism. A number of whitefeminist theorists found her guilty of biological essentialism. Others saw the French theorists as offering significant resources for enabling more adequate engagement with differences between women, even when the theorists themselves sometimes fell short of this potential. Irigaray's work played an important role in Anglophone feminists' development of a pluralizing, multiple concept of woman.

Potential dangers arising from too close an association with Derrida may immediately come to feminist theologians' minds, but suspicions about Irigaray as a potential source for a cure should now be arising given the account of feminist theory that I have just offered. If Irigaray *were* a biological essentialist, then turning to her work would constitute a giant leap backward. Furthermore, I just criticized whitefeminist theorists' deployment of a multiple woman for failing to produce much

in the way of race awareness. How can I be serious in suggesting Irigaray as an ally if this is all she offers? Irigaray can be successfully
defended against charges of essentialism, as a number of her interpreters have argued and as my discussion of her work will show.[67] Handling the second (and more dangerous) question about Irigaray's value
for my project is more complicated. While I will argue that her concept
of woman/women as bearing difference within/between them is central to her value for my project, Irigaray's own work with this multiple
woman exhibits failures similar to those witnessed in this chapter. Irigaray loses track of woman's multiplicity in her later work, and never
puts questions of race into play. Situating Irigaray's woman within the
context provided by this book will allow that woman to go in more
fruitful directions. I will argue that getting race to register consistently
as a factor in the constitution of multiple women requires supple-
menting Irigaray with explicit discussions of race.

In what follows, then, I am not proposing Derrida and Irigaray as
the truly inclusive theorists, nor do I see them as constituting together
the panacea to whitefeminism's exclusionary tendencies. In fact, what
follows is as much an intervention *in* deconstruction as an intervention
using deconstruction—in several senses. The paragraphs above show
that my reading will intervene in what counts as "deconstruction"
within feminist theology, theology in general, and in certain corners
of feminist theory. My reading of Derrida and Irigaray also intervenes
in *their* work with race and gender. That is, it will confront them with
some of the same questions that I have posed to feminist theologians
and theorists. Only when they are read with these questions in view
will their ability to help whitefeminism past this impasse come to light.

My aim, then, is not primarily to produce a better account of Derrida
or Irigaray and their relationship to each other than other scholars have
offered. As the following chapters will indicate, my reading of them
largely supports those accounts that are now recognized by philosophers and feminist theorists as setting the standards for understanding
these two complex thinkers. My aim is, rather, to put Derrida and Irigaray to work on a thorny problem within whitefeminism. In the
course of carrying out this aim, my own views of what these thinkers
do and how they can be read in relation to each other will emerge,
though only insofar as such accounts are necessary to my larger project.
Let me explain what I understand "putting Derrida and Irigaray to
work" to involve. In *Positions*, Derrida describes deconstruction as a
"method" that "is not a voluntary decision or an absolute beginning,
does not take place just anywhere, or in an absolute elsewhere. An

incision, precisely, it can be made only according to lines of force and forces of rupture that are localizable in the discourse to be deconstructed."[68]

This project takes its mark from the lines of force that rupture feminist discourse's claim to theorize and theologize on behalf of women. The divide between race and gender uncovered by this chapter constitutes a rupture in feminist discourse. Feminism's claim to work on behalf of all women founders upon it. In the remaining chapters, I will follow the lines of force that constitute that rupture to their point of exhaustion. This book takes its trajectory from the divide between race and gender. Since feminist theory and theology prioritize gender to the exclusion of race, I will first follow that side of the divide to its end; that is, to the point where the divide between gender and race comes to a close as woman opens onto race (chaps. 2–4). I will turn next to the other side of the divide, race as exclusive of gender, and follow that exclusionary gesture to its end—to the point where race opens onto woman (chaps. 5–6).

The individual chapters within this book take their mark, in turn, from more specific lines of force that lead into and out of the race/gender divide. Each of the levels of questioning opened up by my analysis of feminist theology and theory represents a line of force or rupture that these chapters will follow. Following these lines of force as they emerge sets a specific trajectory for the way I present Derrida and Irigaray. The first lines of force to appear involve questions about authors and texts, texts and contexts. For this reason, I begin the following chapters with a discussion of the Derrideanism, "There is nothing outside the text." Following this line of force allows me to contest certain misreadings of this phrase as I unpack its significance for my project. At the heart of Derrida's "text" lie sexual, gendered, and raced dynamics that I will argue are integral to my project. Chapter 2 will argue that woman and God are linked together in and by the general text that Derrida uncovers. Following woman to her end requires a third chapter on Derrida's woman. At the end of that chapter, Derrida's woman has reached its point of exhaustion and opens onto its *supplément*, Irigaray's woman. Irigaray's woman, in turn, reaches its point of exhaustion/closure where race finds a point of entry. At the end of that chapter, the divide between race and gender is shown to be a hymeneal membrane rather than an absolute barrier. That a hymeneal membrane can be so successful at preventing race and woman from coming into contact in whitefeminist thought still leaves unanswered questions about what grounds the elision of race in whitefeminist thinking. Having carried one side of the divide to its end, it will then be time to pick up the other side and follow it. In chapter 5, I turn back to Derrida's work with race as *supplément* in order to uncover race's place within the context that shapes whitefeminist theorizing and theologizing. While I find the work of Derrida and Irigaray uniquely able to get to the roots of whitefeminism's exclusionary tendencies and to offer strategies for overcoming them, their work can only lay the groundwork for letting the difference race makes to woman really register. The book's final chapter goes over the ground that reading race and woman through Derrida and Irigaray has prepared. It closes by indicating directions for following up on this work as indicated by African American feminist theory.

Before I embark on this journey, a word about cures. The outcome of this project remains to be seen. I do not aim to heal the rupture this chapter has exposed in feminist discourse (in the sense of covering it over with new skin) but to follow that rupture to its closure / opening onto something else. Thus, this project will not accomplish a cure, properly speaking, of whitefeminism's exclusionary gestures. Insofar as it offers a remedy, it does so in a double sense. The next chapter will feature Derrida's discussion of *pharmakon*, the Greek root of English words connected to the idea of cure. *Pharmakon*, Derrida argues, plays undecidably between two meanings; "remedy" and "poison." Neither meaning can be absolutely forbidden in the name of the other. What follows may seem like a poison insofar as it falls short of bringing all women together in a united theoretical, theological, or political front. However, as this chapter has argued, feminism has never been a happy whole. It is my belief that feminism's future requires that it investigate its ungrounded ground. Its best hope lies in finding ways to build on the ever-shifting ground of women's diversity.

2

"Nothing Outside the Text"?

Introduction

The previous chapter uncovered a divide between race and gender at work in whitefeminist theology and theory. This divide affects texts written by whitefeminist theologians and theorists that exceed, resist, and even work against their authors' explicit intentions. I suggested at the end of the previous chapter that moving beyond this impasse, which has constituted whitefeminism's dealings with race, requires exploring the contours of the divide. This chapter launches that task by following the first lines of force that emerged as symptomatic of the divide. These lines center on questions about the relationship between authors, their texts, and their larger contexts. What is it about textuality that enables the divide's persistent and resistant inscription of whitefeminist texts? The divide registers within whitefeminist texts but does not seem to originate there. What does this say about the relationship between the inside and outside of texts?

I turn to the work of Jacques Derrida to begin exploring the race/gender divide because the questions mentioned above figure centrally in his work. Moreover, woman also constitutes a centrifugal axis in the dynamics of textuality that Derrida uncovers. Derrida's woman, like whitefeminism's woman, is not explicitly racially marked. Thus, the issue of textuality links up quickly with the central element of the divide, woman as separate from race. At the same time, following Derrida's woman points beyond the race/gender divide.

To those under the sway of certain popular conceptions of Derrida's work, it may seem strange (if not impossibly absurd) to suggest a connection between his work and critiques of oppression. According to most of its theological press, deconstruction is the latest version of nihilism. Some African American and whitefeminist theorists have cautiously embraced certain aspects of deconstruction as helpful, but only up to a point.[1] Many of these theorists argue that feminism ultimately must leave Derrida behind and go its own way. Whitefeminist theolo-

gians, in particular, exhibit considerable skepticism about the degree
to which an alliance with Derrida is possible, much less fruitful, for
feminist theology. Thus, the next two chapters will also have to consider these views of Derrida's work. In this chapter, in particular, I will
contend with certain readings of Derrida's work that underlie negative
assessments of its value for feminism or theology. I will argue that
dismissals of his work as nihilistic on the grounds that it reduces everything to textuality rest on a complex set of misconstruals. In addition,
I will argue against those who approve of certain elements of deconstruction but exempt their own theological or feminist projects from it.

What Text? Where Is "There"? What "Nothing"?

Whitefeminist theologians are skeptical about the value of Derrida's
work for feminism in general and for their projects in particular. While
most whitefeminist theologians refer to specific Derridean writings,
their depictions of the import of deconstruction seem to be mediated
by the history of its reception in theology and, to some extent, in whitefeminist theory. Encounters between Derrida and theology, in particular, have been dominated by multifaceted and multilayered misconstruals of his work. These misconstruals are multifaceted in that they
target several aspects of his thinking / discourse. They are multilayered
in that few theologians' dealings with deconstruction are based on
firsthand readings of Derrida's own work. Rather, most discussions of
"deconstruction"—insofar as they discuss Derrida at all—rely on the
texts of some appropriation or interpretation, at best, of Derrida and,
at worst, of issues or questions that are purported to be "Derridean."[2]
The terrain of this problematic encounter between theology and deconstruction can be explored by following what coalesces around what
has become a key Derrideanism, "There is nothing outside the text."
This phrase also centers feminist theorists' stances toward Derrida, pro
and con. Paying careful attention to what Derrida means by "nothing
outside the text" will allow me to challenge misconstruals of deconstruction and to begin making my case for its value for my project.

   Theological and whitefeminist responses to deconstruction rest primarily on two readings of "there is nothing outside the text" that can
appear singly or in combination. Perhaps the most common response
takes this phrase to mean language refers to nothing outside itself; thus
everything is "text" in some sense.[3] Rather than accurately revealing
"reality," texts open onto "nothing." If texts do not refer to reality,
then "truth" (understood as correspondence to reality) is an illusion.

Without this extratextual referent to serve as the standard, so the story goes, it is impossible to distinguish between good and bad interpretations, good and bad texts—indeed, good and bad in general. This reading dominated early assessments of deconstruction's impact on theology. In the opening essay of *Deconstruction and Theology* (1982), Carl Raschke claimed that deconstruction exposed the founding concepts of theology as mere discursive forms that refer to nothing real. "Deconstruction," Raschke writes, "is in the final analysis *the death of God put into writing*" (3; author's emphasis).[4] Many theologians simply dismissed Raschke's claim (and with it, deconstruction) as too reductionistic to have a real target. Other theologians since Raschke have argued against it, but this view of deconstruction has maintained a hold on the theological imagination.[5]

Extending the phrase to "there is nothing outside the text *of metaphysics*" yields a different reading. Deconstruction is said to proclaim the end of a *particular* text, the corpus of western philosophy. In its most dramatic form, this reading argues that deconstruction exposes the goals of philosophical inquiry—truth, knowledge, an all-embracing account of reality—to be illusions.[6] A less dramatic version of this school of thought reads "metaphysics" in a more traditional way as the science of being. This version interprets deconstruction as arguing that philosophy has been dominated by the illusory assumption that full presence lies at the heart of reality.[7] More recent assessments of deconstruction's relevance for theology adopt this view of deconstruction's target. Rather than seeing deconstruction as spelling the demise of theology, theologians like Kevin Hart and Jean-Luc Marion see deconstruction as a necessary discipline for theology. They concede deconstruction's veracity as an account of the limits of language and philosophy, but view these insights as old news to theology. Unlike philosophy, which concerns itself with pure reason, theology has always been an *apologia/ interpretatio* of faith, Hart argues. It uses reason as a tool, but knows reason will eventually meet its limit and there exhaust its usefulness for the life of faith.[8] Marion sees deconstruction as providing resources to carry theology beyond its last idol, thinking God in terms of being. In both cases, deconstruction causes problems for particular *concepts* of God inherited from philosophy, but not for the true God to whom Christianity witnesses.[9] These theologians argue that exposing theology to the purifying fires of deconstruction will remove its metaphysical dross and restore theology to its more pristine form.[10]

Whitefeminist readings of deconstruction inside and outside theology have followed a similar route of interpretation. Whitefeminists often embrace the linguistic reading of "nothing outside the text" as exposing the tentativeness of all linguistic constructions. Similarly, they view the philosophical reading of deconstruction as providing ammunition against claims of universal referentiality for philosophical structures that have served to oppress women.[11] Thus, many whitefeminist thinkers see deconstruction as a potentially useful tool for critiquing male privilege and the systems that perpetuate it, but they rarely see feminism *itself* as touched by deconstruction's challenges.[12] Like more recent theological readers, they see deconstruction as confirming insights already realized by their home discipline.

The strongest resistance to deconstruction from whitefeminist theory and theology alike follows from both readings of "nothing outside the text." Whether viewed as describing linguistic entrapment or philosophical limitation, deconstruction is criticized for cutting the ground out from under ethics and politics. As Elizabeth Grosz and Nancy Holland note, many of Derrida's whitefeminist critics see deconstruction as concerned with reading and writing texts. His work is, thus, totally without political import and therefore of limited value at best for feminism.[13] Other readers raise even stronger objections. If the distinction between good and bad is merely linguistic play, if the philosophical concepts that ethics presupposes are questionable or illusory, then ethics in any form other than playful noncommitment seems no longer possible.[14] If deconstruction spells the demise of ethics, its critics say, then neither feminism nor theology will survive in its rarefied atmosphere.[15] Not surprisingly, this critique dominates whitefeminist theologians' view of Derrida's work. Rebecca Chopp cites Derrida approvingly as one of several thinkers who call attention to the historical and philosophical issues involved in recognizing that language shapes reality, but turns to French whitefeminist theorists for the same insight but without Derrida's ethical ambiguity.[16] Sallie McFague appreciates Derrida's "highly perceptive critique of Western metaphysics," but argues that his work cannot provide criteria against which to determine the relative value of conflicting constructions. Sharon Welch aligns Derrida, Foucault, and Irigaray together in her assessment. Welch appreciates their insistence that emotion, power interests, etc. shape thinking, but finds it troubling that they assert "the death of the author and the self just as women and other marginalized people begin to write and assert their identity politically and culturally." Wendy Farley provides more positive comments about Derrida. She applauds him for providing a critique of the desire for plenitude and presence, and she acknowledges an ethical dimension to his work. However, she seems to see that dimension as separate from "nothing outside the text." Mary McClintock Fulkerson appropriates the Derridean trope of the gra(ph)ft to name the complex process of reading/writing produced by the interplay of readers, their communities, and texts. She distinguishes her use of this trope to examine specific and highly determined sites of reading and writing from Derrida's use of the same trope to emphasize the endless play of interpretation.[17]

If these accounts of deconstruction and its implications were able to stand unchallenged, the project I have set for myself would indeed be doomed from the outset. However, a more accurate reading of "nothing outside the text" shows them to be misconstruals. Several of Derrida's interpreters have refuted the interpretations of this phrase that I have argued underlie those responses. Rodolphe Gasché's *The Tain of the Mirror* offers an especially strong defense of Derrida against both readings of "nothing outside the text." Gasché argues that understanding what Derrida means by this phrase requires, first of all, rethinking what "text" means within it. According to Gasché, readers have taken text to mean at least one of the following things: (1) the "sensibly palpable . . . transcription of an oral discourse" that transmits the speaker's original intention (text as sensible object), (2) a combination of signifiers and signifieds that can be intellectually apprehended (text as intelligible object), and (3) a "dialectical sublation" of both previous meanings (the concept of text).[18] In each case, the definition of text posits it as a self-enclosed whole with clearly demarcated borders between inside and outside. That is, text as sensible object is fully contained within the covers that constitute the border between the inside and outside of a book. Text as intelligible object is apprehensible because it constitutes a clearly marked totality. Text as the sublation of both sensible text and intelligible text is the once-and-for-all total disclosure of intelligible content through its sensible form.

None of these definitions of text fit what Derrida means by the text outside of which there is nothing, according to Gasché. Rather than reducing everything to a totality outside of which nothing exists, "there is nothing outside the text" calls attention to what lies at the boundaries of totalities and of clear demarcations. Gasché first notes that Derrida explicitly rejects each of these definitions in turn as describing what he means by text. Instead, Derrida sees these three definitions as "forming the running border of what used to be called a text."[19] It is this "running border" that interests Derrida and that Gasché calls the "general text." What gives rise to distinctions between inside and outside? What enables closure? Properly speaking, nothing gives rise to these

distinctions and expectations, yet they recur again and again. Gasché
calls attention to the French phrase itself: il n'y a pas de hors-texte; that
is, there is no pre-text, no outside-text.[20] This general text is, properly
speaking, neither "text" in its ordinary senses or "reality." That is, as
a running border it is not a totality (and therefore cannot have an inside
or outside); as a running border, it does not, properly speaking, occupy
a fixed place. It belongs to the order of the es gibt, Gasché writes—not to
the order of being. To say "there is nothing outside the text" means, in
its most general sense, that this general text that funds and founds distinctions between inside and outside, desire for closure, and so on, structures our thinking, writing, and doing without our asking it to do so.

This general text carries implications for ordinary texts, but not those
implications assumed by deconstruction's critics. Rather than reducing
everything to literature or textuality, the general text funds the distinctions that we draw between text and reality, between literature and
philosophy, between a particular text and other texts. To be sure, the
general text lends an abyssal quality to the relationships among ordinary texts as well as between them and itself. There is nothing (properly speaking, given the status of the general text) standing outside
texts to bring the process of referentiality to a halt in full plenitude of
meaning. However, as a careful reading of Derrida's texts will show,
this state of affairs does not result in a collapse into a black hole; rather
it renders legible the chains of intertextuality that constitute reading
and writing. Those chains involve links between texts and between
texts and their contexts (including the general text) that both ground
and unground texts' claims to wholeness. As Geoffrey Bennington puts
it, rather than "flattening everything into a single homogeneous text,"
readings framed by this understanding of nothing outside the text
"multipl[y] differences within the text, whose unity and closure were
given only by the context supposed to surround it."[21]

Several scholars, including Gasché, have offered potent correctives
to the common perception of Derrida's relationship to philosophy.[22]
Critics of deconstruction operating out of that perception accuse Derrida of reducing the entire philosophical tradition to one homogeneous
text. Bennington's description of what Derridean reading accomplishes
also applies to Derrida's readings of the philosophers. Derrida's questions to philosophy are directed toward exposing what lies at the margins of philosophy's inscription by the general text, thereby constituting the limits of philosophy. Uncovering those limits requires
"de-construction": taking philosophical texts apart in order to uncover
the structures that undergird them. Thus, as a number of his philosoph-

ical defenders point out, Derrida continues philosophy's traditional interest in uncovering foundations.[23] Gasché uses the term "infrastructures" to name the (non)founding (non)concepts employed by Derrida (*différance, supplément,* re-mark, trace, etc.) in order to highlight their productive and foundational (quasi-transcendental) status. The foundations uncovered by deconstruction, however, refuse fixity.[24] They give rise to distinctions between inside/outside, philosophy and its others (e.g., literature), but unsettle absolute boundaries between these distinctions. Each infrastructure is a chain of referentiality that cannot be brought to rest in plenitude of meaning. Similarly, the infrastructures together constitute a chain in which each supplements the other; that is, each supplants and stands in for the other, but not without remainder. This same structure holds for the chain of the philosophical tradition. As Gasché argues in another context, deconstruction carries philosophy's aims to their opening/closure in dissemination—a dispersal of those same founding aims and concepts. This opening/closure makes it "impossible to establish *what,* in the end, rules the exchanges between the universal and the disseminating Othering" (*Inventions of Difference,* 78) because dissemination is as foundational to philosophy as its aim toward closure and completion.

Does this mean deconstruction is really destruction, a method of violent reading that obliterates any distinctions between philosophers? Does deconstruction destroy philosophy by tearing off the flimsy veil it has produced to disguise the Nothingness at the heart of reality? No, Derrida offers careful readings of the philosophical tradition that attend to the chains of intertextuality that constitute it and that reveal each philosopher as distinctive. These readings uncover, first, a persistent pattern in the tradition of philosophy, which is what Derrida means by the text of western metaphysics. These readings also take this text to its limits in what lies outside it. Is this "outside" an Absolute Nothing (vs. an Absolute Presence)? Gasché offers a particularly effective answer to this question. Nihilism (as Nietzsche pointed out) is itself a metaphysical position. Asserting that an absolute absence lies at the heart of reality renders absence in terms of presence; that is, in terms of metaphysics. As Gasché argues (and as I will show in the following pages), "there is an Absolute Nothing outside the text" describes the fruits of Derrida's reading of philosophy as inaccurately as "there is an Absolute Something outside the text." Gasché describes Derrida as a "heterologist"; as a thinker directed toward radical alterity.[25] But the otherness Derrida seeks is neither the otherness of absolute founding principles nor the otherness of negativity or opposition.

The alterity Derrida uncovers "has nothing of an essence or truth" about it. In Gasché's words,

> It is irretrievably plural and cannot be assimilated, digested, repre-
> sented, or *thought as such,* and hence put to work by the system of
> metaphysics. . . . Derrida's Otherness is, consequently, neither a lack,
> a substantial void, an absence susceptible of determination. . . . [It is]
> more and less than negativity. It is *less* because it has no meaning, no
> signification; . . . It is *more* than negativity because it is the "medium"
> (the nonmediating medium) in which philosophy comes to carve out
> its (dialectical, and hence sublatable) contradictions. (*Tain,* 103–4)

Programmatic statements about Derrida's work are simultaneously helpful and dangerous.[26] While the guides they establish warn against certain misinterpretations, they can play into the hands of reductionist readings of Derrida. Describing Derrida in quasi-transcendental terms threatens to turn him into a philosopher of the most traditional sort. On the other hand, it is difficult for claims about a vertiginous chain of referentiality to register as anything other than nihilistic when presented as programmatic statements.[27] The only cure for both ailments lies in careful readings of Derrida's work itself, to which I will now turn. Understanding what Derrida means by "nothing outside the text" is important to my project because its dynamics explain whitefeminism's apparent lack of control over its own texts. Also, his work renders abyssal structures not as nihilistic but as pointing toward a "beyond." In that sense as well, reading Derrida can indicate directions in which whitefeminism might travel to go beyond its current impasse. The content of Derrida's general text is also important to my project. My reading of Derrida argues that sexual and gendered dynamics lie at the heart of this general text and mark the boundary between its inside and outside. My reading will confirm elements of other accounts of Derrida's work by philosophers and theologians, including those discussed up to this point. Because it is funded by a distinctive agenda, my reading will develop these dynamics in Derrida's work that others either mention in passing or miss altogether. Most of the philosophical apologias for Derrida's work take note of its implications for feminist concerns or for theological concerns, but they do not link the two. Furthermore, where philosophical apologias locate these implications at a secondary level, my reading makes them central issues. Similarly, theologians have offered accounts of God's place in Derrida's work while ignoring or misconstruing woman's place. Whitefeminist theorists attend to woman's place in Derrida's oeuvre while ignoring God's place.[28] My reading of Derrida argues that the figures of woman and

God go together in Derrida's work. To miss one or the other is to miss central implications of Derrida's work for feminism and theology, respectively. The remainder of this chapter will focus on three essays from one of Derrida's early volumes, *Dissemination*.[29] Like other interpreters of Derrida, I find this volume a particularly effective place to ground an investigation into the meaning and ramifications of "nothing outside the text."[30] My reading of *Dissemination* will concur with and expand upon the general parameters of Gasché's interpretation of this phrase. In addition, my reading elicits the stakes that whitefeminist theology has in "nothing outside the text." This, in turn, points toward the importance of feminist deconstructive theology for feminism in general.

"This (therefore) will not have been a book": *Dissemination*

One of the first of Derrida's books to appear in English translation, *Dissemination* focuses on the status of writing, literature, and the book in relation to truth. It traces the trajectory of the careers of writing and the book through western history beginning (though not absolutely or at first) with Plato and ending (though not absolutely or exclusively) with Stéphane Mallarmé. The sense in which these two figures mark the "ends" of the book's inscription within the economy of truth for Derrida requires clarification. He does *not* claim that Plato originates the pattern and Mallarmé eliminates it. Insofar as Derrida's argument proceeds chronologically, a certain reading of Plato founds a structural pattern that Derrida exposes in much of subsequent western assumptions about books and writing. Likewise, Mallarmé marks a culmination point of disruptions of this pattern that accompany the book's career in western thought.

Dissemination opens with an essay bearing many titles, all of which resonate with "Il n'y a pas de hors-texte." "HORS-LIVRE" (announced in large type, all capitals) immediately troubles distinctions between inside/outside and assumptions about texts as self-enclosed wholes. The title announces that what follows is "outside the book," yet that outside appears *within* the book's covers. The second title, "HORS D'OEUVRE" (translated as "Outwork"), carries on the disturbance inaugurated by its predecessor. "Hors d'oeuvre" sets what follows outside the work proper, but as a tantalizing morsel designed to whet the appetite for the main course. "Outwork" sets itself up as a literary hors d'oeuvre; a preface, in other words. But the last title offered in the smallest print announces the topic to be discussed: "prefacing." Thus the "Hors d'oeuvre" announces its intent to take *itself* (or what it appears to be) as a topic.

The text of "Outwork" carries forward the disruptions of inside/outside announced by its titles. It immediately begins to breakdown expectations for "Outwork" as a preface as well as expectations for *Dissemination* as a book. Derrida writes:

> This (therefore) will not have been a book.
>   Still less, despite appearances, will it have been a collection of *three* "essays" whose itinerary it would be time, after the fact, to recognize; whose continuity and underlying laws could now be pointed out; indeed, whose overall concept or meaning could at last, with all the insistence required on such occasions, be squarely set forth. I will not feign, according to the code, either premeditation or improvisation. These texts are assembled otherwise; it is not my intention here to *present* them. (D, 3)

Derrida has refused the genre of the book and the gestures of prefacing, but in the name of what? In what sense does the "Outwork" constitute the outside of "work" and of "book"? In what sense does *Dissemination*, despite appearances to the contrary, constitute an hors livre? The intentions signaled here are borne out by the content of "Outwork" and the (non)book it opens. *Dissemination* begins, not with Plato, but between Plato and Mallarmé—with the history of medieval encyclopedistics. "Outwork" deals not with preliminaries but with serious and close readings of philosophy (notably, Hegel and Marx). The refusal of prefacing opens toward hors livre and hors texte through an investigation into the problematics of the preface and the book.

According to Derrida, medieval encyclopedias aimed toward a complete cataloguing of all that was known about all that existed. This ideal reflected a larger cultural notion, that of the Book of Nature whose author is God. Since Nature is God's handiwork, it can serve as a cipher through which God can be understood; it is a book in which the secrets of the divine ordering of the cosmos can be read. The ordered unity of nature mirrors the mind of the supremely intelligent being behind it. Encyclopedists wanted to produce a book that reflected its subject matter (all that is) as accurately as nature reflected the mind of its Author. Like Nature, the encyclopedia would be a self-enclosed whole written by an author in control of what he says.

It is crucial at this point to understand what Derrida is doing with the notion of book. He is not attempting to expose the aim of encyclopedistics as inherently flawed because it is an impossible aim. He is not making judgments as to the feasibility (or lack thereof) of such a project. Nor is he going to line up specific attempts and judge their relative success or failure. He is, rather, *soliciting* the idea of the book (in French, *solliciter* means to question, to disturb, to exacerbate, to shake up, to cause to tremble) in order to reveal what constitutes it and what exceeds it.[31] The first step in shaking up the concept of the book involves an archaeological move, coaxing out the "deep structures" of a cultural imagination that would allow the *idea* of the pursuit of a universal book of truth to occur. The conditions of possibility for even *thinking* of encyclopedias arise out of a specular economy of truth. Truth is grounded in God, the one being in whom perfect union between knower and known occurs. Since God created the cosmos, its truth and its value lies in its identity as its creator's reflection. Thus, the central speculum or mirror in this economy is the cosmos. The encyclopedia constitutes a second set of mirrors reflecting both sides of the relation between the cosmos and its creator. The author's relationship to the encyclopedia mirrors God's relationship to the cosmos. The encyclopedia itself attempts to mirror the cosmos, as the cosmos mirrors God. Yet that ideal is never realized; encyclopedias are begun but never completed. Derrida shows that the failure of encyclopedists to produce such a book is not accidental, but intrinsic to the structure of the book itself. The ideal of the book as a perfect mirror and a self-enclosed whole carries the possibility of its own failure within it. The faultline in the concept of the book also runs through the specular economy it reflects. The fissure appears as Derrida follows the history of the book/preface through the work of Hegel, Marx, and Novalis.

At first glance, Hegel appears simply to perpetuate the aim of encyclopedistics though with a trinitarian twist. Hegel's philosophy of totality aims to comprehend reality in an ultimately self-contained whole. He uncovers a trinitarian pattern of development in all the different arenas of human existence (from religion, to history, to logic itself) that come into his field of vision. The pattern of Hegel's speculative logic governs all of his analyses and indeed proves to be a rich heuristic device for comprehending the world. Hegel insists, however, that this logic is no mere pattern; rather, it is the dynamic that constitutes reality. It comes to be in and through its articulation in the world. Hegel names this fundamental reality *Geist* (spirit). *Geist* comes to be itself through three moments—the in-itself, the for-itself, and the in-and-for-itself. In the first moment, it exists as mere idea. In the second, it comes into actualization through being realized in some aspect of history, human experience, and so forth. In its final moment, the complete union between ideal and real is achieved as the real is taken up into the ideal—

the Concept Itself (*Begriff*). Each moment involves the *Aufhebung* (pres-
ervation and supersession) of the previous moment. Thus, the in-itself
is preserved and superseded in the for-itself, which is in turn preserved
and superseded in the in-and-for-itself. The present moment is shaped
by/reflects the prior one but also incorporates it.[32]

Each of Hegel's books codifies a piece of the whole but the very
existence of a preface in each book troubles each book's claim to totality. As a self-enclosed whole, the book should need no introduction
because it can speak for itself. Yet Hegel continues to write prefaces.
The rhetoric of Hegel's prefaces dismisses them as unnecessary excess
baggage; as mere preliminaries to the *real* matter, the book itself. Paradoxically, however, what he dismisses as excess baggage he also uses
to shore up the book-as-a-whole. Hegel's prefaces aim to protect the
book's insides from what lies outside it. In laying out parameters for
reading the book, the preface guards the book's borders against excess
in the form of misinterpretations. Thus, prefaces exhibit a desire for
authorial mastery over the book-as-a-whole even as they constitute the
excess of that desire/aim.

It is important to note that Derrida is not offering a psychological
account of Hegel's motivations as a philosopher; Hegel's intentionality
is not in question here. Derrida's questions aim at a level that lies below
or outside Hegel's intentions: the level of the structural necessities governing Hegel's text. Derrida's double reading of Hegel's work reveals a
double writing in several senses. Derrida argues that the preface plays
between absolute oppositions, such as those between book and subject
matter, text and reality. It writes doubly; viewed as an Hegelian in-
itself, it is the seed out of which germinates the real discourse, the book
(or philosophy) itself. Insofar as it is textual excess, Derrida suggests,
it is the seed that escapes the mastery of its father/author. In both of
its roles, the preface elides any absolute division between itself and the
book, the ideal and the real, preliminary and real philosophy, textuality
and reality. Even as it brings these divisions into view, it refuses fixation within them.

Derrida's reading also uncovers something larger than Hegel at
work in Hegel's texts; namely, the specular economy and its double,
the ideal book. That ideal doubles back on itself insofar as fissures appear in it. Hegel's prefaces are symptomatic of the preface/book relationship in general. Prefaces double back on the aim of completion.
They acknowledge a lack even as they attempt to fill it. They reflect
the text, even as they disturb its wholeness. These dynamics are not,

properly speaking, under Hegel's control; they are not, properly speaking, either inside or outside Hegel's texts. Alternatively, they are as much inside as they are outside. To recall Gasché, they constitute a running border that disrupts completion and calls divisions between inside and outside into question.

The fissure in the book and in the specular economy is reflected in the larger pattern of Hegelian thinking. The dynamics attending textuality are repeated and reflected in Hegel's version of reality, further confirming Gasché's interpretation of "nothing outside the text." According to the conventional notion of book, Hegel's books should reflect their subject matter, the tracing of the movement of *Geist* through all realms of human endeavor. Hegel's prefaces suggest that he wants his books to fulfill that function. However, the very movement of *Geist* troubles the conventional notion of book even as Hegel enacts that notion. As previously noted, Hegel dismisses prefaces as preliminary to the real matter at hand. Derrida argues that the trajectory of Hegel's speculative logic problematizes this offhand dismissal of prefaces. Given that the three moments exhaust reality on the macrocosmic and microcosmic levels, it is difficult to see just what "preliminary to philosophy" would mean. If nothing escapes the movement of absolute spirit, the preface should either be the in-itself of philosophy / the book or it should not be writable.

The fissure brought into view by the preface extends into Hegel's philosophy as a whole. Derrida argues that, even as each book reflects the movement of *Geist* in a discreet field, each book also anticipates *Geist*'s next movement. Thus, each book serves as a preface to the next, allowing Derrida to argue that Hegel's oeuvre can be read as a series of hors d'oeuvres leading to the main course, the *Science of Logic*.[33] However, the *Science of Logic* can no more do without its hors d'oeuvres than its predecessors could do without their prefaces. Thus, the dynamics of prefacing problematize the accomplishment *without remainder* of the movement of *Geist*. They resist sublation in reasserting the preface / book dynamic with each of Hegel's inquiries. Their resistance, Derrida argues, opens up a fissure in Hegel's speculative logic that itself resists the closure *Aufhebung* tries to accomplish. Thus, on the one hand, Hegel carries out the legacy of the medieval encyclopedists by attempting vast sweeps over the landscape of western thought and culture. On the other hand, the pattern of the sweeps disrupts the distinct separations between the thing surveyed and the survey itself. Furthermore, the smooth trinitarian logic of these vast sweeps finds *itself* disrupted by

what eludes its grasp and yet sets it in motion. The questions raised
for Hegel's speculative logic by prefaces reveal and reflect a fissure in
the notion of book and its specular logic, and vice versa.

Marx's reversal of the Hegelian dialectic reduplicates in another field
a certain continuity with the notion of book even as it exacerbates the
disruption set in motion by Hegel. In the preface to the second edition
of *Capital*, Marx defends himself against charges that he is perpetuating
Hegelian idealism. Instead of Hegel's vision of the ideal realizing itself
through the material, Marx views the ideal as the real transposed by
the mind into thought. He goes on to distinguish between the relationship of the ideal and the real in the order of inquiry and their relationship within the order of presentation. Within the order of inquiry, the
ideal *appropriates* the material. Within the order of presentation, if the
presentation is successful, the ideal *mirrors* the material.[34] The reflections that appear in *Capital* are not, however, whole and perfect images.
Capital moves in fits and starts. The preface, like the other texts of *Capital*, exhibits the same markings. Rather than being a map that sets the
parameters for reading, Marx's preface to *Capital* mirrors the breaks,
tangents, and revisions that characterize the main body of the work.
On the one hand, then, Marx's dialectic keeps specular logic alive (the
book mirrors the matter). On the other hand, Marx's reprioritization
of the ideal and the real arises from an awareness that what he names
"materiality" eludes specular logic to some degree. This sets a task for
Derrida; namely, "to find out what it is that, written under the mask
of empiricism, turning speculation upside down, *also does something else*
and renders a Hegelian sublation of the preface impracticable" (*D*, 33;
author's emphasis).

Like Hegel, Marx's dealings with prefaces are symptomatic of larger
forces at work in his writing. Derrida claims that the logic that divides
ideal and real constitutes one of the instituting gestures of metaphysics
(and, insofar as philosophy is metaphysics, of philosophy, too). Philosophy, like the book, is understood to be on the side of the ideal; it
reflects reality, which is understood as its "other." Derrida argues that
philosophy deals with its others by appropriating their negative image
via the mirror of its specular logic. Yet the resistance of this other to
appropriation marks both Hegelian and Marxist dialectics. Marx has,
in Derrida's view, further opened the fissure in the relationship between text and reality.

The career of encyclopedistics takes one more notable turn in the
attempt at exhaustive cataloguing made by Novalis. Novalis envisions
his encyclopedia as a "scientific Bible—a model both real and ideal—

and the germ of all books" (*D*, 52). However, rather than the book perfectly reflecting its object (nature), Novalis envisions his encyclopedia as *completing* nature. Nature is in need of a supplement, and the text provides it. This major shift in the concept of the relation of book to nature repeats and carries forward what Marx and Hegel set in motion. Novalis starts from the recognition of a lack of a pregiven unity of nature and book. Rather, the unity has to be created/produced through the book. The book is a *supplément* that completes nature. What Derrida names the "closure of the book" hinges on this graphics of *supplémentation*. Derrida writes, "With the appearance of a book that, even if it passes for nature's double, is added to it in that duplication of the simulacrum, there is broached or breached a scientific or literary text that goes beyond the always-already-constitutedness of meaning and of truth within the theo-logico-encyclopedic space" (*D*, 53).

The possibility of a book as a perfect reflection of a "Nature" that precedes it (and itself reflects the mind of its own creator, the Father God) has come to its closure in Novalis's encyclopedia. The idea of literature, admitting a plurality of books rather than aiming to write *the* book, emerges out of the fissure that marks the closure of the book.

Hors D'Oeuvre, Hors Livre, Hors Texte

I noted at the beginning of my discussion of "Outwork" that its very title resonated with "il n'y a pas de hors-texte." I want now to consider briefly what "Outwork" has accomplished in terms of my previous discussion, via Gasché, of "nothing outside the text." First of all, what "Outwork" has revealed about texts in the ordinary senses of the word fits Gasché's description. The dynamics of prefacing trouble distinctions between inside and outside and call into question books' claims to completion and plenitude. Prefaces point toward the general text (and the meaning of "outside") by resisting incorporation into "text" in each of its three ordinary senses. First, in terms of text as sensible object, prefaces appear between a book's covers; physically, they reside inside the book or text. However, they are written to be effaced by the real matter at hand, the book itself. Thus, insofar as they are properly extraneous to the book, prefaces interiorize the book's outside. Prefaces always appear at the front of the book but are usually written afterward. In that sense, too, they trouble the book as sensible object with a beginning, middle, and end. Second, in terms of text as intelligible object, prefaces refuse easy assignation to the inside or outside. Prefaces are extraneous to the content of the book, properly speaking, and yet they serve as mirrors reflecting that content and pointing the reader toward it. Prefaces also trouble the third meaning of "text," that is, the idea of the book-as-a-whole that communicates meaning-as-a-whole. Prefaces simultaneously constitute and guard against any excess (misinterpretation, especially) that would disrupt the book-as-a-whole.

The roots of the conditions that render texts' closure possible lie outside any particular text. Derrida traces the problematics of book and preface to the idea of book and, in turn, to the specular economy that gives rise to it. Within the terms of this economy, books reflect nature, which in turn reflects its author, God. The conditions that prevent the completion of the book also cut through the specular economy. The mirrors that constitute the economy reflect and refract one another thereby perpetuating a chain of referentiality that cannot be brought to closure. Rather than denying texts' ability to refer to reality, Derrida's analysis has shown that both "reality" and the texts attempting to represent reality accurately are *both* inscribed by a similar pattern. In that sense, texts represent reality rather well.

Has Derrida's reading of Hegel and Marx reduced philosophy to a homogeneous text? No, in fact, quite the contrary. Derrida's reading faithfully reproduces the differences between Marx and Hegel and between Novalis and other encyclopedists. On the other hand, Derrida's reading has uncovered a larger context that links these diverse texts together in a chain of referentiality or intertextuality. The medieval idea of the book and its relationship to reality is sublated—but not without remainder—in and by Hegel's books and their relationship to reality. The closure of the book is simultaneously an opening onto literature; the ideal of the single text opens onto multiple textualities.[35] The shift to Marx perpetuates the ideal book's aim toward closure even as it follows what exceeds that aim. The dynamics of reflection and refraction that constitute the specular economy are further reflected and refracted by Hegel and Marx; thus, their texts also reflect reality and its fissures rather well.

What about the "nothing" that is said to lie "outside" the text? Has Derrida's reading exposed an Absolute Nothing at the heart of reality where Absolute Presence was supposed to reside? What constitutes the running border of what counts as text? Rather than collapsing into a black hole, the general text opens first onto a chain of differences that make possible distinctions between inside and outside, text and reality, preface and book, Hegel and Marx. This is what Gasché calls the general text and what I will characterize in the next section as the text of metaphysics. That text, properly speaking, has no existence outside the particular instances of text/reality that it grounds and ungrounds; it becomes visible only through its effects. This general text, in turn, opens onto what funds it; what Irene Harvey calls the economy of *différance*.[36] A neologism created by Derrida that combines "difference" and "deferral," *différance* grounds and ungrounds this economy.[37] *Différance* is as far from being an absolute nothing as it is from being an absolute presence. It is the nonoriginary origin (neither present nor absent) of the text of metaphysics and its specular economy of truth. It is origin because it funds the distinctions between the various mirrors that make the specular economy go. The specular economy requires "difference-between" its various mirrors in order to function, but "difference-between" also defers the economy's closure and wholeness. *Différance* is a nonoriginary origin because it does not exist, properly speaking; we "know" it only through the traces it leaves in the effects it produces. It is never fully present to itself (How can difference as such be fully present?), and its (non)presence defers the full presence of what it originates. Thus, the economy of *différance* is both productive and disruptive; it grounds and ungrounds that to which it gives rise.[38]

Implications for Whitefeminist Theory and Theology and the Problem of Race

What import does this discussion of "nothing outside the text" hold for whitefeminist theory and theology and their troubled history with race? Contrary to some feminist's assumptions, Derrida's work does more than confirm insights already present in feminism; it opens feminism itself to questions about its place in relation to the general text, its specular economy, and the economy of *différance* that funds them. Reading whitefeminism's history with race against the background of "nothing outside the text" helps explain that history. It would appear that whitefeminism is as susceptible to the conditions of textuality and the specular economy as any other oeuvre. My discussion of whitefeminist theology and theory in chapter 1 showed that whitefeminism's dealings with race exceeded authorial intentions. Over and over again, strategies designed to take account of the difference race makes to woman go astray. This is not to say that whitefeminist writing on race all amounts to the same thing. On the contrary, feminist theology took account of concrete differences between women's historical and social locations, but an essential woman tempered and limited the effects of this attention. Critiques from African American women launched the debate over essentialism within whitefeminist theory, but whitefeminist theorists' failure to attend to the concrete differences race makes contributed to antiessentialism's failure to address white solipsism. Whitefeminist theory's turn to a multiple woman has yet to realize its potential, as well. It seems clear, then, that whitefeminist theory and theology are always already afflicted by *différance*. More specifically, however, it appears that race writes whitefeminism through *différance*. Race as *différance* grounds and ungrounds whitefeminist writing. The answer to white solipsism will not be papering over racial *différance*, but, as later chapters will argue, allowing racial *différance* to do its productive work.

Chapter 1 closed with (or opened onto) an invocation of the race / gender divide as an abyss that seems to threaten the end of feminist theology and theory. My argument so far in this chapter suggests more positive valences to that abyssal structure and to thinking about the "end" of feminist theology and theory. The abyssal structure of *différance* and of intertextuality may, paradoxically, provide the way beyond the race / gender divide. Moreover, taking that path may mean bringing whitefeminist theology and theory to their "ends" in several senses—as limit, as death, but also as goal and beginning. What registered initially as limit and death may also be a new beginning, or rather a return to the beginning. Let me address the "end" of feminist theology more specifically here. The figure of God has made its appearance as a central element within the text of western metaphysics and its specular economy. While attention to the next essay in *Dissemination* will add considerably to a sense of what Derrida shows us about God's place, "Outwork" already challenges Raschke's association of deconstruction with the death of God. "Outwork" does not support claims that God is a mere linguistic construct with no referent in reality. As shown above, both "text" and "reality" are products of a general text (which is not "mere language") and its specular economy. God (understood to be fully present to himself) constitutes the standard of value and truth within the specular economy. This economy is simultaneously produced and disrupted by another economy, the economy of *différance*. Its processes of differing and deferral—the spacings it engenders—fund the specular economy even as they prevent its closure in plenitude. The figure of God, as the center of the specular economy, also exhibits the effects of *différance*. The idea of God rests on the "difference-between" God and the world (God is the plenitude of presence that the cosmos reflects) and the chain of differences that follow from this difference funds the productive machinations of the specular economy. The play of *différance* also defers plenitude and closure thereby undercutting God's claim to mastery. *Différance* produces God as much as it undercuts his mastery.

To encourage whitefeminist theology to engage with Derrida on theological territory is not to bring it to its end in the sense of death. It is, rather, to bring whitefeminist theology to an end that is also *its* beginning. Feminist theology has a stake in undercutting the mastery of this God perhaps in order to make room for other manifestations of the sacred. Whitefeminist theory, in turn, has a stake in seeing white-feminist theology engage with deconstruction on this particular terrain. Insofar as God constitutes the center of the specular economy and its valuing of sameness, then undercutting his mastery will be an important aspect of breaking through the specular economy toward an economy rooted in *différance*. This is not to say that deconstructing God will bring about such an economy on its own, or that it will bring about an end to white solipsism on its own. Once again, the governing presence of the race/gender divide as a site where feminism meets its end as limit makes itself felt here. The importance of thinking the end of *white*feminism as limit in several senses also confronts us. Insofar as whitefeminism constitutes the end of *feminism* (i.e., it limits feminism to white women), then bringing it to its end (in the sense of limit or death) is to return to feminism's original end (as goal).

I want to turn now to the next essay in *Dissemination*, "Plato's Pharmacy." This essay begins where "Outwork" leaves off, in one sense—with the question of writing. However, it begins with issues of Plato and Platonism, suggesting that the book has always been accompanied by its closure/opening into writing. Reading through it will add to an understanding of the general text, or the text of western metaphysics, in several ways. First, where Gasché's discussion of the general text focused on two issues (inside/outside and plenitude), my discussion of "Plato's Pharmacy" will fill in a number of its other attributes. Second, it will show that, while philosophy constitutes a site where this text becomes legible, it is not the sole locus of the text's inscription. Thus, I will further specify the relationship between the text of metaphysics and philosophy. Reading this essay will also show why Derrida speaks in terms of a *text* of metaphysics. In addition to advancing these general goals, reading "Plato's Pharmacy" will also carry forward my particular project. It will allow me to develop a fuller account of God's place in relation to writing and, thus, in relation to the text of metaphysics. It will enable me to show that God's place and questions of woman's place are intimately connected.

The *Oikos* of Writing

The next section of *Dissemination*, "Plato's Pharmacy," focuses on the question of writing's value in western thinking through an exploration of its status in the Platonic corpus and the history of its interpretation.[39] Derrida's strategy of double reading does not seek to simply correct misinterpretations of Plato's texts (although this does go on), to refute Plato, or to refute Plato's critics. Derrida seeks to uncover certain structural necessities at work in Plato's discourse on writing (and the tradition of its interpretation and translation). Derrida concentrates on Plato because of Plato's locus as the founding moment in the tradition of western philosophy. In his words, Plato serves as a marker of one end of metaphysics. The structures of western thinking that Derrida wants to question coalesce here insofar as they trace their heritage to Plato. Derrida does *not* say that these structures "originate" here.[40] The shape we understand as belonging to Plato's text emerges from a complex network of previous thinkers (e.g., Socrates) and subsequent interpreters. This network plays the central role in the transmission of these structures.[41] The Platonic text *also* exhibits traces of the resistances to those structures Derrida wants to solicit. Derrida is not importing a foreign object into Plato's discourse on writing in order to destroy it but is calling our attention to aporias, convolutions, and contradictions that disrupt the smooth surface given to it by the tradition of its interpretation. This double reading and writing of the Platonic text through the history of its interpretation—a reading for both the roots of the text of metaphysics and what resists the text's mastery—reveals Plato's "anagrammatic" writing.[42]

Traditionally, the discussion of writing in the *Phaedrus* (and elsewhere in Plato's corpus) has been read as a condemnation of writing. Derrida argues for a more complex interpretation. His reading reveals, on the one hand, the attempt by the *Phaedrus* and other texts to master writing, understood as "other" to philosophy, by inscribing it in a certain "economy of truth," which, I believe, is a deliberate and apt metaphor. The question of the truth of writing is bound up in questions of "proper"/propriety/ property. Socrates and Phaedrus discuss writing's propriety (Is it good to write?) and its properties (What are the qualities of writing that determine its capacity for truth?).

The answers to these questions are governed by a logic of oppositionality. A collusion of oppositions—inside/outside, life/death, essence/ appearance, presence/absence—separates philosophy from myth, reality from textuality, speaking from writing. However, writing resists this attempt at mastery and thereby exposes the limits of this logic of oppositionality. In this instance, Derrida's double reading exposes both writing's circumscription by these oppositions and its resistance to their mastery. When Phaedrus asks Socrates about the truth of writing, Socrates responds by reciting the myth of its origin. Writing's truth, he says, is only available to us through a recitation of its history. This is particularly interesting because, at the beginning of the dialogue, Socrates dismissed myth from the scene both to allow it its own space and because it has nothing to do with the task of philosophy—the pursuit of truth/knowledge, especially self-knowledge. Myth, like writing, is philosophy's other. Now, writing calls him back to myth. Plato's inclusion of this myth is more than a simple borrowing. Derrida's analysis will show that the myth's structural elements coincide with certain features of Plato's thinking. What might seem to be an infection of philosophy by myth is possible because both are inscribed in this larger text. This coincidence, Derrida argues, calls any simple division between philosophy and mythology into question.

The myth goes as follows: Theuth, a minor god in the pantheon, presents the king of the gods with his invention, writing, in order that the king may determine its value. He presents it to him as a "recipe," according to the translation, for memory; a "remedy" for forgetfulness. The king, however, exposes Theuth as a deceiver. Rather than a cure for memory, he states, writing is a "poison." The king's diatribe against writing defines it according to clear-cut oppositions: good/evil, inside/outside, true/false, essence/appearance. It produces a bad thing, forgetfulness. It equips students with only a semblance of wisdom. However, Derrida's double reading of the Platonic text brings to light the interruptions of these oppositions that subvert this attempt to master writing.

Derrida highlights two particularly striking features of this myth: (1) writing's invocation as recipe/remedy and its nearly simultaneous dismissal as poison and (2) the play of father/son dynamics in this scene. When one turns to the Greek text of the *Phaedrus,* one finds that "remedy" and "poison" are translations of the same word, *pharmakon.* The translator has not made an error; according to the Greek lexicon, "remedy" and "poison" are two poles of this term's possible meaning. This translation even seems to fit the context.[43] However, it obscures the significant fact that Theuth and the king "remain within the unity of the same signifier. Their discourse plays within it" (*D,* 98). This translation of *pharmakon* obscures the play *of* that signifier within and between the oppositions of good/evil, inside/outside, and so on.[44]

The passage between these two poles of meaning also characterizes *pharmakon* in other locations within Plato's texts. The *Protagoras* classifies the *pharmakon* in the context of medicine with those things that are mixtures of good and bad. The *Philebus* spells out this ambiguity: the "good" of cure is offset by the ambiguousness of the curative agent. The *pharmakon* is suspect because it is artificial; it comes from the outside of the body. It interferes with the natural life of the disease and of the patient. Moreover, rather than eliminating the disease, it often encourages it to metastasize; the disease proceeds on its natural course—dislodged from its original site, dispersed but still alive.

To return to the scene of our departure, writing in the myth of its origin, retold by Socrates and as otherwise dealt with in the Platonic corpus, coincidentally enough, bears these same marks. The king in our myth casts suspicion on writing on the same grounds. Writing is artificial; it promotes reliance on marks outside the self for memory. Rather than curing forgetfulness, it actually provides fertile soil for its metastasis. However, insofar as the ambiguity of the *pharmakon* of writing remains in play, the strategy of mastery is marked by resistance. This is as much a part of the Platonic text as the strategy of mastery itself. Derrida's double reading exposes a double writing *about* and *of* writing that is Plato's text.

Following this play of the chain of significations in which *pharmakon*/writing is caught confirms and illustrates "nothing outside the text" as a description of intertextuality (a point developed earlier in this chapter). Texts are not written or read outside the contexts set for them by other texts. Put another way, texts are always already inscribed by other texts; the very condition of possibility of reading and writing *is* intertextuality.[45] In a certain sense, all reading and all writing doubles readings and writings that have gone before. That doubling is constitutive of reading and writing.

The first layer of this contextuality links various Platonic dialogues. *Pharmakon*'s inscription in the *Philebus* and the *Protagoras* resonates when it appears in the *Phaedrus*. The Platonic corpus is itself inscribed by larger texts (including its cultural/linguistic milieu). Plato does not invent *pharmakon*'s play. It is not even, strictly speaking, under his control. In fact, the effects of its play are not a question of Plato's meaning-to-say. Sometimes it seems that Plato deliberately exploits the duplicity of *pharmakon*'s connotations. At other times, he seems to leave it impracticable; at still other times, this play occurs regardless. Any clear answer to a question of who bears responsibility for the play of connotations quickly runs aground. The text of metaphysics inscribes as much as it is inscribed.

The limits placed on this textual play by the *translation* exhibit another layer of this contextuality. As I said, "remedy/recipe" and "poison" are not at all inaccurate, although they do block the play of the chain of significations. This blockage, Derrida says, is an effect of Platonism; another term for the logic of oppositionality that characterizes metaphysics. Clearly this logic does not come to an end once we move beyond Plato's location in time and space. In fact, Platonist readings of Plato exacerbate that logic in Plato's text. The translators essentially take the king's side, in this instance, but the king does not have the last word. The translators' efforts violate the *pharmakon's* undecidability, which withdraws into its reserve to be coaxed out at a future point. All of this is possible only *because of* the play of *pharmakon*.[46]

The second striking feature of the myth of writing is the play of father/son dynamics. This exploration reinforces the significance of contextuality and double reading/writing. Most important, it reveals the specular economy of truth (which governs the text of western metaphysics) to be patro-, logo-, heliocentric. The two characters in this mythical scene are father (the king/determiner of value) and son (Theuth). Derrida argues that it is no coincidence that writing is presented to this *father* so that he may determine its value, or that *writing* is presented to this father so that he may determine its value. Theuth (or a parallel figure) is found throughout different Near Eastern pantheons. His role is that of displacement, replacement, and difference. He is the god of writing, of linguistic differences, of death, of medicine, of counting. In Egyptian mythology, he is the god of the moon, invited by his father, the sun god, to ascend to the sky in his own nightly absence.

The trope of "father" figures prominently in relation to writing and beyond in the Platonic corpus. The relationships of fathers and sons in many instances parallel the relationship of the king and Theuth. I will look first at writing, which is understood to be a derivative form of *logos* (speech, but also reason, the organizing principle of being). Socrates images *logos* (in both senses) as a living organism, a *zoon*. A good speech, Socrates tells Phaedrus, should have an organic unity—it should flow naturally from the beginning, through the middle to the end. Like other living things, *logoi* have fathers. Socrates frequently refers to speakers as fathers of their speeches. Good speeches are of noble birth. Speech is preferable to writing because its father is there to watch over it, to prevent it from going astray. When *logos* is committed to writing, this benevolent paternal relation is somewhat compromised. Writing inscribes the absence of the father.

On the surface, this could seem like a trivial argument. However, patrocentrism plays a much larger role in Plato's logic. The economy of truth turns out to be ruled by fathers and their figures. The Greek word for father, *pater*, carries with it a polysemic network of its own. "Father," "capital," and "goods" are all meanings that resonate within *pater*. The metaphor of fatherhood marks discussions of the Good elsewhere in Plato's corpus. In the *Republic,* for example, Socrates declines to speak of the Good itself, offering instead to speak of its *offspring,* which are made in its likeness. He describes this as *counting up the interest* on capital. The offspring he goes on to discuss is the visible sun; it illuminates vision just as the Good illuminates the intellect. As analog, the sun stands in for the Good. This deferral, it turns out, is not a temporary avoidance. Socrates says one can no more speak directly about this Good/Father than one can look directly at the visible sun.[47] A similar movement occurs in the *Phaedo*. Direct contemplation of *ta onta* (beings) is impossible because it is too dangerous to the mind's eye. Socrates turned, therefore, to the realm of "ideas," according to the translator; although the Greek says *logoi*—to seek truth. *Logoi* in this broader sense protect our metaphorical eyes from the blinding metaphorical sun (*Republic*) *and* serve as our resource in its absence (*Phaedo*). These paternal relationships parallel the relationships of Theuth and the king. The locus of origin of *logos,* of the Good, and ultimate value is accorded to the paternal position. The sons replace the absent or deferred father.[48]

"Nothing outside the Text of Metaphysics"

Where "Outwork" focused on inside/outside and plenitude as constitutive features of the general text, this discussion about *pharmakon* and fathers reveals others. Plato's pharmacy is an economy of truth composed of a set of hierarchical oppositions—good/bad, natural/artificial, and the like, all revolving around presence/absence but not reducible to them. This economy of truth attempts to master what it deems as "other" (in this case, writing) according to a logic of oppositionality. Writing is opposed to wisdom and speech because writing lacks the presence that characterizes speech, the truth writing claims to assist is mere appearance, it defers memories for monuments, and so on. However, if *logos* (which metaphysics espouses as its own) is *also* affected with deferral, difference, and absence, then it, too, shares the characteristics that make writing suspect and other; the distinction between writing and speaking founders. Speaking does not get outside the text of metaphysics, nor does it escape the economy of *différance* that circumscribes the text.

Has Derrida simply replaced the presumed superiority of speech with the superiority of writing? Derrida's intervention in the network of hierarchical oppositions that constitute the text of metaphysics i not a simple overturning, a revalorizing of the devalued sides of thos oppositions. It is, rather, a double reading that accomplishes a vei specific displacement, folding back, a *re*mark. Derrida's work wi Plato's texts and their doubles (the myths, linguistic structures, a conversations with Socrates that precede them, the interpretations t issue from them) reveals that these oppositions, which attempt to m ter writing, are separated by permeable boundaries. Plato's texts what precedes and issues from them are likewise separated by pei able boundaries. The general text is constituted by and opens ont play of *différance* and undecidability.

What is the relationship between the text of metaphysics and p ophy? Has Derrida brought us to the end of philosophy? I would no, not "end" in any final sense. First of all, Derrida is not sayi Hegel, Marx, or Plato are wrong or mistaken. In each case, th reflect responsiveness to the situation of the economy of truth questions them because their writings are symptomatic of larg Derrida's double reading uncovers certain structural nec these philosopher's texts that shape their lines of investigati gumentation. The set of hierarchical oppositions that make of metaphysics inscribes Plato, Hegel, and Marx (as writer jects of reading) as does the economy of *différance*. The t physics is legible in the philosophical tradition but neit the meaning of the other. Thus, Derrida's analysis brings of philosophy in the sense of limit. Each philosopher r in a chain of intertextuality, in the text of metaphysics, a omy of *différance*. "Nothing outside the text" mean marked by a patterning that lies outside it, that is not v that reappears at different times, in different places (ar ent—Hegel is not Marx, Plato is not Hegel), and in

I would argue that Derrida's reading of Plato an the end of philosophy in multiple senses, none of t the end/goal/aim that, in Aristotelian metaphysic when anything comes into being. The instituting phy (ideal/real, essence/accident, etc.) play themselves out in Plato, Hegel, and Marx but do not, properly speaking, originate with them. Each reinstitutes those founding gestures, but never in precisely the same way. Derrida has also brought us to philosophy's end as limit. "Plato's Pharmacy" uncovers the boundary that distinguishes philosophy from its others (myth and literature). This boundary, however, turns out to be permeable. Literature and myth find their way into philosophy's domain at the very points where philosophy exhausts its own resources.

Though Derrida's readings bring these dynamics to light, they do not bring them into existence. "Plato's Pharmacy" shows that philosophy's end was present in its beginning. Derrida brings philosophy's instituting gestures to a close that is also a permanent opening. Philosophy is constitutively unable to bring its gestures of mastery to completion; philosophy is revealed as a site of perpetual conflict between mastery and resistance.

Have we arrived at the nihilist core of Derridean deconstruction? I would argue that we have not. Writing's truth is undecidable because it disrupts the economy of truth that tries to decide it. The structures of this economy (good/bad, natural/artificial, presence/absence, etc.) show themselves to be afflicted by undecidability when they try to fix this *pharmakon*, writing. Derrida has not shown truth to be an illusion or absence to be the fundamental level of reality. What he *has* done is reinscribe the economy of truth in its larger context, the economy of *différance*. The text from which the economy of truth emerges (and it does emerge) is one of undecidability—like the *pharmakon*. Just as the possibility of a decision in favor of "remedy" or "poison" emerges from what it tries to master (the undecidable ambiguousness of the *pharma-kon*), so the economy of truth emerges from a text constituted as much by what *it* tries to master (difference, deferral and absence) as by sameness and presence. Because the characteristics of writing or textuality (difference, deferral, etc.) are more foundational, Derrida chooses *text* to name these constitutive structures of metaphysics.

Coming to this understanding of "nothing outside the text" has important implications for my project as a whole. Those who remain skeptical about the possibilities of an alliance between feminist theology and deconstruction cite feminist theology's necessary dependence on the discourse that grounds ethics; that is, notions of goodness and evil. Deconstruction, these skeptics argue, promotes a radical relativism where free play rules and anything goes. I would argue that the displacement produced by Derrida's double reading does not replace a unitary truth with radical relativism. Undecidability is not indeterminacy. The play of *pharmakon* is not random. That is, *pharmakon* does not play between "star," "remedy," and "pizza," but between remedy and poison. Its meaning cannot be decided between those terms. Thus, *stable* meaning is differed/deferred. This situation is hardly synonymous with saying meaning is impossible. Derrida's reading of Plato gives a highly determinate account of the meaning of Plato's texts. While this instability can seem to be an affliction, one must recognize that it is also definitive and productive. Without instability, there would be no truth or meaning. Thus, the condition of truth's possibility is also the condition of its affliction; one never has meaning unattended by destabilization.

Deconstruction and Feminist Theology

Reading this essay confirms and expands on implications for my project drawn from the end of "Outwork." First, it challenges views of deconstruction's import for theology offered by many of the deconstructive theologians. Announcements of God's death appear to be premature. God is certainly circumscribed by the play of *différance*, but God is also produced by that play. To be sure, to circumscribe God's power as guarantor of truth, as full presence, and so on, is, in a sense, to call into question a certain notion of God, but deconstruction hardly originates that challenge. Moreover, deconstruction also suggests that this notion of God will not be so easily dismissed from the scene. Insofar as we continue to think we can mean what we say, we are, in some sense, keeping that god alive.

Rather than spelling the end of feminist theology, I would argue that deconstruction offers considerable potential for deepening its critical and constructive aims. The theologian Kevin Hart, among others, challenges any alliance between deconstruction and feminism on the grounds that deconstruction cannot take stands. Hart claims deconstruction can show only how a text or meaning is constituted. Two aspects of "Plato's Pharmacy" militate against this view: the outcome of Derrida's double reading and its gender dynamics. Derrida's textual interventions do more than uncover structures of meaning; they show that those structures depend on what they dismiss/define as "other." Doing so displaces the mastery of those structures and renders legible the trace of the text's "other." Writing is the *pharmakon* (remedy/poison) that "cures" this economy of truth and opens it up toward another economy. Derrida's textual interventions are not neutral be-

cause the texts he reads are not neutral. The text of metaphysics sides
with the king; Derrida gives voice to what is rendered "other" by the
text. Derrida's analysis reveals the text of metaphysics and its economy
of truth to be patro-, logo-, heliocentric.

It is here that my reading of Derrida on "nothing outside the text"
aims to expand and deepen that provided by most of his philosophical
and theological interpreters. A number of Derridean scholars attend to
God's place or to the gender dynamics in Derrida's work. However,
they tend to miss either the link between the two issues or the breadth
and depth of their place in what Derrida's readings produce.[49] I would
argue that sexual marking is intrinsic to the metaphysical text; as intrinsic as its other hallmarks like presence/absence, inside/outside, plenitude, and closure. In fact, the text's sexual markings are bound up with
these other hallmarks. Speech is deemed good because its metaphorical
father is there to watch over it to ensure that it says what he means.
Writing's distance from such a guardian renders it problematic. Its father's presence has been deferred; its words differ from those that came
out of the father's mouth. The standard of value against which writing
is measured is proximity to the father. Can it be mere coincidence that
the father is the determiner of value in this economy of truth and that
fathers occupy such high status in western culture—including the
throne of the divine?

Feminist theology would surely recognize an ally in Derrida's *solicitation* of God the Father. Critiques of this construal of the divine constitute the bedrock of feminist theology.[50] Where feminist theologians
have tended to read God's masculinity as a matter of image or metaphor, they have been very aware of the effects of that metaphor on
real women's lives, on humanity's relationship to the earth, and so on.
Derrida can be read as carrying feminist insights to the foundations of
philosophy and beyond. Derrida's reading of the problematic of writing shows that the effects of the Father God reach to the level of basic
presuppositions of western thinking, the distinction between writing
and speaking. Indeed, as later chapters will show, "nothing outside
the text of metaphysics" also means that institutions, economies (in
the narrow sense of the word), families, and such, also bear marks of
inscription by the text of metaphysics, its economy of truth, and its
Father God.

My reading of the relationship between philosophy and the text of
metaphysics also challenges the exemption from deconstruction's
questioning that some theologians claim for theology. The end of philosophy that Derrida effects is not an exposure of the limits of reason;

thus, theology's traditional location at the limits of reason will not exempt it from deconstruction's solicitations. The reading I have provided of "Plato's Pharmacy" also suggests that the text of metaphysics reaches far beyond the boundaries of philosophy. One would expect to find marks of its presence even in theology that is not explicitly philosophical, in liturgy, in church practices, and so forth. One would expect to find evidence of the economy of *différance* at those sites, as well. Locating sexual markings at the heart of the text of metaphysics also sounds a warning to deconstructive philosophers and theologians; failure to attend to these aspects of Derrida's work risks leaving vestiges of the system of metaphysics in place.[51]

Nor can whitefeminist theology and theory claim exemption from deconstruction's questions. Indeed we should expect to find marks of the text of metaphysics and the economy of *différance* in these fields, as well. Whitefeminism's dealings with race are symptomatic of its inscription in and by an economy of sameness. Explaining why the *particular* difference of race is so elusive remains a task for a later chapter; however, reading "Plato's Pharmacy" further confirms a deconstructive theology's importance to the work of overcoming whitefeminism's white solipsism. Insofar as God the Father founds the economy of sameness, the route toward opening whitefeminism to difference will lie through the *solicitation* of this god.

One more essay in *Dissemination* remains to be read. This essay, "The Double Session," takes the idea of the book to its end in what Derrida calls "literature," as exemplified by Mallarmé. Reading this essay will confirm even more strongly the points that I have made here about the relationship between textuality and reality as framed by Derrida. It will also allow me to anticipate dealing with another layer of whitefeminist critiques of Derrida's work with woman. A number of whitefeminists have criticized Derrida for taking up figures associated with women's bodies and putting them to deconstructive use.[52] These critics argue that Derrida is repeating the ancient philosophical gesture of appropriating the female body to serve masculine ends while exhibiting callous disregard for embodied women. Thus, to enter into a consideration of Derrida's use of such figures as the hymen, invagination, and so on, is again to appear to enter an abyss that threatens to swallow feminism. I will argue, however, that my project has a stake in Derrida's work with the figure of the hymen as deployed in "The Double Session." The hymen figures herein as the gateway between the book and literature, between textuality and reality, between the specular economy and the economy of *différance*. Marking these boundaries with a female figure carries woman toward the other side of these oppositions and toward *différance*. Since the hope for overcoming the race/woman divide also lies in that direction, I will argue that Derrida's use of these terms in this context, at least, works to feminism's benefit.

From the Book to Literature, from Plato's Sun to Mallarmé's *Lustre*

What Derrida names "literature" emerges out of the closure of the "book" and makes its appearance with Mallarmé. Literature comes out of the book in two senses; it emerges out of the book's closure and it represents the book's heir. Like the encyclopedists before him, Mallarmé also dreams of a Book—the one book that he thinks all writers and poets are attempting to write. However, he admits the impossibility of its realization. "We know . . . that there is nothing but what is . . . nature takes place; it cannot be added to."[53] At best authors can hope to adequately reflect some portion of it. Mallarmé names his goal as merely "showing one fragment of [the book] executed"[54] or "lift[ing] one corner of the veil"[55] which covers its impossible possibility. This is, Mallarmé writes, both his pleasure and his torture. The one mirror of the book becomes the multiple mirrors of literature. Literature's appearance on the scene bears the marks of its inscription by the specular economy of truth even as it disrupts that economy. Like writing, literature is relegated to a subsidiary place in the scene of truth. However, its power to disrupt this scene reveals literature as constitutive of truth. Derrida asks, if all that is (the world) is always already constituted, what is literature's status with regard to being? It would seem that it cannot properly be said to exist. However, setting literature outside "reality" constitutes the wholeness of "reality" as the effect of its reflection in literature's mirror.

"The Double Session" illustrates this blurring of the line between literature and reality by playing on the border between those distinctions. It returns to Plato in recalling the division between myth/story and philosophy, which occupied Derrida's attention in "Plato's Pharmacy." "Double Session" records the proceedings of a seminar on mimesis featuring a text by Mallarmé entitled *Mimique* and an excerpt from the *Philebus* where Socrates' discussion of the soul illustrates Plato's assignment of mimesis. The seminar's focal question is, where does "reality" end and "the text" (as literature) begin? Mimesis grounds the distinction between literature and reality within the specular economy of truth. Literature, like the book (and like other arts) mirrors reality. Its truth *is* mimesis; its truth is measured in terms of the adequacy of its reflection. Plato's dealings with literature exhibit this conception and resistance to it. Derrida reminds us in "Double Session" that Plato exiles Homer from his republic on the grounds that mimesis is dangerous. Yet this dismissal is not Plato's final word on mimesis. Mimesis, like writing, plays between good and bad depending on what it copies and whether it copies accurately. Mimesis is at work in contexts other than written texts. In the *Philebus,* Plato describes the relationship between the soul and truth in terms of mimesis. Like a book, the soul is only capable of truth insofar as what is written on it truly reflects what is. Plato's invocation of soul-as-book recalls the scene in the *Republic* enacted between writing, myth, and truth. There, Plato/Socrates dismissed myth from philosophy only to have to call it back in order to determine the truth of writing. Myth's return undoes the opposition between myth and philosophy on the grounds of truth. Similarly, in the *Philebus,* Socrates is asked whether the writing on the soul can anticipate what is yet to come. He concludes that it can and indeed does. This metaphor ends up undoing the distinction between mimetic truth (*adequatio*) and truth itself. According to the logic of mimesis, the imitated precedes the imitation. The economy of mimesis slips out of the grasp of the specular economy through the fissure in the order of imitated and imitation enacted here. The division between "text" and "reality itself," the imitation and the imitated, turns out to be undecidable. "Text" and "reality" are separated not by an absolute break, but by a transparent and permeable membrane.

Through another instantiation of double reading/writing, "Double Session" renders legible a different relationship between text and reality. From the opening sentences, Derrida plays on the border between text and reality, mimesis and truth. The proceedings of the seminar—down to a copy of what Derrida had written on the board (e.g., copies of the passages from Mallarmé and Plato, plays with titles)—are duplicated in these pages. Already the lines are crossed between the reality of the seminar and its supposed reduplication by reduction to writing within *Dissemination.* The texts discussed in the seminar further disrupt the stability of this border. Mallarmé's *Mimique* gives an account of a pantomime in which it appears that nothing described in the pamphlet about the pantomime ever happens/ed on stage, much less "in reality." The pantomime involves the murder/orgasm of Pierrot's wife, Columbine, brought on by her husband's tickling. Pierrot himself subsequently dies of a similar spasm. The reality of this event is continually in question. First of all, the characters of the pantomime, Pierrot and Columbine, are not and have never been "real." As stock pantomime characters, they occupy a place somewhere between real people and mere characters. On the one hand, while they do not represent real people, they are not simply figments of Mallarmé's imagination, either. Plot is similarly problematized in *Mimique*. First of all, *Mimique* recounts the plot of a pantomime that may or may not have ever been performed. Already one has moved a few steps back from "reality"—even the reality of a staged performance. Furthermore, the reader cannot conclude for certain that the murder ever happens in the script that the pamphlet recounts. Pierrot, the victim, narrates the story after both his wife's murder *and* his own death. Both deaths take place offstage.

Mimique exacerbates what already came to the fore in the *Philebus.* Platonism (which is not to be confused with Plato) tries to separate textuality and reality. Literature's truth is measured in terms of the adequacy of its reflection of reality. To maintain control over mimesis, the specular economy requires a firm distinction between text and reality. In *Mimique*, however, reality recedes from view and yet the structure of mimesis remains. It continues to work its differentiating magic but without the absolute certainty of a referent outside the mimetic system. Derrida reads *Mimique* doubly, and *Mimique* doubles the Platonic economy. These double readings displace the specular economy of truth. Rather than being comprehended *by* truth, *Mimique* disrupts its mastery by reflecting a mimesis that is neither "something" nor "nothing." *Mimique* performs what should be impossible, according to the specular economy of truth. Mimesis should *require* a clearly real referent in order to function. *Mimique* renders that assumption null and void. Mimesis does not require a constant influx of the currency of the specular economy that supposedly gives rise to it. As a consequence, the division between ideal and real, textuality and reality, truth and mimesis looks less absolute. In Derrida's words, *Mimique* enacts "a simulacrum of Platonism or Hegelianism, which is separated from what it simulates only by a barely perceptible veil, about which one can just as well say that it already runs—unnoticed—between Platonism and itself, between Hegelianism and itself. Between Mallarmé's text and itself" (*D,* 207). In other words, *Mimique* only makes more explicit dynamics that are already in play in Plato's texts (as the discussion of both the *Philebus* and *pharmakon* shows), Hegel's texts (see the previous discussion of "Hors Livre"), and elsewhere. What separates text from reality, one text from another text, is not the hard cover of a book or an impermeable boundary but something much more delicate and fluid; a hymeneal membrane.

Conclusion/Opening

What is the import of Derrida's solicitation for books, literature, and philosophy, for conceiving textuality and reality, and, ultimately, for my project? Does the closure of the book mean books can no longer be written because their claims to refer to anything outside themselves are not legitimate or because all we have are endless chains of random mirrors? I would argue that the import of closure is multiple: the book in the sense of perfect mirror of nature is closed because of the cut/ *coup* that Derrida shows attends it. We will never have that perfect mirror; we never have had it. In a sense, the book was always already closed. But the closure of the book is also its opening; what closes it is also what makes it possible in the first place. Books could not and would not have been written without a cut that called for covering over. The emergence of literature out of the closure of the book does not constitute the emergence of chaos or an endless chain of random reflections. Pierrot does not suddenly become Lassie in the next reflection down the line. Thus literature constitutes a perpetuation of the book but a perpetuation that Derrida shows to be disrupted. The sun of Plato's myth of the cave becomes the many-faceted *lustre* of Mallarmé's texts.

The implications of "Double Session" reach beyond books, literature, and textuality in their ordinary senses. "Double Session" exposes fissures in the specular economy of truth, whose reach extends to the limits of the West. Previous essays in *Dissemination* uncovered the specular economy's persistent patro-, logo-, heliocentrisms. "Double Session" adds an important dimension to our understanding of the gendered and sexual dynamics of this economy. The fissures in the specular economy bear feminine markings. Derrida, picking up on one of Mallarmé's tropes, figures the membrane covering the fissure separating text and reality as a hymen. Like *pharmakon*, hymen plays between two poles of signification. If pierced, it signifies conjugal union; if unpierced, it signifies virginity. With the addition of this trope, the economy of truth shows itself to be not only specular but possessed of an erotic bearing. The dynamic of the author's relationship to the book and its referent, nature, is shaped by the sexual economy of what I will call man's-desire-for-woman.[56] The author's desire for mastery over the book reads simultaneously as a desire to cover over the split's exposure of undecidability *and* a desire to pierce the membrane or lift the veil. Either way, the desire for the book-as-unified-whole and for perfect reflection is set in motion by the undecidability of the cut/hymen. That same membrane frustrates this desire because the separations it engenders are not absolute. The splits between ideal/real, book/nature, and so forth, emerge from a context of undecidability. The hymen eludes piercing.

When read in the context of the rest of *Dissemination*, Mallarmé's trope is more than a mere figure of speech. The fissures in specular logic constitute their own (a)logic. The membranes at stake here go beyond the distinction between text (book, literature, or writing) and reality. Derrida extends the metaphor of hymen/veil to include the permeable boundaries between the hierarchical oppositions that constitute the basis for the distinction between text and reality—ideal/real, essence/appearance, and so on. Specular logic both depends upon and is undercut by the logic of the hymen. Rather than reenacting the desire for masterful piercing or overarching wholeness, Derrida wants to stay with the hymen's resistance to both projects.

"Double Session," then, adds important dimensions to deconstruction's significance for my project. My reading of the previous essays in *Dissemination* exposed gender markings at the heart of the text of metaphysics. "Double Session" carries woman to the end of that text and suggests that she participates in what lies beyond it. "Double Session," like the essays that preceded it, calls the specular economy into question in the name of a differing and deferring that funds it. To be sure, there is an abyssal quality to this mimetic economy, but it is the abyss of a set of many-sided mirrors bouncing reflections off one another to infinity; it is not a dark, empty hole of nothingness. Making explicit connections between the specular economy and race will have to wait until we have followed woman's separation from race to its end. But connecting her to the other side of the specular economy will turn out to be important to subverting the race/gender divide. In the meantime, the full scope of her connection to the specular economy and what lies beyond it has yet to emerge. The next chapter will follow the path from the woman's side of the race/gender divide through openings created by this discussion.

3

Deconstruction's Alliance with Feminism: Possibilities and Limits

Introduction

Chapter 2 began this project's inquiry into the contours of the race/gender divide uncovered in whitefeminist theology and theory. It took off from the first line of force that came into question as a result of the first chapter's investigation into whitefeminism's dealings with race, the relationship of author, text, and context. An inquiry into what Derrida means by "nothing outside the text" showed that whitefeminism's dealings with race are symptomatic of the larger conditions of textuality. Those dynamics turned out, however, not to be limited to textuality in its ordinary sense. Reading *Dissemination* uncovered a specular economy at work in the West's idea of the book, the history of its understanding of the relationship between texts and their contexts, textuality, and reality. This specular economy exhibits gendered markings and possesses an erotic bearing. These markings are not extraneous addenda to the text of metaphysics, but fundamental to it. God the Father stands at the center of this specular economy as its standard and guarantor of truth. The specular economy and its God do not exercise undisturbed mastery over authors and texts, textuality and reality, and so on. Another economy, that of *différance,* funds the specular economy. I suggested that whitefeminism's dealings with race reflect whitefeminism's inscription within the specular economy as an economy that values sameness. Fully developing this claim will require investigating race's relationship to the text of metaphysics and its economy of sameness, a task taken on in chapter 5. Insofar as whitefeminism's dealings with race are shaped by this specular economy, then it has a stake in that economy's overcoming.

Reading *Dissemination* also suggested that overturning the specular economy has a stake in feminism as well. Many of the sites where the economy of *différance* breaks through the specular economy carry female markings. Hence, following woman through the text of metaphysics to its end is integral to my project. First, it stays aligned with the agenda set by the race/gender divide. In considering woman apart from race, it follows the direction laid out by whitefeminism. Taking this route would appear simply to freeze woman forever in isolation from race; however, the previous chapter suggests that this is not necessarily the case. It seems clear that whitefeminism's dealings with race exhibit its inscription by the specular economy of sameness. If woman represents a route toward what lies beyond the economy of sameness, then following her in that direction also heads toward the other side of the race/gender divide. Getting to the end of the divide requires, first of all, following woman to her end, which is, among other things, the point where she can no longer keep race at bay.

This chapter picks up where chapter 2 ended, with the inquiry into the place of woman in relationship to the text of metaphysics and its specular economy. Specifically, it follows the erotic bearing of man's-desire-for-woman that began to emerge in *Dissemination*. In chapter 2 I found the path to woman's place in this larger context; this chapter will expand awareness of her place by excavating other sites where woman figures prominently in the specular economy. The path leading to woman's place comes to its end at the point where woman marks a rupture within the text of metaphysics and its specular economy. This point of rupture will occur at another end of authorial mastery; in this case, that of Derrida's Nietzsche. Following Derrida's woman to that end will also take her to the limits of the text of metaphysics and toward this project's stake in what lies outside it.

This chapter's trajectory will also revisit the question of Derrida's import for feminism. I noted earlier some feminists' objections that pertained to "nothing outside the text." My reading of Derrida suggested that, rather than undercutting feminist projects, Derrida's solicitation of the text of metaphysics offered potential for carrying them to deeper levels. However, feminists' resistance to his work comes from sites beyond debates about "nothing outside the text," sites that this chapter will explore. Let me summarize the critiques briefly here before launching into further readings of Derridean texts.

Some of Derrida's whitefeminist critics argue that Derrida sees woman as devoid of content; in Rosi Braidotti's words, "the feminine . . . is a perennial empty set." Others argue that Derrida fails to draw connections between the figure of woman in his texts and the material conditions of flesh-and-blood women's oppression.[1] Feminist critics often read Derrida's view of feminism as articulated in interviews like "Women in the Beehive" and "Choreographies" as exclusively critical.[2]

Some of his feminist critics charge that Derrida is only interested in woman insofar as she aids his deconstructive project. They read his work with her as business-as-usual among men. As noted in the previous chapter, Derrida's use of terms like *hymen* and *invagination* registers as an appropriative gesture in many whitefeminists' eyes. Derrida's claim that deconstruction needs to start from woman's place (and his professed aim to write from that place) also registers as an appropriative gesture in many feminists' eyes. Derrida takes from woman what suits his needs but bypasses any consideration of what she might need, be, or want. These readings would suggest that to turn to Derrida's work with woman in order to cure whitefeminism of its exclusionary tendencies is playing with poison. Many of these same theorists would no doubt urge me to drop Derrida in favor of the thinker whose work will appear in the next chapter, Luce Irigaray. In their view, she appropriates some useful elements from Derrida but leaves behind the serious problems that attend his work with woman.[3] I will persist in following Derrida's woman as far as she can take me for a number of reasons. First of all, as I argued in the introduction to this chapter, the project that I have set for myself requires that I stay with Derrida as far as he can take me. Second, while the argument in this chapter will end up confirming certain critiques of Derrida, I will also argue against dismissing Derrida prematurely.[4] I have argued elsewhere that opting for Irigaray in opposition to Derrida closes off ways of reading them *together* that are more productive for feminism.[5] Derrida's work with woman has its limits, but so does Irigaray's work, as I will argue in chapter 4. Moreover, Derrida prepares the way for Irigaray both in what he accomplishes and where he falls short. What Irigaray offers my project (and feminism in general) will register much more clearly against the screen this chapter offers than it would without it, both in what these thinkers share in common and where they diverge.

Freudian Figures

Intertextuality emerged early in this project as one of the multiple meanings of "nothing outside the text." As I demonstrated in the previous chapter, texts are written and read within the contexts set for them by other texts. One of Derrida's central strategies involves exploiting/exploring textual intersections and exacerbating their effects within particular texts undergoing solicitation. Gayatri Chakravorty Spivak describes this aspect of Derrida's work as making use of a Freudian intertextuality.[6] The invocation of Freud's name in this context points to an important stream of Derridean intertextuality. Freud (along with another hermeneut of suspicion, Nietzsche) is central to the specific intertextual context of Derrida's work.[7] The project of deconstruction becomes possible at this particular historical nexus—after Hegel, Nietzsche, Husserl, Heidegger, and Freud.[8] This is not to say that the specular economy ruled in unquestioned mastery until now, but that its deconstruction (disrupting its mastery by unearthing and exacerbating resistances internal to the economy) becomes possible only now.[9]

Derrida draws on the funds of this heritage in many ways. The style of Derrida's attention to texts is reminiscent of Freud. Derrida takes no text at face value but carefully interrogates each one to elicit what it represses, what exceeds its mastery. Some of the tropes that he exploits have Freudian roots. While in many ways Freud's texts reinstate the text of metaphysics, they also present challenges to some of the text's governing presuppositions. At particular points in what Derrida terms Freud's "itinerary," Freud resorts to the metaphor of writing to describe the dynamics of the psyche. Derrida argues that this choice of metaphor is more than accidental. Derrida focuses on a comparison Freud draws between the psyche (in particular, the relationship between the unconscious and consciousness) and a new toy, the mystic writing pad. This pad consists of a wax tablet covered by a plastic sheet on which one writes with an inkless stylus. Writing appears on the surface of the plastic sheet by virtue of the impression made on the wax beneath. Lifting the plastic sheet erases images from the surface, but their traces remain embedded in the wax beneath. If we could imagine one hand writing and another hand simultaneously lifting the sheet, Freud writes, we would understand the way the unconscious and consciousness work on each other to produce memory. With this turn to the metaphor of writing and the topology of the trace in interpreting the psyche,[10] Freud prefigures the closure of the Platonic topology of the subject in the *Phaedrus* (in all the various senses of "closure" discussed previously). Derrida describes this accomplishment of Freud's text as follows:

> The subject of writing is a *system* of relationships between strata: the Mystic Pad, the psyche, society, the world. Within that scene, on that stage, the punctual simplicity of the classical subject is not to be found.
> . . . That which, in Freud's discourse, opens itself to the theme of writing results in psychoanalysis being not simply psychology—nor simply psychoanalysis. Thus are perhaps augured, in the Freudian breakthrough, a beyond and a beneath of the closure we might term

"Platonic." In that moment of world history "subsumed" by the name of Freud, . . . a relationship to itself of the historico-transcendental stage of writing was spoken without being said, thought without being thought: was written and simultaneously erased, metaphorized; designating itself while indicating intraworldly relations, it *was represented*.[11]

The place in the history of western thought marked by "Derrida" (whether as writer, reader, or object of another's reading and writing) emerges out of this representation. Like "Freud," Derrida as interlocutor is historically, socially, culturally embedded. I read Derrida as exploiting his situation in as many ways as possible without ever claiming to escape it. This locatedness marks both the value and the limitations of his work for my project. Investigation of the scene of woman's place in Derrida's work will map Derrida's location and explore both its productive effects and its limits.

Derridean/Freudian intertextuality plays itself out in notable ways in what circulates between Derrida and Freud's recent French interpreter, Jacques Lacan. Derrida's reading of Lacan is more critical than appreciative, at least on the surface, but engaging in conversation with Lacan is clearly productive for Derrida. Indeed, Derrida identifies Lacan as the figure whose work his own encounters "more than any other today."[12] Much of what circulates between them revolves around the figure of woman. A detailed interrogation of Derrida's relationship to Lacan would, no doubt, be fruitful for feminism, but it lies outside the scope of my current project. Subverting the race/gender divide that governs whitefeminism requires something different. Following woman into and through the text of metaphysics until she opens onto race requires following her to the depths of Derrida's work and to its limits. Reading Derrida against the background of Lacan's work with woman will help with that process. Furthermore, Irigaray also works out of a Lacanian background; thus, taking up Lacan here will prepare the ground for reading Irigaray in the next chapter.

The "French Freud" on Woman's Place

Freud's position on woman is well known. The role of what Freud identifies as the Oedipus complex, the castration complex, and penis envy in the production of a "normal woman" remains a subject of controversy in feminist theory as well as in psychoanalytic theory and practice to this date.[13] It is interesting to note the role that geography plays in this debate. In America, a certain reading of Freud has found its way into both psychoanalytic practice and into our intellectual milieu. The American reading of Freud posits a biological cause (anatomy) for the intrapsychic dynamics his patients exhibit. The difference between male and female anatomy determines femininity and sets the often-tragic course of women's lives. In American feminism's terms, Freud grounds woman's nature in sex rather than gender. The French reading of Freud (via Lacan), by contrast, locates the origin of man and woman in a cultural discourse that runs below the division between sex and gender and its correlates (nature/culture, body/psyche). The difference between man and woman is not first anatomical, but discursive. Sexual difference precedes the division between sex and gender.[14]

The significance of these different readings of Freud comes to the fore in discussions of the place of woman in western culture. The American Freud defines woman in terms of her lack of a crucial piece of male anatomy, the penis. Since this lack sets the stage for her development into a woman, anatomy appears to be destiny, for one is born either male or female. Lacan rereads Freud's focus on the penis as phallocentrism. Lacan insists (as do his interpreters, critics and partisans alike) that the phallus is not to be equated with the penis. It is a discursive term, not a biological organ.[15] Penis envy becomes desire for the phallus; the castration complex becomes fear of the loss of the phallus, and the Oedipus complex becomes *truly* complex. Through a survey of the scene of Lacan's rereading of penis envy, the castration complex, and the Oedipus complex, I will elucidate the position of both the phallus and woman in Lacan's rereading of Freud.[16]

My reading of *Dissemination* in chapter 2 exposed gender markings and man's-desire-for-woman at the heart of the specular economy of truth. Reading Lacan and Derrida together will uncover further symptoms of those markings and expand our awareness of their reach. Lacan and Derrida both explore and exploit the convergence of sexuality, truth, and language within western culture's discourse and its specular economy. The topology of the economy that governs linguistic truth, assignations as man or woman, and sexuality reflect and engender each other. Language and meaning are marked by gendered and sexualized positions. Becoming a human being involves coming into language; coming into language is a "sexual affair" in many senses of the term. Lacan rewrites yet reaffirms Freud's most notorious (and hotly contested) interpretive moves (the Oedipus complex, castration complex, and penis envy) in moving the scene of their performance to language.

The entrance into language occurs as the resolution of a primal drama involving the mother, father, and the child. In the beginning, mother and child coexist in a symbiotic economy of need and satisfaction. The child has needs and endows the mother with the power to fulfill those needs. The mother needs the child (as a result of her own passage through this same drama), and the child wants to fulfill that need for the mother. The drama is directed toward its denouement by seeming accidents: glimpses the child gets of its sibling's and its parents' genitalia. The consequences of these sightings are significant and vary depending on the gender/sex of the child. The little girl sees her brother's penis and immediately realizes she does not have one. She sees her mother's genitalia and realizes her mother does not have one either. The little girl wants it, gets angry at her mother for not giving it to her, knows her father has it, and begins to want her father to give it to her in the form of a baby. The little girl now transfers the object of her desire from her mother to her father. The dynamics set in motion by these glances set the little girl on the path toward becoming a woman—which means, in part, one who desires the thing of value (or at least a chain of acceptable substitutes) that she believes only the man can give her.

For the little boy, the glimpse of his mother and his sister yield different immediate consequences. The little boy assumes both females at one time had penises and did, in fact, lose them. Their apparent loss arouses his fear that he will lose his, too. Thus the little boy, like his sister, switches his allegiance from the mother to the father. That allegiance, however, is of a different sort. The little boy comes to identify with the father. The mother remains the object of his desire, but that desire is now forbidden by the incest taboo imposed by the father's intrusion on the primal scene. The little boy is on his way to becoming a man—which means, among other things, one who both fears and desires the woman. The man fears her because she embodies the castration he fears. He desires her because she desires what he fears to lose. He thinks he can give it to her thereby reaffirming his belief that he still has it.

Anatomical differences figure so highly in this drama because of the particular shape of the western cultural context. The sexual economy reflects and figures a linguistic economy and vice versa. The penis is endowed with such value because it points to (via its resemblance to) the phallus, which constitutes the standard of value in this context, according to Lacan.[17] The entry into manhood or womanhood, and into directed sexual desire, is simultaneously entry into that discourse which is *the* language of western culture. The discourse of western culture is, for Lacan as for Derrida, dominated by fathers and father figures. The father's cut into the symbiotic relationship with the mother via the incest taboo and the "resolution" of the castration and Oedipus complexes brings the (male) child into language. The (male) child is then able to take up the position of the subject, the one "with" the phallus.[18]

That this drama constitutes the threshold of language is reflected in/ reflects the structure of language itself. The drama revolves around the penis—and lack thereof. This reveals/reflects the center of value in this linguistic economy, the phallus. The grounding provided by the phallus turns out to be rather unstable. Like God the Father, the phallus's status in relation to truth and to presence is complex. The phallus is always lacking; it "has" no referent in reality. It is not the penis, it never "is" itself, it is not "to be" or "to be had." In other words, the phallus is always already castrated, but its absence is also always already veiled by the desire for its presence. In structuralist terms, the phallus is a signifier without a signified. If truth is supposed to be the union of signifier and signified, then truth is brought up short by the absence of the phallus (by castration). At the same time, the possibility of truth (as the union of signifier and signified) is figured by castration. If the phallus can be completely lacking, then it could potentially be completely present.

The overlapping features of the sexual and linguistic economy uncovered by Lacan and the specular economy revealed by *Dissemination* are striking. Both economies circulate around the presence/absence of the thing of value (phallus, for Lacan; *pater*/father and *logos*/son, for Derrida). Each economy presupposes the presence of the thing of value; yet the circulation of currency in each economy requires its absence. The standard of value is figured as masculine in both Lacan's rereading of Freud and in Derrida's reading of the text of western metaphysics. The position of subjectivity is undercut in both economies because it is afflicted with absence. The subject's perpetual lack of its object of desire means the Lacanian subject is always split. Similarly, the Derridean subject's position as master of discourse is undercut by what eludes it.

Moreover, positions of mastery, afflicted with absence and split as they are, are accorded to man in both economies. Because of their different positions in relation to the phallus, accession to the subject position varies according to gender/sex. The little boy's access to that position is relatively unimpeded, but the little girl must masquerade as the one who "has" it—or "is" it (and is therefore desirable to the man)—in order to accede to subjectivity. The Law of the Father rules the symbolic order in Lacan's scheme. The father is both arbiter of value and guarantor of meaning in the text of western metaphysics. The reign of the fathers in both economies is also always perpetually undercut. Most important, both economies follow the trajectory of man's-desire-for-woman/the phallus.[19] That is, their currency circulates between man and woman, not between man and man or woman and woman.[20] Moreover, even though both man and woman are afflicted by lack or absence, such goods as this sexual economy provides are figured as masculine—thus, man has the upper hand.[21]

And what of woman? Woman's problematic relationship to subjectivity governs what Lacan has to say about her and, as I will argue shortly, what Derrida says about her as well. For both thinkers, "woman does not exist."[22] At first glance, this would seem to render their work completely antithetical to any feminist agenda. As Linda Alcoff argues, "What can we demand in the name of women if 'women' do not exist and demands in their name simply reinforce the myth that they do?"[23] The meaning of this phrase requires considerable unpacking before its significance for feminism can accurately be assessed. Because what Derrida does with this depiction of woman's place rests on Lacan's articulation of it, I will begin by tracing some of its connotations within Lacan's work. "Woman does not exist" recalls Freud's assertion that the libido is always masculine, whether embodied in a man or a woman. On Lacan's reading, it becomes a description of the discursive situation of men and women. Because the object of desire for *both* sexes is the phallus, there is only one libidinal economy, and one libido—and it bears masculine marks. Within this economy, woman's desire is not hers in several senses: it is not hers because it aims for a figure marked as masculine, and it enacts its desire via a man. Her desire neither issues solely from her or returns to her, properly speaking. She desires him to desire her, her desire awakens his desire, her desire for the phallus is his desire for the phallus, and so on. Thus, her desire is his desire in many senses. "Woman does not exist" also situates her at the limit of being and of truth. Because woman embodies the absence of the phallus, she also embodies the truth of the phallus; that is, castration.[24] To recall another of Lacan's famous lines: Woman is *pas tout* (not all). That is, she marks the limit of plenitude in marking the limit of truth as castration.

When read against the background of what *Dissemination* revealed about the economy of truth, Lacan adds more layers to the reach of the text of western metaphysics. The terrains of psychoanalysis and philosophy overlap at the points of their inscription by the specular

economy. Neither the central role of the father in the inaugural moments of the text of metaphysics nor the phallus's appearance at the
center of the sexual and linguistic economy are coincidental. Patro-,
logo-, heliocentrism is *phallogocentrism*. In Derrida's words, "Phallogocentrism is neither an accident nor a speculative error that can be im-
puted to any given theoretician. It is an old and enormous root that
must also be accounted for."[25] Philosophy and psychoanalysis also
overlap in exhibiting symptoms of the specular economy's limits. In
both cases, the source or standard of value is afflicted by absence and
lack. This affliction bears directly on questions of truth. Truth is not
revealed as illusion, but is rather inscribed within a larger context. That
context also turns out to have important ramifications for woman.

Derrida criticizes Lacan, though, on several fronts having to do with
Lacan's route through this intersection of philosophy and psychoanalysis. Rather than staying with the side of resistance to mastery, Derrida
argues that Lacan reinstantiates it at every turn. In "Le facteur de la
vérité,"[26] Derrida follows out several symptoms of Lacan's bondage to
phallogocentrism through a reading of Lacan's seminar on Poe's short
story, "The Purloined Letter." I will focus only on those symptoms that
revolve around the position of the phallus in Lacan's work.[27] Derrida
argues that Lacan attempts to "fix" the phallus in several senses. First,
the lack of the phallus has determinable outlines, in Derrida's opinion.
Lacking the phallus fixes it in its proper place—that of absence, and
an absence that takes a particular shape. Second, the phallus in Lacan's
scheme remains subject to the economy of truth both as *adequatio* and
as *aletheia*. The phallus may have no real referent, but as such, it embodies an absolute negativity. Total absence is just as metaphysical as total
presence.[28] Truth in a standard sense also governs Lacan's project as a
whole, Derrida claims. The truth of castration embodied by woman
gets the process of signification (union of signifier and signified) underway and continues to mark the possibility of a full return of truth.
Derrida argues that the seminar follows the same trajectory as the short
story; Lacan's concern in the seminar (and everywhere) is to ensure
that Freud's "letter" (his oeuvre) is returned to him. Derrida reads Lacan as taking up various positions in relation to this project; detective,
correspondent, and postman. In asserting himself as the source of the
authentic Freud, Lacan reserves the place of mastery for himself, Derrida argues.

One could cut through the psychoanalytic/philosophical landscape
another way, according to Derrida. Lacan's analysis identifies places
of resistance to the mastery of phallocentrism, but his texts keep them

in submission and under control. Thus, in Derrida's eyes, Lacan ultimately preserves rather than undercuts phallogocentrism. Derrida, on the other hand, wants to follow the resistances to phallogocentrism. This means following the disturbances engendered by woman and by castration.[29] It remains to be seen, however, the extent to which Derrida's work is able to achieve significant disruption of this state of affairs. In fact, I will argue that Derrida comes closest to Lacan where his attempt meets its limits.

The Question of the Truth of/as Woman: Nietzsche's *Spurs*

A prime example of Derrida's own intervention within this scene occurs in his reading of Heidegger's reading of Nietzsche in *Spurs*.[30] *Spurs* recapitulates the gendered and sexual dynamics of *Dissemination*. It also establishes strategies for dealing with woman that Derrida uses elsewhere. *Spurs* is also one of the texts frequently criticized by feminist readers.[31] *Spurs* follows the play engendered in Nietzsche's work by the question of woman; a play Heidegger overlooks. Once again, issues of woman and truth intertwine with one another on terrain where philosophy and psychoanalysis overlap. Once again, Derrida's readers find themselves in a sexual economy reflective of man's-desire-for-woman. Man and woman initially line up on the same sides of the economy in *Spurs* as in *Dissemination*. The strategies Derrida follows to disrupt this economy's mastery again involve the exacerbation of woman's resistance to mastery by man.

Spurs weaves together at least three strands of questions: one strand continues *Dissemination*'s solicitation of books and authors as *Spurs* takes on the questions of the truth of a text. This strand overlaps with a second strand of questioning that follows woman and truth figured as woman through Nietzsche's writings. The third strand involves the play of the particular tropes in which woman and truth are figured (e.g., *le coup* [cut], *le don* [gift], *le coup de don* [the cut of the gift], *l'hymen* [hymen], *le voile* [veil], *la voile* [sail], *l'éperon* [spur]). While *Spurs* directs questions to both Nietzsche and Heidegger, I am going to focus on the figure of Nietzsche produced by Derrida's reading as counterpoint to Heidegger's Nietzsche. According to Derrida's reading of Nietzsche, as the movement of woman goes, so goes truth (and vice versa), and so goes Nietzsche. I will start by pulling out the strand dealing with the question of woman per se then follow it to the larger terrain of the Nietzschean problematic.

Derrida knows Nietzsche's misogynist reputation; however, his reading of woman through Nietzsche's writings uncovers a complex pattern in Nietzsche's dealings with woman. Derrida identifies three positions taken by Nietzsche with regard to woman. Each position takes a particular place with regard to truth. Quite frequently, Nietzsche takes the position of truth and condemns woman as the figure of falsehood.[32] At other points, Nietzsche condemns woman as the figure of truth *rather* than falsehood. Both of these positions toward woman remain solidly entrenched within the phallogocentric economy. However, Derrida also identifies a third position of woman in Nietzsche's work, which shows her disrupting the phallocentric economy of truth. In these places, Nietzsche affirms woman as dissimulator, as the supreme artist, as Dionysiac. As I will show, it is this third position that interests Derrida.

Derrida does not conclude, from woman's refusal to be "fixed" in these texts, that Nietzsche is a protofeminist rather than the misogynist he is reputed to be. He argues that none of the three positions constitutes the truth, according to Nietzsche, of woman. Rather, the circulation of all three through Nietzsche's writings renders such a definitive statement regarding woman impossible, even when it seems Nietzsche is trying to make such statements. Derrida is interested in Nietzsche for the same reasons he explored Plato, Hegel, Marx, and Mallarmé in *Dissemination*. He found their work—and finds Nietzsche's work as well—symptomatic of larger issues. The significance of this discovery of woman's elusiveness is important for what it says about disruptions in that larger text of which Nietzsche remains a part, the text of western metaphysics. Here, the other strands of Derrida's reading come to the fore. In Nietzsche's texts, truth is figured as a woman. In fact, Nietzsche identifies this figuring of truth as a historical epoch that he wants to question. At this intersection, philosophy and psychoanalysis overlap. Lacan's connection of woman and truth intersects with a history older than the discipline of psychoanalysis. As woman went in Lacan, so went truth. Derrida's analysis of Nietzsche's text will reveal a similar dynamic.

The play of woman in Nietzsche's texts sets in motion significant concentric disruptions within his writings and in the larger context that circumscribes them, the text of western metaphysics. Like *pharmakon* in Plato's texts, woman constitutes an undecidable in Nietzsche's texts. Her play with his attempts to "fix" her disrupts conventional notions of author (as master of his text) and of book-as-a-whole. Derrida's Nietzsche names neither an author nor a discrete body of books. Second, woman's refusal of place in Nietzsche's texts disrupts attempts to philosophize or ontologize her. Woman escapes the trajectory of metaphysics' attempt to determine the whatness of things. Thus, that woman does not exist also means that she has no determinable fixed essence.[33] In resisting these metaphysical restraints, woman's play disrupts the phallogocentric economy of truth that governs the text of metaphysics. The economy of truth attempts to fix her, but she eludes subjection.[34]

Both the attempt at circumscription and symptoms of its failure are read in Nietzsche's text, but they cannot be assigned simply to its inside or outside. This strand of *Spurs* returns to the surface of the Freudian figures I discussed previously; in particular, castration. In the phallocentric economy of truth, the phallus is that around which the economy of truth/sexuality circulates. Castration plays a crucial role within that economy. Woman as the mark of castration sets that economy in motion. The first two positions Nietzsche takes toward woman are *the* two authorized positions on her available in the phallogocentric economy. On the one hand, Nietzsche takes the position of the would-be possessor of the phallus (the signifier of the possibility of truth) and condemns woman as the one who does not have truth or the phallus. On the other hand, Nietzsche puts woman on the side of truth and the phallus and condemns her for that (woman as phallus). The third position, however, matches neither of the first two, nor can it be contained between them. Here woman dissimulates; in phallic terms, she pretends to have it and pretends not to have it. Castration does not take place and she knows it. "Of man—she knows, with a knowledge against which no dogmatic or credulous philosopher is able to measure himself, that castration does not take place/has no place (*n'a pas lieu*)" (*SP*, 60; my translation). Because "woman" means "castrated one," one consequence is again that there is no such thing as woman . . . really. Woman withdraws from this attempt to fix her as either a mark of the presence of the phallus or a mark of its lack. She occupies a position of undecidability with regard to the determining factor of this economy. She withdraws behind veils to a distance. And yet she is not castration's opposite. Rather, she plays between castration and anticastration simulating castration, but by simulating it, keeping it at bay.

This position of undecidability occupied by woman disrupts the phallogocentric economy as economy of propriation (in all its senses of property, propriety, proper). What occurs around woman's supposed castration (or belief in it) set Lacan's phallocentric economy in motion. Value in that economy works according to the location of the phallus; how close one is to having it determines one's proper place and determines what one can appropriate as one's own. Similarly, what occurs around woman's not-castration in Derrida's reading of Nietzsche initiates a complicated system of exchange that Derrida claims disrupts the economy of propriation. As goes woman, so goes truth in this epoch. The play among the tropes that figure the issues in this text illustrate the economy of propriation (and its disruption) in action. The place of woman's elusion opens onto another order, Derrida argues, and he tries to evoke that different order/terrain through this play with/of tropes.

The two primary tropes at work in *Spurs* are that of the hymen and of the spur. Both bring with them a multivalent network of meanings. Both are initially associated with one gender or the other but, as written/read by Derrida's Nietzsche, move from one gender to the other. This exchange disrupts the economy of propriation in that what is proper (the property of, in the sense of ownership and in the sense of attribution of qualities) to each gender refuses fixation. I begin with the figure of the hymen as it plays through this text and then move to the figure of the spur.

Undecidability is the (a)logic of the hymen, as Derrida argued in *Dissemination*. In *Spurs*, the hymen reprises its role as that which enables and marks woman's dissimulation of castration. *Spurs* also draws on the surplus of hymen's associations with "veil" (*le voile*) and, in turn, veil's association in French with "sail" (*la voile*) by exacerbating the play of two of Nietzsche's metaphors for woman/truth. At times, Nietzsche figures truth as a woman modestly withdrawn behind a veil. In other places, he describes woman/truth as a sailing ship gliding calmly across a smooth sea. *L'éperon* (spur) means, among other things, style/stylus (with many phallic resonances), mark, trace, prow of a ship, rocky promontory at the head of a harbor, and so on. All of these associations are pertinent to Derrida's deployment of "spur" across Nietzsche's text. The metaphorical economy of *Spurs* involves exchanges and interactions between hymens/veils/sails and spurs (of all types) across the terrain of Nietzsche's woman, woman-as-truth, Nietzsche's text, and, finally, Derrida's Nietzsche (or Nietzsche's styles).

Spurs opens and closes on a seascape figured by masculine and feminine tropes. The resonances of *le voile/la voile* that come most immediately to mind are feminine. Likewise, those that come most immediately to mind around *l'éperon* are masculine. Derrida uses these resonances, but also picks up on others that reverse this gendered pattern. Veil is associated with woman but gendered masculine in French (*le voile*), as is its associate, hymen. *Voile* means "sail" when used with the feminine article (*la voile*), moreover. In the opening pages of *Spurs*, Derrida calls to mind Nietzsche's figure of woman as a sailing ship, appearing on the distant horizon gliding quietly across the harbor. But sailing ships also have prows (spurs) that cut (*coup*) through the waves as the ship makes its way toward the harbor (of truth? the ship's home?). The harbor has feminine resonances—it conjures up the image of a round, calm, passive place waiting to receive and to embrace approaching ships. Yet the harbor can be guarded by a promontory (spur)—indeed this one is—for the harbor's protection. The ship returns to the harbor only to be rebuffed by its promontory; the harbor withdraws itself and eludes the ship's approach.[35]

Spurs also images the terrain of Nietzsche's work as text. In this context, Derrida calls on spur's meaning as stylus/style. As stylus, the spur represents a long phallic column that aims to perforate the virgin writing surface of the paper (hymen). Like the harbor, this virgin writing surface also resists inscription (its margins remain unpenetrated). Furthermore, the stylus wants to write in a certain style, but style, though gendered masculine, belongs to "her." Thus, "*Elle (s')écrit. C'est à elle que revient le style*" (she writes [herself]/is written; style returns to her/is hers [by right] [*SP*, 56; my translation]). That return is also a withdrawal; a falling of the veil which is masculine. So when Derrida writes "*le voile/tombe*" (*SP*, 58), "*l'érection tombe*" (*SP*, 104), "*le signature/ tombe*" (*SP*, 126),[36] he plays on *voile*'s feminine and masculine registers. These dynamics affect the text of metaphysics and its phallogocentric economy. The falling of the veil covers the absence of the phallus. Read in this way, it recalls woman as the mark of castration and the hymen as the veil over the uterus's opening. On a second reading, the veil (as masculine/feminine) *takes the place of* the phallus; that is, the veil stands in for the nonexistent phallus. Because the veil itself does not properly exist, it succeeds and fails as stand-in. As nonexistent, how can it stand in for anything? On the other hand, since the phallus itself does not exist, the veil is its ideal stand-in. With this reversal of roles, the determination of what is proper to both genders/genres is disrupted. The phallus no longer stands erect at the center of the economy of propriation (*l'érection/tombe*, "the erection/falls"). Because the phallus is also the signatory of the author, the signature as the author's proper mark and his property falls with the phallus. As goes the phallus, so go all questions of the proper—whether philosophical, economic, or linguistic. The phallus's erection is founded in and foundered by the (a)logic of the hymen, undecidability. The proper, too, is founded and founders here. Does this mean that propriation is dead? Once again, Derrida is not arguing that propriation is dead; propriation will continue to recur, but insofar as this analysis of its ground is recalled with it, its emergence will be called into question by its nonoriginary (because it is undecidable, not-one, not an origin, etc.) origin. "The stylate spur traverses/passes through the veil, not tearing it only in order to see or to produce the thing itself, but undoing the opposition in itself; the opposition bent upon itself of the veiled/unveiled, the truth as production, unveiling/dissimulation of the product in presence" (*SP*, 106; my translation).

What has Derrida's invocation and evocation of the play of truth as woman/woman as truth accomplished on this highly figured landscape? What of its accomplishments might aid feminism and aid my project? Many of Derrida's feminist readers would say that *Spurs* gets feminism nowhere. Kelly Oliver, in *Womanizing Nietzsche*, mounts a particularly strident critique of this text. She accuses Derrida of appropriating female figures to serve typically masculine ends. *Spurs*, she argues, writes only man's desire. Woman figures in the text only as the object of his desire while her own specificity and materiality never register. Derrida never gets outside the economy of castration and of the proper. Rather than opening subjectivity to woman, *Spurs* effectively closes off any access she might have had to it.[37] When read against the background of *Dissemination*, a more positive assessment of *Spurs'* significance for feminism—and ultimately for my project, begins to appear. First, *Spurs* shows once again that metaphysics (in this case, its desire for truth) is founded on, and works by means of, a trajectory of desire that is not gender neutral. The position of the seeker-of-truth is masculine and is figured as man's-desire-for-woman. At the same time, Derrida's reading shows that metaphysics' desire for absolute truth remains unfulfilled. The root of this unfulfillment lies in something prior to metaphysics: the movement of what Derrida has elsewhere called *différance* plays a constitutive role in this economy. Equiprimordial with the (always lacking) phallus is the hymen; the veil that simultaneously sets the economy in motion and disrupts it. As goes woman, so goes truth, in this epoch. Derrida's reading also reveals the failure of this economy to fix gender permanently. The phallogocentric economy assigns woman the task of giving and man the task of appropriation, but Derrida's reading of woman through Nietzsche's corpus disrupts the economy's drive toward fulfillment. But to what degree do his interventions disrupt the phallogocentric economy? *Spurs* shows that woman and truth exceed the economy's attempts to fix them, thus Derrida's project disrupts the economy's achievement of mastery over her/truth. However, a significant aspect of phallogo-centrism remains relatively undisturbed by Derrida's solicitation.

I noted earlier that, in addition to being marked by particular gender positions, the economy of truth followed the trajectory of man's-desire-for-woman. Derrida's solicitation of the text of metaphysics by way of Nietzsche leaves that *trajectory* in place even as it follows the movement of woman, the phallus, or truth beyond the text's reach. Leaving the trajectory in place limits the efficacy of Derrida's interventions. Follow-ing the signs of this trajectory's ability to hold its own allows the limits of Derrida's work with woman to emerge. I am going to suggest that the limit arises from the very thing that makes Derrida's intervention possible; namely, his own inscription as a man in this phallogocentric economy. Surveying this limit will leave women asking for something more, but can a man give it to women? Should a man give it?[38]

The feminine figures that appear on the terrain just covered are those aspects of woman that are of significance for the trajectory of man's-desire-for-woman. Within an economy structured by this trajectory, the hymen serves as the mark of woman's value. Unpierced, it marks her value as virgin, as unspoiled goods. Pierced, it indicates that she has been appropriated by a man.[39] Outside such an economy, what would its value be? Moreover, the hymen may elude the spur's desire to pierce to infinity, but that does not deter the spur from likewise pursuing its course to infinity. If anything, it may make it more determined. Simi-larly, woman as sailing ship gliding across the sea at a distance, while elusive, also serves to keep phallogocentric desire in motion. There is nothing like the tantalizing almost-absence of a woman to get man's-desire-for-woman going. Indeed, this has been woman's function in the phallogocentric economy all along, and Derrida's Nietzsche does little to disturb it.

What of the reversal of man and woman that Derrida's reading keeps in motion? Woman does have spurs (prows/promontories/styles) and man is sometimes the veil. However, even if man and woman switch positions, the positions remain determined by the same tra-jectory. Spurs are for piercing or parrying; veils are for disguising/dissimulating/sailing away from that which aims at appropriation. A clear mark of the limits of Derrida's solicitation appears when one follows out the consequences of the play of woman and truth for Nietzsche. I noted earlier that the play of woman/truth among three positions disrupted Nietzsche's position as author with mastery over his texts. As woman goes, so goes truth, and so goes Nietzsche. I would argue that disrupting Nietzsche's claim to mastery does not dislodge

Nietzsche from a master*ly* position. Let me quote two passages from
Spurs. Early in the text, Derrida forecasts the position in which Nietzsche will find himself as *Spurs* draws to a close:

> *Nietzsche aura pratiqué tous les genres.*

> Nietzsche must have practiced all the genres [and taking advantage
> of a complicity in French] / genders. (*SP*, 38; my translation)[40]

Later, Derrida writes,

> *Il était, il redoutait telle femme châtrée.*
> *Il était, il redoutait telle femme castratrice.*
> *Il était, il aimait telle femme affirmatrice.*

> He [Nietzsche] was, he dreaded such a castrated woman.
> He was, he dreaded such a castrating woman.
> He was, he loved such an affirming woman. (*SP*, 100; my translation)

And immediately following this triad:

> *Tout cela à la fois, simultanément ou successivement, selon les lieux de son*
> *corps et les positions de son histoire. Il avait affaire en lui, hors de lui, à tant*
> *de femmes.*

> All this at once, simultaneously or successively, depending on the
> places of his body and the positions of his story / history. He "had
> affairs" (had dealings) with so many women within himself, outside
> himself. (*SP*, 100; my translation)[41]

Nietzsche may have been displaced from his position as author *of* his
texts by the play of woman *in* his texts, but he manages to come out
on top, nonetheless. Derrida's Nietzsche remains the one in whose
hands the plural styles converge (or out of whose hands the plural
styles diverge). This Nietzsche occupies both the displaced position of
man-who-desires-woman (a different woman, to be sure, than the
usual object of phallogocentric sexuality) and of woman in all three
positions. To be sure, identifying Nietzsche with the three women in
his texts calls this Nietzsche's gender into question, but not without
resistance. To the degree that Nietzsche remains indelibly marked in
a reader's mind as male, Derrida's Nietzsche reincorporates this disruption of phallogocentrism within himself and within his dealings
with women. The figure of Nietzsche, the man-who-desires-woman,
persists through the multiple positionings of his gender and authority.
To the degree that the conjunction between Nietzsche and man-who-
desires-woman reasserts itself, having the masterly position occupied

by even a residual man is not fully satisfying no matter how unstable the "top" may be.

Nietzsche's marking as male gains the upper hand because the *trajectory* of man's-desire-for-woman passes through Derrida's solicitation of Nietzsche relatively undisturbed. The symptoms of its persistence appear in Derrida's discussion of the economy of propriation's governance of sexuality in Nietzsche's texts and woman's disruption of its mastery. The same dynamics of attempted appropriation and resistance to that appropriation that culminated in woman-as-truth's withdrawal also govern sexuality.[42] The interactions between man and woman are governed by the economy of propriation in all its variety (appropriation, expropriation, giving oneself, taking someone else, etc.). The two figures assume typical positions at the beginning; the man takes, the woman gives. However, Derrida's Nietzsche suggests that her giving sometimes reverses the positions of mastery in the text of sexuality.

> Across numerous analyses . . . it appears according to the law formulated already, that sometimes woman is woman in giving, *in giving herself* [*se donner*], while man takes, possesses, takes possession. Sometimes to the contrary, woman in giving herself *gives* (herself) *for* / *gives for* (herself) / *is* (herself) *given for* [*se donne-pour*], simulates and consequently assures herself possessive mastery. (*SP*, 108; my translation)

Derrida quotes Nietzsche, who writes, "Women have known, by their submission (*Unterordnung*), how to assure themselves the greatest advantage, even domination (*Herrschaft* [master-y])" (*SP*, 110; my translation). Derrida concludes that *se donner pour*, an ambiguous reflexive verb whose play between meanings will not translate easily into English ("she gives herself / is given for" an unnamed party, "she gives for herself") sets in motion a disruption that cannot be stopped in the stereotypical dynamics of gift / possession. Another economy, that of gift *without* exchange, peeks through the crack in the economy of propriation, but is all too quickly recaptured in an economy of exchange.[43] "Man and woman change places, exchanging their masks to infinity" (*SP*, 110; my translation). The place of mastery is no longer assignable strictly or simply to the man, but is sometimes occupied also by the woman. The place traditionally assigned to woman is also available to man.[44] The foundation of the economy of propriation is shown to rest on an undecidable assignation of gendered positions, but the positions circulate in an economy still governed by exchange. The other economy of gift appears only briefly before it recedes from view.

The strategies Derrida has used here to intervene in the phallogocentric economy are those he will follow elsewhere.[45] Having uncovered woman's elusion of the trajectory of man's-desire-for-woman, he will proceed to give her lots of opportunities to so maneuver in other contexts. Having uncovered man and woman switching masks to eternity, he will enact that switch in other places. Where does Derrida's Nietzsche leave woman on this disrupted terrain of phallogocentrism? In my view, Derrida's disruptions of the machinations of phallogocentrism leave women asking for more.

Insofar as the positions in the trajectory of desire remain the same (that of mastery and elusion of mastery), what difference does it make that the position of mastery can, from time to time, be occupied by a woman?[46] As long as the trajectory of desire remains the same (one giving, one appropriating; one on top, one on bottom), do the genders of the positions really change? The occupants of the positions seem to switch genders, but have they really? Is the top really available to woman-as-such or does she become him upon gaining the upper hand? Gayatri Spivak reads this "final (non)resting place" of (hetero)sexuality as Derrida's affirmation of the possibility of genuine love between the sexes.[47] I would argue one could just as easily read the dance between the positions in terms of the proverbial "war between the sexes." Can women aspire only to give themselves to man in such a way that holds the self in reserve and thereby gains mastery over him? At the same time, can Derrida—or any man, for that matter—offer women something more than this dance/war?

These limits to the efficacy of Derrida's interventions arise from the position from which Derrida intervenes. Derrida, like Nietzsche, remains figured as a man who by his own admission continues to desire woman (see, e.g., *SP*, 71). I have described the import of *Spurs* as showing that as goes woman, so goes truth, and so goes (Derrida's) Nietzsche. Let me suggest another twist to this line of thinking: as goes Derrida's Nietzsche, so goes Derrida. Derrida, like his Nietzsche, remains entangled in this same trajectory. The sign of Derrida's own inscription (and arguably of his awareness of it) appears in "Women in the Beehive," the report of an interview with Derrida on the question of feminism by two feminist scholars. The interview discusses Derrida's acknowledged desire to write like a woman as a step toward rendering gender obsolete, a move some feminists have found objectionable. In the course of the conversation, Derrida also acknowledges the impossibility of fulfilling his desire. To my mind, the most telling sign of this desire and its impossibility lies not in what Derrida says about it but in the form that "Women in the Beehive" as text takes.[48] In "Women in the Beehive," the discussion of feminism and deconstruction is reproduced almost literally as it happened, according to the editors, with one difference. The speaking positions are not autographed with anyone's name—neither Derrida's nor his (female) interlocutors, at Derrida's request. Moreover, a disclaimer appears at the beginning of the report:

> The speaker referred to as "Response" is not the writer Jacques Derrida, but is rather our account of his responses. . . . Due to the improvised nature of the seminar's dialogue and the vulnerable philosophical position M. Derrida is placed in [no] quotation marks appear in this edited text. We thank M. Derrida for allowing us to publish this transcript—this text, authorized but authorless. ("Beehive," 189)

Refusing the editorial privilege and the signatorial privilege can be read as Derrida's attempt to relinquish mastery over this text, a significant gesture given the topic under discussion. Abdicating that privilege in favor of "our account" of his responses—where "our" is constituted by two women—enacts the reversal of positions *Spurs* uncovers. Derrida's abdication offers a gift; it allows his words to be appropriated by women. This reading suggests that the interviewee, Jacques Derrida, is very much aware of the effect his position as a man (and "the *writer* Jacques Derrida*") will have on the weight of his words. However, the gift only accomplishes so much and only goes so far. It is clear from the flow of the text who the interlocutors are and who the subject responding to questions, no matter how vulnerable, is. Even in the official absence of the author, the reader's recollection of Derrida will sign off in Derrida's place on such a text.[49]

The effects (and the limits to their efficacy) as set in motion around the figure of Derrida are strikingly reminiscent of the effects and limits that attend Derrida's Nietzsche. As was the case with Nietzsche, it is difficult for Derrida to shake his attachment to/by the position of mastery. The figures of Nietzsche and Derrida continue the old game of give and take by appropriating woman's place and style. To be sure, exposing the essential unfulfillability of that desire to appropriate carries the trajectory of man's-desire-for-woman toward exhaustion. However, that bearing meets its limit. Neither Nietzsche nor Derrida manage to bring the economy of propriation and its gendered system (which accords the position of mastery to man and the position of property to woman) to the point where gender is no longer pertinent.

I am not arguing that Derrida's work with woman in *Spurs* and in

"Beehive" (as well as elsewhere) recapitulates the phallogocentric context's gender dynamics in the same old way. In this, my evaluation differs from that offered by Oliver and others. The text's strategies for keeping woman in her place may reassert themselves in Derrida's readings of woman and the trajectory of man's-desire-for-woman, but the disruption his readings engender remains a fissure in phallogocentrism. That the text's strategies reassert themselves *despite* Derrida's intervention is a tribute to their strength and pervasiveness. In other words, to identify this limit to Derrida's disruption of the trajectory of man's-desire-for-woman is not so much to criticize Derrida but to unearth the intransigence of phallogocentrism. It is clear from other texts that Derrida claims no exemption from inscription by the text of metaphysics. Certainly "the reader Jacques Derrida" would not be surprised by such an excavation of his own indebtedness to the phallogocentric shape of this terrain with the text of metaphysics. Taking man's-desire-for-woman to its limit may even be the best that Derrida—or any man—can do. However, Derrida's intervention leaves women hungry for something more. We need to have attention paid to the larger context of our situation. As his feminist critics rightly insist, our oppression occurs in multiple loci beyond (though not outside) the bed constituted by man's-desire-for-woman (and its most immediate context, the *oikos*/household in the most literal and traditional sense). Nor are our multiple oppressions the end of the story. We also need to broach the question of our own pleasure.[50] We yearn for the thematization of trajectories of desire other than assertion of mastery and resistance to it.

That none of these sites appear in Derrida's reading of woman is significant both for an evaluation of what double reading/writing from the side of the man-who-desires-woman can accomplish and for what it leaves undone.[51] For "the writer Jacques Derrida" as (unforgettably) a man to have broached these topics would have been to make a grossly appropriative gesture.[52] That he fails/refuses to do so suggests again his awareness of the hold the text of metaphysics has on him and his awareness of its/his limits. It is, I think, appropriate that Derrida remains with the task of bringing man's-desire-for-woman to the brink of exhaustion. Yet leaving woman unexplored means she remains the dark continent. To be sure, the boundaries keeping that continent in its place have been breached, but the continent remains unexplored. Derrida's *solicitation* of the trajectory of man's-desire-for-woman has opened the door to another order, but it remains for others to come through this opening and to uncover the many other loci of woman's inscription in and by the text of western metaphysics and to move toward an intervention from the side of woman.[53]

Conclusion/Opening

This chapter took its mark where chapter 2 ended, from the point where woman's place in relation to the text of metaphysics began to appear. It followed woman as object of man's desire, the erotic bearing constitutive of the text of metaphysics, as far as Derrida takes her. This traversal began at the intersection between deconstruction and psychoanalysis. The patro-, logo-, heliocentric specular economy that chapter 2 excavated turned out to be phallogocentric, as well. Symptoms of phallogocentrism appear not only in the sexual economy in its narrow sense, but in the larger discursive economy as well. Within that economy, as Derrida's reading of Nietzsche in *Spurs* reveals, woman and truth go together. Both elude capture by the economy of propriation and, in so doing, point to something beyond or outside it. Derrida's *solicitation* of woman-as-truth carries man's-desire-for-woman to its end as limit and goal, if not quite to its death. Its end as point of exhaustion appears where man and woman exchange masks to eternity. Derrida's solicitation looks toward another sexual economy in pointing beyond the economy of propriation toward the economy of the gift.

While Derrida's work with woman stops short of engaging with women's concrete situations of oppression, it breaks open a space in which such an engagement can occur in recognition of women's variety. As Gayatri Chakravorty Spivak argues, Derrida exposes woman as undecidable, as resistant to fixation by the specular economy.[54] *Spurs* suggests, then, that woman offers a particularly potent site from which to deconstruct that economy; a site that prefigures the economy of gift rather than propriation. Taking woman to this point in the text of metaphysics and its sexual economy deepens my claim that woman has a potential life on the other side of the economy of sameness at work in the race/gender divide. At the same time, especially when sighted from the divide, it also questions feminism's claim to an exemption from deconstruction in ways that are valuable for my project. Some whitefeminists find this connection of woman with undecidability problematic because it risks losing sexual specificity.[55] I see positive potential in this connection, especially when viewed from the perspective of overcoming the race/gender divide. Peggy Kamuf argues that, in disrupting man and woman as determinedly fixed identities, Derrida renders impossible a certain return of the self to itself, of self-possession. Rather than rejecting Derrida on this point, Kamuf argues for this point's importance in carrying feminism beyond identity politics.[56] She notes that feminists have welcomed challenges to the notion of a universal subject within masculine philosophy while wanting to hang onto some kind of general subjectivity for women. She suggests, instead, that feminist aims might be enhanced by relinquishing such projects since they inevitably rest on exclusionary grounds. I am sympathetic to Kamuf's suggestion. It seems to me that feminism's history with regard to race could be read as symptomatic of precisely these dynamics. Let me hasten to point out, however, that I am not suggesting relinquishing woman altogether; rather, I would advocate holding to her *as* a figure of undecidability. Thought and practiced in this way, woman could make room for a fluid give and take between multiple positions that could take up residence in that category. In other words, Kamuf's suggestion seems to me to be compatible with whitefeminism's turn toward conceiving woman as multiple. At the same time, invoking that most recent turn in whitefeminist theory also calls to mind the limits of its efficacy in subverting the race/gender divide. While woman as undecidable carries *potential* for thinking women as multiply raced, it does nothing to *ensure* that such thinking would occur at such a site. Once again, the limits of this line of inquiry into the divide (that of following woman to her end) exhibits its limit as a strategy for subverting the divide between race and woman.

One further step remains to be taken, however, in following woman to her end. Reading Derrida's woman left women calling for more. Luce Irigaray, whose work I address in the following chapter, offers "something more" in several senses. She shares Derrida's view of woman's place in relationship to the text of metaphysics, but she intervenes in that place from woman's side. More successfully than Derrida, she disrupts the current sexual economy in favor of another economy. Central to this achievement is bearing woman toward her end in multiple senses. When chapter 4 comes to its conclusion/opening, woman will no longer be able to keep race at bay.

4

Irigaray: Thinking Difference(s)

Introduction

The previous two chapters have followed particular lines of force that constitute the divide between race and gender within whitefeminist theory and theology. Chapter 2 began with questions about textuality raised by the persistence of white solipsism in whitefeminist thought. Following those issues through an inquiry into the Derrideanism "There is nothing outside the text" suggested that whitefeminist thought's difficulties are symptomatic of the field's inscription by the context of metaphysics and its specular economy of sameness. Tracing the contours of this context also entered the race/gender divide itself from the side of woman. Analyzing woman's place in Derrida's work uncovered gender marks and an erotic bearing at the heart of the context of western metaphysics. In contrast to those who would dismiss Derrida from feminism, I argued that, while his own work with woman is (properly) limited, deconstruction is compatible with feminist aims. Moreover, Derrida's work also points in directions that whitefeminism might follow as it attempts to move beyond this impasse in its dealings with race.

In eluding fixation by the specular economy, woman fissures that economy and points toward the economy of *différance* that funds it. Insofar as this economy is implicated in whitefeminism's own inability to break with sameness, then following woman through those fissures toward the economy of *différance* should aid in moving beyond the race/gender divide. Following woman through Derrida's work also argues for whitefeminist theology as a critical site for whitefeminist engagement with such a project. God the Father constitutes the center of value in the economy of sameness uncovered by Derrida. Thus, disrupting his mastery is integral to disrupting that economy in order to make room for alterities. Whitefeminist theology would be a logical place to engage deconstruction toward that aim. Deconstruction offers resources for carrying whitefeminist theology's critical and constructive work to ever deeper levels. By following woman and God together toward what they might become on the other side of the specular economy, whitefeminist theology could, in turn, provide important resources for moving whitefeminism beyond the race/gender divide.

Locating a self-differing woman on the other side of the specular economy holds out hope for a feminism beyond the race/gender divide. However, familiarity with whitefeminism tempers any confidence that sighting the other side of this economy through such a woman will, on its own, subvert the divide. My analysis in chapter 1 showed that deploying a multiple woman provides no guarantee that the difference race makes to woman will register. It will not, in and of itself, ensure that whitefeminism holds itself accountable to African American feminism, nor does it obligate whitefeminism to investigate whiteness as a racial mark. Thus, even as reading Derrida indicated a route beyond an economy of sameness, reading Derrida also took us into the race/gender divide. His work with woman also proceeds as though she were racially neutral. It becomes even more imperative to follow this racially neutral woman to her end—to the point where she can no longer keep race at bay.

Following woman to her end requires turning to the work of Luce Irigaray, a French philosopher, linguist, and psychoanalyst. I turn to Irigaray as Derrida's *supplément* here for a number of reasons. First of all, I turn to her as *supplément* because of her proximity to Derrida. A number of feminist theorists have given varying accounts of this proximity. Virtually all of Irigaray's readers mention Derrida as an important influence on Irigaray's work. They note affinities between their strategies of reading and writing, parallels in the texts that they discuss, and similarities in their approach to philosophy. They also note that, although Irigaray never directly refers to Derrida in her work, much of it can be read as a critical address to Derrida.[1] Tina Chanter aptly describes Irigaray as "reading Derrida as a woman—and not merely as a woman, but as a woman who has understood the importance of his work and tried to go beyond it" (*Ethics of Eros*, 249). Irigaray revisits many of the sites Derrida traverses, but her visitations engender different effects because her point of entry into those sites is different. Like Derrida, Irigaray uses double writing and reading to expose attempts at mastery and resistances to it. However, she enters the texts she reads and writes from the side of the woman-desired-by-man. Thus, she can be productively read as Derrida's *supplément*.

Let me say a few words here about what I understand reading Irigaray as *supplément* to Derrida to entail. First of all, what follows does not aim to give an account of Irigaray's relationship to Derrida, though it will produce a proximity between them. Rather, in and through a reading of Irigaray, I aim to solicit the disruption of the divide between gender and race uncovered in chapter 1. The resources Irigaray offers for this project are made available by reading her through the opening created for her work by my reading of Derrida. Thus, I turn to Irigaray at this point for specific reasons. The failure of Derrida's disruption of man's-desire-for-woman opens the way for intervention from the side of the desired woman. This is, in fact, the position from which Irigaray begins. In this sense, the closure of Derrida's dealings with woman opens onto *woman's* dealings with woman. Reading Irigaray as Derrida's *supplément* will entail following Irigaray through some of the same territory covered by my reading of Derrida. However, like all supplemental readings, to cover the same territory is not to retrace the same steps. The reading of Irigaray that follows will supplement Derrida's readings of woman in exhibiting her everywhere. Under Irigaray's gaze, the specular economy exhibits woman's reflection in every mirror.

I also turn to Irigaray as Derrida's *supplément* because of her relationship to the problematics in whitefeminist theory and theology discussed in chapter 1. Irigaray's work came onto the Anglophone feminist scene in the early 1980s, the decade of the so-called problem of essentialism. As Tina Chanter and Kelly Oliver have both argued, the issues dominating the American scene definitively shaped early Anglo-American readings of Irigaray's work. For many, Irigaray came to epitomize the evils of biological essentialism. Others have come to see Irigaray's insistence on woman's multiplicity as laying the theoretical groundwork for dealing more adequately with differences between women, an assumption Patricia Huntington has recently called into question.[2] Either way, Irigaray is clearly implicated in the dynamics of whitefeminism's dealings with race as analyzed in chapter 1. In fact, it may appear at first that turning to Irigaray would carry my project astray. If Irigaray is an essentialist, then she offers my project virtually nothing. If she is not an essentialist but rather a theorist of woman-as-multiple, she may still offer my project next to nothing. Indeed, given the career of multiplicity in recent whitefeminist theory, she may offer my project false hope. Huntington argues that Irigaray ends up "reinstating the very 'white authorial presence' that some U.S. feminists believe French psychoanalytic feminism can help them avoid"

(187). It is precisely this situation that constitutes Irigaray's value for my project of deconstructing the divide between race and gender in whitefeminism. As I have noted throughout, my project is deconstructive in that it takes its mark from the lines of force in whitefeminist theory and theology. Essentialism and multiplicity constitute significant lines of force within whitefeminist theory and theology and their dealings with woman and race. Reading Irigaray, then, will repeat whitefeminism's gestures toward dealing with race, even to the point of repeating its exclusion of race. It will revisit the question of essentialism and carry it to its end in Irigaray's concern with sexual difference. Sexual difference, in turn, comes to its end in Irigaray's insistence on differences within and between women. This multiple woman / women comes to her / their end, in turn, in Irigaray's failure to think through the specific difference race makes for woman. Reading Irigaray also takes us to the point where the exclusion of race from whitefeminism's woman reaches its end. Its inability to keep race at bay also leads whitefeminism into the terrain of race. Significantly, its closure within Irigaray's oeuvre takes place in a theological scene. Thus, its closure also constitutes a call for whitefeminist theology as a necessary site of intervention if whitefeminism is to move beyond its exclusionary tendencies.

Irigaray's Reception in Anglo-American Feminism

The question of the role of essentialism in Irigaray's work has formed the centerpiece of debates over Irigaray's usefulness for feminism in Anglo-American contexts. The first generation of assessments of her work often argued that she posits an essential femininity that is grounded in female biology. Those who read her this way (and they were numerous; the bulk of the early secondary literature on Irigaray followed this line of interpretation) understood Irigaray to be positing an essential difference in how women think that is grounded in their autoerotic experience.[3] That these readings entrap Irigaray within the scene of Anglo-American feminism of the 1980s is also borne out in defenses of Irigaray against these charges. As Tina Chanter argues, a number of factors contributed to this reading of Irigaray, including being read through a number of vectors that shape Anglo-American feminism, but have no analogue in Irigaray's context. As this chapter will show, the female body figures prominently in Irigaray's work. Chanter argues that this aspect of Irigaray's work got read through the sex /

gender distinction that governed American feminism in the 1980s. Within that paradigm, any reference to the body would seem to be a reference to "sex"; that is, to an unchanging biological given. Hence, Irigaray's deployment of terms of embodiment registered as biological essentialism.

A number of Irigaray's earlier interpreters defend Irigaray against charges of essentialism. Two recent accounts of Irigaray's work by Margaret Whitford and Elizabeth Grosz have taken a middle position on the question of her essentialism.[4] No, they argue, Irigaray is not positing an essential difference between women and men *that is grounded in biology*. She is, however, a theorist of "feminine specificity," to use a common phrase. Investigating this terrain, they argue, seems to require that Irigaray take the risk of *some* kind of essentialism. Evaluations of exactly *what* kind of essentialism she risks, the degree to which she risks it, and her reasons for doing so vary among her interpreters. Nonetheless, they seem agreed that, as long as essentialism does not ground itself in biological claims, it poses little risk to feminist projects. It may even be necessary to their success.

While I find much in Grosz and Whitford to applaud, I also think they close off many of the most significant possibilities that Irigaray's woman offers feminist theory. Although both of these theorists recognize that Irigaray is challenging western culture's domination by an economy of sameness, I find that their accounts of Irigaray's work remain bound by that logic. Grosz and Whitford tend to align the economy of sameness exclusively with a masculinity disguising itself as generic. In their eyes, Irigaray's value for feminism comes in her exposure of the falseness of this neutrality and her insistence on women's *self-defined* difference.[5]

Whether intended or not, this reading of Irigaray comes too close to what I would argue is a gyno(phallogo)centric feminism—that is, a feminism that sets up femininity as the standard for sexual difference. If one thinks that only men are likely to confuse neutrality with sameness, then one might not view this leaning as problematic. If, however, one remembers that feminism has shown itself to be as vulnerable to an economy of sameness as any other aspect of western culture, one is disturbed by this slippage. At the same time, the fact that Irigaray's work can be held captive to this foreign scene suggests the need to revisit these questions once again. My exposition of Irigaray's work will start with the question of essentialism for two additional reasons. Although these charges against Irigaray have largely been laid to rest

in feminist theory, feminist theology has yet to register fully that accomplishment.[6] Furthermore, what Irigaray offers my project becomes
clear against the screen of this misreading of her work.

The Question of Irigaray's Essentialism

Irigaray's first two books, *Speculum of the Other Woman* and *This Sex
Which Is Not One*, launched the debate over the place of essentialism
in her work.[7] Though ably translated, the complexity and density of
Irigaray's writings presented a significant barrier to American readers.
Indeed, Chanter and Whitford both suggest that lack of familiarity with
this background contributed to essentialist readings of Irigaray. The
background against which Irigaray writes is a distinctively French convergence of psychoanalytic theory (Freud via Lacan), the tradition of
continental philosophy from Plato to Derrida, and Marxist analysis.
This convergence is still foreign to American thinking, with its roots
in pragmatic philosophies of various sorts, its suspicion of Freudian
psychoanalysis and Marxism, and its relatively recent (and no less suspicious) acquaintance with Derrida, in particular. Most Anglophone
accounts of Irigaray's work read her primarily through the lens of psychoanalysis (and often a particularly *American* understanding of that
discipline). While familiarity with psychoanalytic theory is critical for
understanding Irigaray, reading her *exclusively* by its light led to a
skewed understanding of her work. These readings understood Irigaray to be one more participant in the debate over woman's *true* nature or essence. Not coincidentally, given Irigaray's proximity to Derrida, these misreadings parallel the nihilist readings of Derrida that I
called into question in the preceding chapters. Their interpreters have
understood these thinkers to be simply reversing the value system they
question. So, for example, many read Derrida's exposure of the aporetic
character of the dominance of presence in western metaphysics as an
identification of an absolute abyss / *nihil* at the base of reality where
we used to think absolute presence resided. Similarly, Irigaray's critics
read her exposure of aporias attending what she will call phallocentrism as an identification of the *essential* woman hidden behind the
mask imposed on her by patriarchy.

One can see where such readings got their impetus. In *This Sex Which
Is Not One*, Irigaray spends a great deal of time describing the plurality
of the erotic areas of a woman's body (*TS*, 28, e.g.), the continuousness
of genital touch that women experience (*TS*, 24), and so forth. She even
seems to assert that this plurality of woman's autoeroticism is reflected

in her thought patterns, which yields a uniquely feminine form of ratio-nality:

> "She" is indefinitely other in herself. This is doubtless why she is said to be whimsical, incomprehensible, agitated, capricious . . . not to mention her language, in which "she" sets off in all directions leaving "him" unable to discern the coherence of any meaning. Hers are con-tradictory worlds, somewhat mad from the standpoint of reason, in-audible for whoever listens to them with ready-made grids, with a fully elaborated code in hand. For in what she *says*, too, at least when she dares, woman is constantly touching herself. . . . One would have to listen with another ear, as if hearing an "other meaning" always in the process of weaving itself, of embracing itself with words, but also of getting rid of words in order not to become fixed, congealed in them. (*TS*, 28–29)

These interpreters read what Irigaray calls the "feminine imaginary" as a kind of subconscious feminine essence, as an account of uniquely feminine sexuality that patriarchy has covered over and that founds a uniquely feminine language characterized by an absence of reason, meaning, and order.[8] Is this as simple as it looks? In positing an intel-lectual difference that is rooted in a physical/emotional difference, is Irigaray simply accepting the traditional reductionistic definition of woman as a creature utterly defined/determined by her body and in-capable of rational thought? A careful reading of her work will show that it is not as simple as it looks.

Such accounts seem to have read right past Irigaray's *repeated* refus-als to answer questions like "What is woman?" and "What is woman's unconscious?" In a transcribed conversation, Irigaray is asked, "What is a woman?" She responds, "There is no way I would 'answer' that question. The question 'what is . . . ?' is the question—the metaphysical question—to which the feminine does not allow itself to submit" (*TS*, 122).[9] She similarly refuses a request to describe the female unconscious on the grounds that to take it on would be to "anticipate a certain his-torical process, and to slow down its interpretation and its evolution by prescribing, as of now, themes and contents for the feminine uncon-scious" (*TS*, 124).

This disclaimer has its roots in Lacan's infamous claim that "woman does not exist," which I discussed in chapter 3. Whitford, along with many other feminist theorists, interprets Lacan as denying any being to woman. Whitford reads Irigaray, by contrast, as claiming that woman does not *yet* exist. I would argue for a more radical reading. I read Irigaray's claim as more Lacanian (and Derridean): woman is outside metaphysics, to put it philosophically; she is outside what passes for love in this culture, to use psychoanalytic terms. Whatever woman means, is, or comes to be, she is not/will not be subject to the order of the "is."[10]

Even by my reading, Irigaray's early critics would have been correct to accuse Irigaray of either solipsism or of failing to carry out her project and falling into essentialism against her will *if* what she writes under the name of woman claimed to be answers to these questions that she so stalwartly refuses. The weight I think should be given to Irigaray's disclaimers alters the way I read what Irigaray writes under the name of woman. I would argue that accusations of essentialism against Irigaray's work came out of the same kind of misreading that characterized nihilist readings of Derrida. These interpreters of Irigaray failed to grasp the *level* at which her critique and construction is occurring. Rather than attempting to rewrite woman/women free from patriarchal taint, Irigaray is moving the problematics of the question of woman (by problematics, I mean critique, construction, ongoing questioning, and problematizing) to a deeper level; that of our cultural discourse. Irigaray's target is the "general grammar of [western] culture" (*TS*, 155) or what Derrida calls the text of western metaphysics. Like Derrida, Irigaray finds this grammar/text at work in our culture's institutions, its economy, its philosophical tradition, in psychoanalytic theory and practice, and in the concepts of male and female found in every aspect of western society.[11] This cultural grammar courses below distinctions between sex and gender and their analogues (body and mind, nature and culture). Prior to sex/gender lies sexual difference; that is, the notion of difference between man and his other, woman.[12] As Irigaray will show, sexual difference amounts to sexual *in*difference as long as woman's alterity is defined in terms of man.

This alternative reading of her work is easy to produce if one situates her reading of psychoanalysis within the other two streams of thought that constitute the Irigarayan milieu; namely, Marxism and the tradition of continental philosophy—especially the critique of metaphysics espoused by Derrida.[13] Like those American feminists who have ventured into these waters, Irigaray finds that psychoanalysis, Marxism, and philosophy shed some light on the situation of women; yet the question of woman also brings to light the limits of these perspectives. It is what appears at the limits of these systems that Irigaray wants to question. All three streams of thought share a common inscription in/ by the general grammar of western culture and its economic system that is built on sameness.[14] Irigaray collects the characteristics of this general grammar as exposed by the convergence of Freudian, Marxist, and philosophical thinking in the terms "scopic economy" (in *TS*) and "specular economy" (in *S*). The logic of this economy is photologic, she writes in *Speculum*. Its system of values and of argumentation is dominated by sight, light, and the gaze. In Irigaray's text, one sees both what we feminists already knew (the equation of man with mind, spirit, idea, logos, and subject while woman equals body, nature, matter, and object) and something more. We come face to face with an uncanny connivance between the dominance of presence, form, and the visual with the definition of woman as lack. *This* is where Irigaray's criticism and construction is directed.

The Questioning of Philosophy

The tradition of continental philosophy provides a privileged point of access to the cultural grammar and its specular/scopic economy. Since it is the master discourse that lays down the rules for other discourses, on Irigaray's account, exhibiting slippages in the scopic economy's grip provides significant leverage against the cultural grammar and its inscription of woman. The bulk of *Speculum of the Other Woman* consists of careful, subtle readings of several major philosophers from Plato to Hegel.[15] As Tina Chanter has shown, Irigaray's readings of each of the philosophers in *Speculum* and elsewhere are complex and well worth exploring in their own right, but such a task is beyond the scope of my project.[16] My interest here is in uncovering the larger pattern that Irigaray reads in and through the philosophical tradition; thus, my account of these essays in *Speculum* will be directed toward that end.

Like Derrida, Irigaray goes after what lies at the limits of the philosopher's control. The play of metaphors and tropes in philosophical texts plays a large role in her reading of the philosophers. Irigaray's analyses simultaneously expose coincidences between the tropes that describe woman in these philosophers' texts and those that describe, for example, the relationship of matter and form in Plotinus's *Enneads* (*S, 168–79*) or the relationship of subject and world in Kant (*S, 203–13*) and Descartes (*S, 180–90*). This coincidence exhibits philosophy's inscription in the larger grammar that is the ultimate target of her critiques.

Her reading uncovers a trajectory directing and locating matter/world/woman that is both made possible and disrupted by a play of mirrors within itself. Like Derrida, Irigaray's questioning is directed not at these thinkers' conscious intentions but at what *inscribes* their thinking about and through woman: Why does their work take, repeatedly, certain directions as opposed to others? Her readings of the philosophical tradition uncover symptoms of a deeper problem. The trail of these tropes exposes a text that winds through the thought of the major western philosophers. The general grammar of western culture inscribes itself as a cultural imaginary. Matter / world / woman are linked together, rigorously controlled and circumscribed by being relegated to the outside of what really counts even as it / they slip away from circumscription. Though rejected, they also serve as the ground, or raw material, of philosophical speculation. Aristotle's metaphysics, for example, dismisses as derivative and controls as suspect both Prime Matter (which is gendered female) and woman. As a result, both occupy peculiar places of resistance and circumscription in the chain of Being. Both woman and matter are dependent on an "other" in order to be. Both are caught between being and nonbeing, lack and unrealizable potentiality, growth and decay. Woman cannot achieve the status of an active subject because she is unrealizable, potential man; yet, insofar as she is the receptacle of male (procreative) activity, she is a condition whereby *man* comes to be (coming to be is a matter of realizing potentiality). Prime Matter forms, in a sense, one end of the chain whose other end is the Aristotelian God, the Prime Mover. In contrast to the Prime Mover who *is* most perfectly and fully, Prime Matter "eludes the question 'what is' " (*S*, 161). Prime Matter requires form to properly exist. Unbounded, it threatens to disintegrate form and order and all that is good.

The same trajectory of control and resistance characterizes Plotinus's dealings with matter. Irigaray's piece on Plotinus, "Une Mère de Glace," consists entirely of quotations of passages from the Sixth Tractate of the *Enneads*.[17] Matter (gendered female) serves as both circumscribed threat to and shifting reflective ground of reality. Plotinus agrees with Aristotle that matter needs to be controlled. Yet, as nonbeing, it is also always in danger of slipping away, and paradoxically, always submissive. Plotinus's identification of matter as utter nonbeing has several consequences for its locus in his account of existence. Matter threatens form / being / reality in that as utter nonbeing, it is evil.[18] Because it is utter nonbeing, matter as raw material of reality has only a tenuous and derivative relationship to being. It serves as the receptacle of form; thus it is the means by which other things appear, but it cannot present itself. Matter seems to participate in being, but it merely reflects it; thus its participation in being is a mere seeming rather than a real involvement. It serves as a mirror, but is in itself invisible and inauthentic.

A shift in this trajectory occurs at the dawn of the modern period of philosophy with the turn to the subject as the centerpiece of knowing and being, instituted by Descartes and reconceived by Kant's critical philosophy. The relationship of the subject to his world in both thinkers continues the trajectory of control over matter and woman, but her/their role as mirror is taken up into the subject. Irigaray's essay on Descartes, ". . . And If, Taking the Eye of a Man Recently Dead, . . . " takes the reader on a tour through Descartes' construction of the problem of the human being's relationship to its world. Her reading reveals a similar circumscription of the messy material world of the senses that seems to threaten the subject and to serve as his forgotten ground. Descartes seeks a firm ground for knowing being by doubting all that he encounters through his senses, then in his thoughts, until he comes to that which doubt cannot erase: the *res cogitans,* the irreducible facticity of the "I think" of self-reflection. This is the ground of the human being's experience, he argues. Whereas in Plotinus and Aristotle matter serves as the mirror reflecting ideals/forms, "in the *wink of an eye*" (*S,* 181), as Irigaray describes it, the subject ingests/incorporates the mirror. Descartes' search for foundations posits a mirror at the back of the subject whose self-reflection constitutes both his own ground and that of his world, which the mirror refracts.

Having established knowing and being on this firm ground, Descartes reverses his direction, moving out from this center back toward its environment. Descartes' rhetoric describes the world with all its incessant bombardment of the senses as surrounding the "I" like a sea that threatens to overwhelm the thinking subject. Though not ostensibly in order to gain control of this sea, Descartes' positing of the world's essence as extension (*res extensa*) achieves this end, at least in part. It establishes the subject as the "ruler" (both king and measure) of all he surveys. The world/nature is laid out before him on the grid of its essence, extension. Where before it threatened to overwhelm him, now the subject has the upper hand. He can divide/cut up nature into manageable pieces in order to put her to use.

Irigaray's reading of Kant attends to the differences between his program and that of Descartes, but finds in it the tracing of a familiar trajectory. Like Descartes, Kant is seeking the ground of knowing, which he finds in the transcendental structures of the subject. Although Kant's transcendental analysis of sensible experience passes through the sensible world (and indeed could be said to be grounded in it, or certainly imbedded in it), it also follows the rhetorical path laid out by the tradition of western philosophy, especially as redirected by Descartes. The transcendental schemata of space and time function to control and subdue what would be, in its raw state (if there were such a thing) a chaotic mass of sensation.[19] Like the Cartesian *res extensa*, the transcendental schemata of space and time function in Kant's critical philosophy to regulate the otherwise inchoate (and unexperienceable) sensible world. Space and time form a window that frames and organizes intuitions of the world. The manifold of intuitions presupposes the synthetic unity of apperception (the location of the object according to a grid constructed by the twin axes of space and time). In turn, apperception ensures that the phenomenal objects of sensible intuition will be "properly conceived" (*S*, 205).

This controlling strategy is also marked/marred by excess. The inaccessibility of things-in-themselves and the materiality that attaches to Kantian objects as afterthoughts both demarcate boundaries of knowledge, in the first case, and indicate an amaterialist trajectory in Kant's program. Kant's transcendental analysis of sensible knowledge is also exceeded insofar as the space/time of the phenomenal world presupposes/internalizes the space/time of specular logic. Irigaray's reading uncovers another forgotten mirror at the bottom of Kant's analysis. She heads the essay with two quotations from Kant's writings that deal with the human being's spatial orientation according to a distinction between left and right.[20] The first quotation concerns ascertaining what our intuition tells us that the understanding (the home of concepts) cannot. When a human being looks at itself in a mirror, it finds there a replica of itself. The concept, "hand," would tell the human being that its real right hand and the hand it sees directly across from it on its double are of the same genre. However, the human being's intuition makes two distinctions: (1) between the useful appendage and its useless, fleshless double and (2) between the left hand and the right hand of the body and those of its mirror image. Intuition takes into account, Kant writes, the paradox of symmetry; a figurative mirror within the subject that doubles the reflection, thereby properly orienting the subject and making proper perception possible. Mirrors are no mere bystanders to this event, Irigaray argues. Rather, they support the apprehension of spatial orientation and therefore the apperception of the objects that present themselves within its spatial/temporal grid.

The second epigraph deals with how the human being orients itself in a dark room. Kant argues that external conditions do not play the fundamental part in this orientation. A human being is able to locate itself in the room even if the objects that also share this space have been reassembled in an unrecognizable order. The human being accomplishes this task of self-location according to its internal compass that constitutes its consciousness of left and right. Just as the Cartesian *cogito* incorporated the Aristotelian/Neoplatonic mirror into itself, so Kant's transcendental subject assumes (consumes and replaces) the role of the mirror in the first epigraph insofar as an internal self-reflection becomes the support of apprehension/apperception and orientation.

This internal play of mirrors is not limited to knowledge proper (in Kant's view, knowledge per se refers only to knowledge of sensible things, but not to intangible aspects of human experience such as religion, morality, aesthetics, etc.). This play of mirrors structures other aspects of human experience; for example, a man's experience/perception of a woman. Although there is more at stake in this perception than mere perceiving, the something more follows the form of perception in the strict sense. Kant argues that a woman can have different effects on a man (from aesthetic pleasure, to sensual pleasure, to simple respect). However, the possibility of any response on his part to her presupposes something always already present in him; namely an inclination toward women. What matters to this having of an object is not something intrinsic to the object but something intrinsic to the object's reflection/framing in man's imagination.

Supplementation's First Fruits

Irigaray's reading of the philosophical tradition follows strategies similar to those practiced by Derrida. Like Derrida, Irigaray reads and writes doubly. Her readings expose both the repeated recurrence of this systematic locating of woman on the side of matter and reservoir and her refusal to remain there. Irigaray's readings, like Derrida's, also trouble easy distinctions between the inside and outside of a text. This play of woman is not, strictly speaking, under the control of the philosophers in question. Their texts are inscribed by a larger context, the specular economy that Derrida's readings also expose. Under Irigaray's gaze, the philosophical tradition becomes a series of distinctive reflections of the specular economy. Each reflection differs from the one before; each reflection defers the closure of the specular economy. Irigaray's reading exceeds Derrida's in what it exposes as lying outside the context of the cultural grammar and its specular economy. Where

Derrida's work produced significant symptoms of woman's place in this economy, Irigaray's work lays bare the full scope of her situation. The cultural grammar excludes and uses her at one and the same time.

Irigaray also supplements Derrida's analysis of what gives rise to the specular economy. The specular economy that governs the cultural grammar is itself funded and founded by a larger context. Irigaray's reading exposes that context to be not simply *différance* in general, but sexual difference. Woman serves as the forgotten resource that, quite literally, funds this economy. Fully exploring the relationship between sexual difference (especially woman) and *différance* will have to wait for further discussion of Irigaray, but some similarities already present themselves. Like *différance*, woman is, properly speaking, neither something or nothing, present or absent. She is not, properly speaking, "there" in the texts or their contexts, nor is she altogether absent. Her image appears for a moment in the mirrors that conduct the economy's business. That (dis)appearance funds the economy, but no woman as such resides at its heart. Thus, woman as such does not exist here, either.[21]

I have claimed that Irigaray offers valuable resources for whitefeminism as it attempts to deal more adequately with differences between women. Thus, I have offered Irigaray as part of a "cure" for what ails whitefeminism. I noted early on the ambivalence of cure in *pharmakon*'s play between poison and remedy. At first glance, Irigaray may appear to be handing feminism a dose of hemlock. If woman's presence is endlessly deferred within a hall of mirrors that has no real center, has Irigaray not effectively killed off woman and brought feminism to an end? Reading Irigaray against a Derridean background allows her analysis to register differently. Neither Derrida nor Irigaray have exposed a *nihil*—whether under the name of woman or of *différance*—at the heart of reality. Irigaray's reading of the philosophers turns upon/ opens into an essay called "L'incontournable volume" (translated as "Volume-Fluidity" in *Speculum*, but more accurately as "Volume without Contours" in Whitford's *Irigaray Reader*).[22] The title bears allusions to the interior of the female body, but also to woman's (non)place within the philosophical tradition.

> Woman has not yet taken (a) place. . . . Woman is still the place, the whole of the place in which she cannot take possession of herself as such. She is experienced as all-powerful precisely insofar as her indifferentiation makes her radically powerless. She is never here and now because it is she who sets up that eternal elsewhere from which the "subject" continues to draw his reserves, his re-sources, though with-

out being able to recognize them / her. She is not uprooted from matter, from the earth, but yet, but still, she is already scattered into x
number of places that are never gathered together into anything she
knows of herself and these remain the basis of (re)production—particularly of discourse—in all its forms. (S, 227)

Irigaray connects the openness of the female body with the cultural
grammar's inability to fix woman in one place. Woman names a (non)-
space whose boundaries cannot be secured. Rather than defining and
fixing woman's place, Irigaray wants to maintain woman's resistance
to circumscription. Rather than sounding the death knell of feminism
and its subject, I will argue that Irigaray's woman holds out important possibilities for feminism precisely because woman refuses boundaries and defers closure and presence. Exposing woman's funding /
foundational role in the specular economy is critical to bringing that
economy to its end in another economy. As Philippa Berry suggests,
Irigaray's *Speculum* effectively uses the mirrors that constitute the specular economy to burn a hole in the cultural grammar, and through this
immolation a different economy might be born.[23] It is this other economy and its woman that constitute the resources Irigaray offers to help
whitefeminism beyond its current impasse. Getting to those resources,
however, requires going deeper into the question of Irigaray's essentialism. Making those resources work on whitefeminism's behalf will
require going beyond Irigaray's own work. It is to those issues that I
now turn.

The "Dark Continent": Woman in Psychoanalytic Theory

Psychoanalytic theory constitutes a second resource for Irigaray's
work. Under Irigaray's gaze, it also reveals its inscription by the specular economy. Her opening essay in *Speculum* argues that woman in
Freud's writings on femininity plays a role analogous to that of matter
in philosophical texts. Rather than standing on her own merits, woman
serves as mirror of what really counts and as its forgotten, abandoned,
threatening ground. On first reading, Irigaray's analysis of Freud in
the first essay in *Speculum* and in *This Sex Which Is Not One* sounds
criticisms perhaps *too* familiar to American ears; too familiar in that
we hear them as identical to ones already raised in our context, thereby
missing other things occurring in her critique. She argues, as many
other feminists have, that Freud's focus on the clitoris (the deformed
penis) and the vagina (the replacement for the little boy's hand) to the
exclusion of any other erogenous zones in female sexuality suggests

that male sexuality provided a hidden lens through which Freud viewed female sexuality:

> The opposition between "masculine" clitoral activity and "feminine" vaginal passivity, an opposition which Freud—and many others—saw as stages, or alternatives, in the development of a sexually "normal" woman, seems rather too clearly required by the practice of male sexuality. . . . In these terms, woman's erogenous zones never amount to anything but a clitoris-sex that is not comparable to the noble phallic organ, or a hole-envelope that serves to sheathe and massage the penis in intercourse: a non-sex, or a masculine organ turned back upon itself, self-embracing. (TS, 23)

American feminists have, on similar grounds, tended to dismiss Freud out of hand and with it, psychoanalysis. Irigaray, on the contrary, still finds Freud and psychoanalysis both far more helpful and far more problematic insofar as they are *symptomatic* of this larger problem of our cultural grammar.[24] They are helpful in that they offer powerful descriptions of the status quo for women. Most important, Freud opens the door to this other realm of forces not subject to our control but at work in us nonetheless. However, even as Freud opens this door, Irigaray exposes his own inscription/prescription/proscription by such forces. Irigaray's account exposes Freud's theories as both inscribing and inscribed in what she calls an "economy of the Same." Freud's account of sexual difference reduces to sameness because the standard of value that governs his account of femininity is not just masculine sexuality, but the phallus.[25] The phallocentrism evident in Freud's texts is not simply or even primarily a matter of his authorial intention or of his own personal beliefs. Rather, the phallocentrism of psychoanalysis reflects/reveals the phallocentrism of the larger text in which Freud and philosophy are inscribed: the general grammar of western culture and of western society. The phallocentrism found in psychoanalysis cannot be isolated from property interests or discursive structures that come together to form this cultural economy:

> So long as psychoanalysis does not interpret its entrapment within a certain type of regime of property, within a certain type of discourse (to simplify, let us say that of metaphysics), within a certain type of religious mythology, it cannot raise the question of female sexuality. This latter cannot in fact be reduced to one among other isolated questions within the theoretical and practical field of psychoanalysis; rather, it requires the interpretation of the cultural capital and general economy underlying that field. (TS, 125)[26]

To accomplish this questioning, Irigaray brings Marxist analysis into play because it offers a path of inquiry left unexplored by Freud (the material conditions that produce so-called normal femininity) and because it presents challenges to the oblivion of both philosophy and psychoanalysis to the ways they are influenced by material interests. Toril Moi, one of the few English language interpreters of Irigaray to mention the Marxist element in her work, finds Irigaray's appropriation of Marx to be entirely conventional and uncritical.[27] I find Irigaray's use of Marx to be, on the contrary, marked by a creative critical engagement with his thought, which yields something other than orthodox Marxist analysis. Irigaray makes it clear that Marxist analysis has its limits. Women make a difficult object for it to pursue because we do not form a discrete class. Our racial differences further complicate matters. However, Irigaray's reading of Marx in "Women on the Market" (*TS*, 170–91) and the Marxist aspect of her reading of Freud in "The Blind Spot in the Old Dream of Symmetry" (*S*, 13–129) reveal intricate interweavings between women's status within the sexual economy and the workings of capitalism. Just as her readings of philosophers revealed coincidences between woman and nature/matter in western philosophy, so her reading of Marx and Freud reveal a similar collusion within patriarchal capitalism.

Irigaray's reading of Marx flows in two directions through an analogy between woman's place in society and the commodity's place in a capitalist economy. On the one hand, women function like commodities on an exchange market in which their value is determined by masculine desire; on the other hand, Marx's description of the workings of capitalism on commodities perpetuates gender markings that Irigaray has argued are characteristic of western thinking. According to Marxist analysis, a natural resource becomes a commodity by being submitted to human labor. Human beings then determine the commodity's exchange value and its use value. These values are not properties of the things themselves; rather, their values are determined by their relation to a third term, which represents the needs and desires of the consumers/exchangers. Irigaray argues that women's development into exemplars of normal femininity as described by Freud involves a passage from natural value to social value (their value as objects for use and exchange). Irigaray argues that the phallus serves as the standard of value that women reflect. Women thus serve to ensure the circulation of phallic currency. Irigaray exhibits this economic inscription of woman through her own double reading of Freud on femininity, shadowed by Lacan's rereading. Irigaray traverses the same territory as Derrida, in a sense, but from a different position and with somewhat different results.

The process of becoming a woman, according to Freud, centers around coming to terms with the lack of a penis.[28] Freud's interpretation of the little girl's movement from recognition of her castration to the Oedipus complex all works to ensure the circulation of a sexual currency whose standard of value is the phallus. Even the little girl's play with dolls is inscribed in this economy. According to Freud, the little girl is not acting out a desire to imitate her mother, but to have a child by her father.

Whether the adult woman is heterosexual or homosexual both her sexual desires and, if heterosexual, her value in the economy of reproduction are interpreted as reflections of masculine desire. A heterosexual woman chooses for her partner the man she wishes she could have been. A homosexual woman is not expressing any desire that resides within a sexual economy whose currency is female. She is, rather, revealing her unresolved masculinity complex by identifying with a male position and desiring the same object that a man would: a woman.

Irigaray identifies three positions for the (heterosexual) woman in this economy; virgin, mother, and prostitute. In each case, women's bodies become commodities by being marked by a supplemental value drawn from their bodies' role in reflecting the phallic standard. Regardless of which roles they assume, women array themselves with jewelry, makeup, and clothing designed both to attract the one who has what they lack and to disguise that lack. In this, too, they resemble commodities. Commodities are natural things in wrappers that both disguise them and increase their value. As virgin, a woman represents pure exchange value; she marks the spot of possible exchanges. Once deflowered, her value is determined by her potential for use and she becomes private property. If she becomes a prostitute, her value on the exchange market is determined by her use. Paradoxically, her value often increases (at least up to a point) the more she has been used. If a woman marries, the marriage contract, Irigaray argues, also signifies a form of exchange between men (the bride's father and the husband). Her assessment of marriage in patriarchal capitalism follows the standard Marxist line. Like Engels and many other Marxist thinkers, Irigaray argues that marriage represents a state of both domestic and sexual servitude.

Marriage also generally leads to motherhood, the third role Irigaray identifies as available to women. As a mother, the woman's value rests in her reproductive capabilities for producing both heirs to the family (paternal) name and new fodder for the labor force. Freud's reading of the woman's own desires for motherhood are again read in phallocentric terms. Her desire for the instrument of sexual pleasure, the penis (which occupies the place of the phallus in the economy of sexual desire), is deflected onto/into her desire for a baby (another stand-in for the phallus). This desire is only fully satisfied with the birth of a son. The new mother's mother has no more positive standing in this economy of reproduction than she did in Freud's interpretation of the little girl's doll play. If the new mother has a daughter, she does indeed represent her mother but, within this phallocentric economy, that position is not a happy one. The new mother is identified with someone who not only lacked the desired organ herself but produced another creature suffering from a similar lack. Having a son allows the new mother at best an identification with her mother-in-law, who is only singularly rather than doubly deficient.

The consequences of this inscription/prescription/proscription of woman are significant and substantial. What purports to be a theory of sexual difference never leaves the starting blocks. It remains solidly entrenched within a preestablished paradigm of sameness. Women (and men) are distanced from a devalued maternal origin. Woman is distanced from both her body and from any pleasure that might follow its shape rather than that of the phallus and its signatory, the penis.

> [Woman's] entry into a dominant scopic economy signifies, again, her consignment to passivity: she is to be the beautiful object of contemplation. While her body finds itself thus eroticized, and called to a double movement of exhibition and of chaste retreat in order to stimulate the drives of the "subject," her sexual organ represents *the horror of nothing to see.* . . . This organ which has nothing to show for itself also lacks a form of its own. And if woman takes pleasure precisely from this incompleteness of form which allows her organ to touch itself over and over again, indefinitely, by itself, that pleasure is denied by a civilization that privileges phallomorphism. (*TS,* 26)

It is crucial to recall again that this problem is not unique to Freud but is characteristic of our culture. This collusion exposed at the intersection of Freudian, philosophical, and Marxist discourses is not grounded in a deeper reality; rather it resides within a specular economy constituted by a series of phallocentric reflections. The phallocentrism of western discourse is reflected in/reflects the phallocentrism of sexual difference, the sexual economy of western society in which only the phallus has value in and of itself. The phallocentrism of the sexual practice and theory of western thinking reflects/is reflected in the phallocentrism of the economy in its narrower sense (job market, monetary system, etc.). Within the specular economy, women are commodities evaluated and defined in terms of their use or exchange value in the eyes of the subjects of this economy, those in possession of the phallus equivalents.[29]

More Fruits of Supplementation

I argued in the second and third chapters that Derrida opens a new level of philosophical interrogation, the text of western metaphysics. Derrida's double reading and writing brings to the fore the scope of the text's governance and the questioning of itself that the text bears within it. Derrida's work further exposed the depth to which gender markings run in the specular economy of truth that governs that text. Thus, deconstruction helped explain how feminism got into the predicament I outlined in chapter 1 and showed possible paths out of it. In chapter 3, I followed the play of woman in Derrida's work to its limits. I argued that Derrida reveals woman as eluding fixation by the phallogocentric economy of truth and of being. Woman eludes its attempts to fix her as essentially the same. I also concluded that Derrida's work with woman left women asking for more. In this chapter, I have turned to Irigaray as an important *supplément* to Derrida's intervention in phallogocentrism. Irigaray uses similar strategies to rework much of the same terrain that Derrida covers. Reading Irigaray against a Derridean background illuminates the level at which her analysis is directed. Like Derrida, Irigaray's readings of the philosophical tradition gain access to its larger contexts, the cultural grammar and its specular economy. Irigaray's readings exceed Derrida's in their exposure of the scope of woman's place in the cultural grammar. Irigaray's analysis shows that woman does not occur only where she is the explicit topic or trope (whether in Nietzsche's treatises or Freud's); rather, she marks the trajectory of the cultural grammar's philosophical accounts of subject and world, nature and spirit, and its economic theory. Woman funds the specular economy—not just in Nietzsche's texts, not just in philosophy, but at every level of the economy's functioning. Moreover, as the next section of this chapter will show, the strategies that Irigaray develops for working woman's way out of the specular economy take seriously the breadth *and* depth of the specular economy's strength and open it up to something truly other. Irigaray's woman not only eludes attempts by phallogocentrism to master her, she bears difference within her—essentially.

Strategies of Resistance

Just as she has taken the exposure of structures implicated in the oppression of women to new depths—that is, to the profound level of the discourse that constitutes western thinking—so also Irigaray's strategies for unearthing and overcoming it take feminist critical and constructive work in new directions. The options available for practical or theoretical resistance to this discursive economy's inscription of woman through its institutions, methods of analyses, or its job markets, are circumscribed by phallocentrism's pervasiveness. In fact, Irigaray's assessment of these options in *This Sex Which Is Not One* runs parallel to Ruether's typology of feminisms. Women can, on the one hand, demand access to the same opportunities and benefits that men have (what Ruether labels the liberal feminist agenda). On the other hand, women can withdraw from phallocratic culture and establish their own society (Ruether's romantic feminist agenda). Irigaray finds both options to be problematic, though necessary as stages. Adopting a strategy of development—perhaps securing places for women on an equal par with men—leaves the phallocentric economy in place. Nonetheless, women must "continue to struggle for equal wages and social rights, against discrimination in employment and education, and so forth" (*TS*, 165–66) yet always keeping in mind that this alone is not enough.[30] While she advocates temporary separatist moves—"tactical strikes," as she calls them—as "necessary stages in the escape from . . . proletarization on the exchange market" (*TS*, 33), she rejects total withdrawal because such a strategy threatens to, in Irigaray's words, "correspond once again to the disconnection from power that is traditionally theirs[.] Would it not involve a new prison, a new cloister, built of their own accord?" (*TS*, 33)[31] Retreating to this cloister, even though it would allow women the space necessary for exploring their differences and would remove them from the commodities market, is not itself the answer. If such a move were undertaken with the goal of reversing the economic order as it now stands, "history would repeat itself in the long run" (*TS*, 33), Irigaray asserts, because the economy would revert to sameness; a different kind of sameness, but phallocratism nonetheless because it would again be based on identity. As long as an economy of the same is in place—even if femaleness replaced maleness as normative model—"What I am trying to designate as 'feminine' would not emerge. There would be a phallic 'seizure of power' " (*TS*, 130).[32]

The options available to women in terms of theory are similarly problematic. The practical options listed above are undergirded by parallel courses in theory. Liberal versions of feminist activism are based on the concept of woman's equality with man. She partakes from the same smorgasbord of human characteristics that he does. Romantic versions of feminist activism accept the definition of woman current in culture but reverse its valuation. As we saw in chapter 1, the texts of both Daly and Ruether remain bounded by the discursive structure of an essential woman. And I have argued that this structure is implicated in critiques of feminist thinking raised by womanist thinkers. What does Irigaray pose as an alternative?

The answer is not a matter of charting corrective courses in Freudian theory, Marxist analysis, or philosophical anthropology. Such theoretical corrections leave the text in which these systems of thought are inscribed in place. To speak about woman is to keep her in the role of object even if a woman speaks as the subject most knowledgeable about that object. In opening her mouth to speak (or picking up her pen to write) in one of these discourses, a woman is always already perpetuating her own oppression. These theories are inscribed by the discourse of western thinking. Because it is structured by phallocentrism, the power or ability of women *sexualized as female* to speak this discourse is limited—even denied. Indeed, within phallocentrism there is no such thing as woman.[33] Phallocentrism does not allow woman as such to speak as a subject. In order to speak and be heard one must speak according to the rules; that is, in accordance with the structures of this discourse (*TS*, 148–49). By definition, speaking woman cannot be subject, have ideas, or even speak her mind.

It is important here to bring Lacan into the picture once more in order to understand what Irigaray is trying to say and to get a fix on the level at which this claim is directed. The three central constructs for Lacan are the symbolic, the imaginary, and the real. These are not only different stages of the individual's psychic development, they are *also* something more like a collective psyche—a context that inscribes both our psychic *development* from infancy to early childhood *and* our adult lives. The Symbolic is the realm of society and subjectivity. It is governed by the Law of the Father. Our entrance into subjectivity comes via submission to the prohibition against incest that is the primal command of the Law of the Father.[34] This breaks the union of mother/

child, but our desire for reunion with the mother continues to be consti-tuted in us as lack (thus, for Lacan, the subject is perpetually split). Irigaray agrees with feminists such as Jacqueline Rose and Juliet Mitch-ell, who want to claim Lacan for feminism, that the position of subject is available to women. They enter the symbolic, as do men. However, because of the phallocentrism of the economy of the symbolic, to be-come a subject is to become male. The "outside" of the symbolic is madness and psychosis. There is no place for a woman *sexualized as female* to become subject. For this to occur will require a revolution, not a theoretical correction.

> In other words, the issue is not one of elaborating a new theory of which woman would be the *subject* or the *object,* but of jamming the theoretical machinery itself, of suspending its pretension to the pro-duction of a truth and of a meaning that are excessively univocal. Which presupposes that women do not aspire simply to be men's equals in knowledge. That they do not claim to be rivaling men in constructing a logic of the feminine that would still take onto-theo-logic as its model, but that they are rather attempting to wrest this question away from the economy of the logos (*TS,* 78).

> So for woman it is not a matter of installing herself within this lack, this negative, even by denouncing it, nor of reversing the economy of sameness by turning the feminine into *the standard for "sexual differ-ence"*; it is rather a matter of trying to practice that difference. . . . Is it possible that the difference might not be reduced once again to a process of *hierarchization? Of subordinating the other to the same?* (*TS,* 159; author's emphasis)

Given her clear resistance to making theoretical corrections, it is more than a little ironic that so many of her critics read her as doing just that. Rather than either creating a realm of the feminine completely outside phallocentric discourse *or* articulating a theory *about* woman within that discourse, Irigaray wants to make a place for the femi-nine—genuinely other, genuinely different—within phallocentric dis-course or within the symbolic. By "make a place for," I do not mean create a space within the enclosure of phallocentric discourse; I mean rather, set in motion a disruption in that discourse that will open it up for a different discursive economy, that of the feminine imaginary.[35] To borrow a phrase from Derrida, Irigaray "uses against the edifice the instruments or stones available in the house"[36] to deconstruct it. She wields the speculum of the specular economy on behalf of woman through her strategy of *mimetisme.*

> To play with mimesis is thus, for a woman, to try to recover the place of her exploitation by discourse, without allowing herself to be simply

reduced to it. It means to resubmit herself—inasmuch as she is on the side of the "perceptible," of "matter"—to "ideas," in particular to ideas about herself, that are elaborated in/by a masculine logic, but so as to make "visible," by an effect of playful repetition, what was supposed to remain invisible: the cover-up of a possible operation of the feminine in language. It also means "to unveil" the fact, if women are such good mimics, it is because they are not simply resorbed in this function. *They also remain elsewhere.* (TS, 76; author's emphasis)[37]

Mimetisme works in her readings of Freud, Marx, and the philosophers in much the same way that *différance* and other undecidables work in Derrida's readings of texts. *Mimetisme* lets loose a "disruptive excess" (TS, 78) that phallocentrism attempts to cover over. As *différance* exceeds systematization, so *mimetisme* shows that woman exceeds attempts to tame or circumscribe her.

Through the jamming logic of *mimetisme,* a place is made *in Irigaray's texts*—not in some reified metaphysical space or language—for the feminine imaginary to speak/write itself. This aspect of her writing provides the primary fuel for charges of essentialism. It is crucial to understand just what Irigaray means by the feminine *imaginary.* I noted earlier that many of her readers understand it to be something like a feminine unconscious: the specifically feminine libido that undergirds feminine subjectivity. To understand both the term and its locus in Irigaray's work requires a return to the work of Jacques Lacan. The imaginary seems to mean two things. One is a kind of collection of tropes that recur throughout western culture. The other is the pre-Oedipal period of symbiotic unity between the mother and child. Our access to the imaginary comes only through its inscription in the gaps and margins of the symbolic.[38] Insofar as this applies to our psychological development, the imaginary is both blocked and made present in its absence by the prohibition. Insofar as the imaginary is a cultural subtext, our access to it comes only through reading its inscriptions in our symbolic discourse. Irigaray's reading of the trajectories of woman/matter/nature in philosophical texts exhibits this inscription. Thus, the imaginary is not a place of absolute anteriority or exteriority, as some of her critics would have it (see S, 142).[39] Irigaray's reading of Lacan parallels her reading of Freud. As a description of the status quo, she finds his work powerful. Her readings of philosophical texts, of the economy in the strict sense, of her patients' lives, confirm that the Symbolic that writes society is dominated by a specular logic that, in privileging the phallus, identifies order with the Law of the Father. Her concern, however, is with the disastrous consequences of this inscription on women's lives. To break the hold of phallocentrism on discourse requires, in Irigaray's view, exacerbating the already-present play of the imaginary in the symbolic thereby exposing the other (economy and sex) it represses.

> There is no simple manageable way to leap to the outside of phallogocentrism, *nor any possible way to situate oneself there that would result from the simple fact of being a woman.* And in *Speculum,* if I was attempting to move back through the "masculine" imaginary, that is, our cultural imaginary, it is because that move imposed itself, both in order to demarcate the possible "outside" of this imaginary and to allow me to situate myself with respect to it as a woman, implicated in it and at the same time exceeding its limits. (*TS,* 163; author's emphasis)[40]

Irigaray is not claiming here (or anywhere) that she has gotten behind phallocentric discourse to the *real* woman or to her *true* language; rather, she is breaking open phallocentric discourse in such a way that the possibility of a new ordering of that discourse (and what it inscribes) might be possible.

> But if the female imaginary were to deploy itself, if it could bring itself into play otherwise than as scraps, uncollected debris, would it represent itself, even so, in the form of *one* universe? Would it even be volume instead of surface? No . . . (Re)-discovering herself, for a woman, thus could only signify the possibility of sacrificing no one of her pleasures to another, of identifying herself with none of them in particular, *of never being simply one.* A sort of expanding universe to which no limits could be fixed and which would not be incoherence nonetheless. (*TS,* 30–31)[41]

This aspect of Irigaray's work recapitulates her mimetic strategy. One might say her work mimes the trajectory of Freudian/Lacanian psychoanalysis. Irigaray's double reading of woman mimes the inscription of man that is the general grammar of western culture. I argued earlier that Irigaray's reading of Freud in the first essay in *Speculum* reveals the phallomorphism of his account of femininity to be both a reflection of and reflected by the phallocentrism of the western discursive and financial economies. These economies inscribe Freud's own reading of femininity. In writing the feminine imaginary, Irigaray is attempting to both write and be written by an economy that appears in the gaps of the economy of the Same, which represses it. This other economy privileges difference rather than sameness and plurality rather than unity. She finds *one* reflection of this economy in a different accounting of women's bodies. She is not claiming that her account of women's

sexuality is finally how women *really* are or how we *really* experience
our bodies. This is not a literal description. She is rather opening up
another possibility for reading/writing women's bodies. The essay
that ends *This Sex Which Is Not One,* entitled "When Our Lips Speak
Together" (*TS,* 205–18), exemplifies the many layers of this new accounting. The essay is a poetic conversation between two who, while
not the same as one another, are not correctly described as completely
separate from one another either. The essay can be read as celebrating
love between a mother and daughter, between two female lovers,
between/within the "two lips" of a woman's labia or mouth, and so
on. This essay imagines what "between woman/women"—this sex
which is not one—would be like in an economy that celebrated difference. Irigaray brings this utopian vision down to earth and speaks to
its *political* promise when she urges each woman to "find the struggles
that are appropriate for each woman, right where she is, depending
upon her nationality, her job, her social class, her sexual experience,
that is, upon the form of oppression that is for her the most immediately unbearable" (*TS,* 167).

This establishment of difference at the core of woman sets the stage
for a very different way of viewing differences between and among
women. Rather than being accidental variations on an essential theme,
differences are reflections of/reflected by an "essential" differing/
deferring that "is" woman.[42] I would argue that the other economy,
which Irigaray's figuring of anatomical differing/deferring allows to
seep through the cracks in the specular economy, figures/reflects a
pluralism of sexual *jouissance,* economic *jouissance,* political *jouissance,*
and so on. If fully explored and exploited, this way of working differences into the picture would disrupt feminist essentialist hegemonies
and open up feminist contexts (politics, groups, academic organizations as well as feminist writing) to alterities.[43] If supplemented with
insights gleaned from African American theorists, the difference race
makes to woman can begin to become legible in and around Irigaray's
woman. The discursive structures that Irigaray exposes as undercur-
rents running through western thought and civilization still stand, but
the workings of its economy are more complex than Irigaray allows.
For example, all women are not *legitimate* objects of exchange to all
men. In many places in contemporary racist society, white women are
still generally considered off limits to black men. From the days of
slavery through the 1960s, white men justified lynchings and other hostile acts against black men on the grounds of the threat they supposedly
posed to white women. Over that same time period, black women (in-

deed, often all women of the servant class) were understood to be sexually available to white men.[44]

Women's consignment to the passive role of beautiful object of contemplation within this economy affects women differently depending
upon their race and class. This image calls to mind the pedestal of the
Victorian ideal of womanhood; a piece of imaginary furniture that still
graces the homes of many white, middle- and upper-class women.
Many feminists and womanists contend that this pedestal rests on the
backs of the domestic and sexual servitude of women of color and/or
lower class. One would have to conclude that, whatever roles women
of color might be consigned to, they are hardly that of an object of
contemplation.[45] More often, women of color have served as exploited
labor—sexual, manual, and domestic. Irigaray's analysis of women's
status as commodities would need to be expanded to account for these
differences in function.

However, because it serves as the ideal in western culture, woman
as passive object of contemplation finds ways to insinuate itself into
black culture. Paula Giddings's book, *When and Where I Enter*, reports
extensively on how the battle over this cultural ideal shaped relations
between black men and women active in especially the more radical
arms of the black liberation movements of the 1960s and 1970s. Many
of the movement's male leaders believed strongly that black women
should assume positions of passive submission in relation to black
men.[46] Needless to say, this caused a great deal of conflict within the
movement.[47] The shadows of this conflict often resurface in current
events. One will still hear rhetoric occasionally that blames black
women for the ongoing difficulties threatening black men's very survival.[48] Behind this rhetoric lies the cultural ideal that Irigaray exposes.

More immediate connections can be made from critiques of racism
to Irigaray's exposure of the dominance of photologic in our scopic
economy. Irigaray's readings exposed the workings of that logic in
our culture's evaluation of women—especially of women's genitalia
which, in contrast to the male organ, present nothing to the eye. Other
scholars have argued that the dominance of light, sight, and the gaze
is at work in racist ideology and practices.[49] The dominance of symmetry and sameness not only determines how western culture views
males and females located inside its boundaries, but also how it views
peoples of other cultures. Those who are asymmetrical with regard
to the standard are sometimes rendered peculiarly invisible. In fact,
evidence suggests an uncanny recapitulation of a connection between a
deviation from the visible standard and a subsequent invisibility. Many

people of color describe feeling invisible in white society; indeed, white
society often looks right past or through people of color.[50] At other
times, as many scholars have noted, their asymmetry is itself quite literally marked. For example, an early text by Cornel West explores the
way the normative gaze of modernity located the "savage" by extrapo-
lating all kinds of character traits from perceived differences in dimension and shape between the skulls of native Africans and those of the
western European cultural ideal, the classic Greek face and head.[51]
Sander Gilman has published a compelling analysis of similar symp-
tomology in medical textbooks and nineteenth century art.[52] The medical textbooks ground African women's ostensibly "savage" (insatiable,
aggressive) sexuality in supposed genital asymmetries between European women and African women. This association of African women
with sexual deviance is repeated in nineteenth-century art.

Irigaray's Woman, Whitefeminist Theory, Whitefeminist Theology: More of the Same?

The connections that I have just drawn between Irigaray's work and
that of African American feminists likely represent the kind of potential
that whitefeminists saw in her work in the 1980s. Importing race into
Irigaray's analysis, however, calls into question any claim that her
differing/deferring woman is racially neutral. Confronting Irigaray's
woman with African American women brings Irigaray's woman to her
end in the sense of limit. She reveals herself as always already raced.
Irigaray's woman can articulate certain issues facing African American
women, but only those issues that conform to or evolve from her woman's predetermined contours. Whiteness remains in the position of
mastery over Irigaray's differing and deferring woman. The concerns
raised by Irigaray's inscription by white solipsism are only heightened
by the fact that this differing and deferring woman virtually disappears
from much of Irigaray's later work. Woman is returned to a logic of
sameness in the name of a larger and, in Irigaray's view, more important project: thinking *genuine* sexual difference.[53] Ironically but not surprisingly, Irigaray loses track of this differing/deferring woman when
her work enters theological terrain.

Invocations of God and other religious motifs appear in much of
Irigaray's later work, notably in essays in *Sexes and Genealogies* and in
An Ethics of Sexual Difference.[54] Much of Irigaray's work with religion
builds on the position articulated by the nineteenth-century theologian
and philosopher Ludwig Feuerbach, who argued that theology was

anthropology. According to Feuerbach, all statements about God are projections of idealized human nature (read "man's" nature) that "man" should internalize and realize. Feuerbach's understanding of religion provides the impetus for Irigaray's critical analyses of connections between God and the subject in the philosophical tradition and her proposals for religion's place in contemporary feminism. In *An Ethics of Sexual Difference*, Irigaray targets God as the ground of male subjectivity. Several of Irigaray's essays in this collection explore the effects of a mutually reflective relationship between a God figured as male and the (male) subject as these effects register in the work of philosophers from Descartes to Levinas. This relationship both founds and funds the epoch of monosexuality that Irigaray sees as coming to a close. The end of this epoch is signified by the demise of traditional conceptions of divinity and the potential emergence of new manifestations of the sacred in a new epoch of sexual difference.[55]

Irigaray's double reading of the relationship between God as male ground and the subject as male opens up the possibility for writing the divine otherwise in the service of writing what has yet to be written, female subjectivity. Essays in *Sexes and Genealogies* seem to argue that women should take Feuerbach by the horns. If God is only a projection of idealized humanity, then women need to seize control of the projector and shine *their* image on its screen. Projecting a female deity will accomplish several things for women. First of all, it will give their subjectivity a ground that it needs.

> If she is to become woman, if she is to accomplish her female subjectivity, woman needs a god who is a figure of the perfection of her subjectivity. . . . Having a God and becoming one's gender go hand in hand. God is the other that we absolutely cannot be without. ("Divine Women" in *SG*, 64)

Second, it will make genuine exchange between the sexes possible as well as exchanges between women.[56]

Whitefeminist theorists are wary of this aspect of Irigaray's deployment of religious discourse. Elizabeth Grosz, one of the few feminist theorists to deal substantively with this aspect of Irigaray's work, notes that Irigaray's readers tend to view with suspicion her bold-faced deployment of deity imaged as female in her project of rethinking woman.[57] Feminists have good reason for being wary of invocations of God; after all, as feminist and womanist theologians have repeatedly argued, women have certainly suffered at religion's hands. Some whitefeminist theorists read Irigaray's call to image God in female form in order to ground women's subjectivity as a recapitulation of the "good old God" (in whose name women were forbidden to speak and relegated to secondary status) in disguise. I share Grosz's wariness for some of the same reasons and for others more pertinent to my current project. Suggesting that women project their own image onto the divine seems to run the risk of setting up an economy of sameness for women that would parallel the current phallocentric economy. Irigaray seems to forget her own warning that changing the gender of the standard from masculine to feminine can still recapitulate phallocratism if a single standard remains in place. The essentially differing/deferring woman is altogether absent from the places where Irigaray advocates projecting a female deity as the ground for female subjectivity. This lapse on Irigaray's part is surprising and certainly disappointing given that she, perhaps more than any other feminist thinker, has exposed the depth of the workings of an economy of sameness.[58]

The course for Irigaray's lapse is set in her early work. Irigaray's critical readings of Freud, Marx, and the philosophical tradition appear to arise in part out of Irigaray's awareness of and concern for women's diversity. However, I do not find evidence that these issues stay at the forefront of her analysis of these streams of thought. Spelman warns her readers that attention to "women" as though other social markers were not pertinent will likely produce insights only about certain women. Spelman shows the necessity for taking all factors into account in her reading of Plato. When read next to Spelman's account, Irigaray's opening piece on Plato in *Speculum* exhibits the very problem that Spelman criticizes. Irigaray's analysis focuses on Socrates' scheme for arranging mating within the ideal polis to ensure that human offspring are of the highest quality. Her reading of Plato is stunning in its revelation of the specular economy at work, but she fails to alert herself or her reader to the domain of her reading's applicability. Socrates is discussing the mating of the polis's free citizens. "Women," in this context, would not seem to include slave women within its domain.

This inattention is not limited to her readings of the philosophical tradition. As I noted earlier, Irigaray recognizes that the purviews of both Marxist analysis and Freudian psychoanalytic theory are limited by women's diversity. Marxist analysis has trouble taking women's situation(s) as its object because women do not form a discrete class. Irigaray further insists that Freud's reading of femininity cannot be taken outside its situation of origin, patriarchal capitalism. However, her own readings of these two figures fail to thematize substantially specific ways in which differences of race and class might complicate the accounts of femininity that she calls into question. For Irigaray, as she makes repeatedly clear, the fundamental problem of our time is that of the West's failure to think sexual difference; a difference that seems to subsume other differences (e.g., of race or class).[59] The power of her insistence that women resist the form of oppression that most affects them is undercut by her own failure to attend to any salient difference in oppression. In the scopic economy her reading exposes, (all) women are (and, by implication, in the same ways) commodities on an exchange market run by and for (all) men (whose powers of consumption and exchange are the same, by implication, regardless of race or class).

Conclusion/Opening

I noted at the outset of this chapter that Irigaray's value for my project lay as much in her repetition of certain whitefeminist gestures as in her difference from them. My reading of her started with questions about Irigaray's relationship to one of those gestures, the critique of essentialism. My account of Irigaray showed that what originally registered within the Anglo-American context as biological essentialism turns out to be something quite different. Irigaray's reading of and through continental philosophy, psychoanalysis, and Marxism exposed the cultural discourse that funds and grounds woman's situation within western culture. The general grammar of western culture and its specular economy simultaneously excludes woman as other and uses her as its resource and currency. Getting to that level of cultural discourse required passing through the terrain of essentialism but ended up reworking the very notion of an essence of woman. Irigaray's interrogation of the general grammar of western culture uncovered woman's resistance to inscription in sameness and her refusal of fixation. The term "essentialism" hardly fits Irigaray's woman given that her essential features are difference and deferral. Woman's (non)essence first appears in her ability to evade phallogocentrism's fixations. Irigaray also reads her differing and deferral off/into a different accounting of her body's morphology. Rather than the oneness of the phallomorphic body (against which woman's body appears as lack), woman's body cannot be counted in single units. Irigaray uses this body morphology to ground a different economy of relationship between women. Relationships between women will not be easily reduced to one-plus-one-plus-one.[60]

Reading Irigaray through the question of her essentialism opened onto whitefeminist theory's more recent strategy of deploying a concept of female subjectivity grounded in multiplicity. Irigaray's woman is "essentially" different from herself and from other women. Relations between women are built upon difference rather than similarity. Such a vision of woman and women holds out substantial promise for allowing the difference race makes to woman to register, and for a different mode of relationality among differing women. However, this vision is not new to whitefeminist theory. In chapter 1, I argued that it largely failed to produce substantial attention to race. Unfortunately, Irigaray's woman exhibits similar symptoms. Following Irigaray's differing/deferring woman to her end in her disappearance from Irigaray's later work appears to have brought us back to where we started. For all her promise, Irigaray's woman appears to be just as inadequate to the task of theorizing differences between women as her Anglophone sisters who were discussed in chapter 1. Deconstruction may not have succeeded in poisoning feminism, but it hardly seems to have cured it of its exclusionary tendencies. Woman seems to be unable to break out of her enclosure within the economy of racial sameness that continues to circumscribe whitefeminism.

These symptoms suggest that white solipsism will not be successfully confronted by an inquiry into the race/gender divide that proceeds solely from woman's side. If it is to be, ultimately, useful to my project, Irigaray's work needs supplementation by an analysis that carries racial difference to the same depth in the specular economy. Several of the questions that emerged at the end of chapter 1 and remain unaddressed now press upon my project with greater urgency. What enables whiteness to masquerade as neutrality? What continues to prevent it from emerging as a necessary point of interrogation? What place does race occupy in the West's cultural grammar/text of metaphysics and its specular economy? Excavating these questions returns me to Derrida, the other side of the supplemental reading I have been engaging. I turn to Derrida as *supplément* for a number of reasons. First of all, as earlier chapters have established, Derrida and Irigaray work at the same level; that of the text of metaphysics or what Irigaray calls the West's cultural grammar. Thus, to explore race's place in Derrida's work is to explore its place within the text of metaphysics and its specular economy.

To put Derrida forward as Irigaray's *supplément* is not to turn to him as a replacement for Irigaray, as the site of plenitude that she somehow lacks. Derrida exhibits symptoms of inscription by the race/gender divide, as well. Derrida does not inquire into race difference and sexual difference together. As in whitefeminism, race comes up as an issue only when Derrida is dealing with those marked as racial others. The reading I will give of Derrida's work will produce whiteness as a legible mark, but Derrida does not take up an inquiry into whiteness. To turn to Derrida as Irigaray's *supplément* is also to play off Irigaray as *his supplément*. Reading Irigaray against the background of Derrida's work with "nothing outside the text" increased the legibility of the effects of her work. Similarly, reading Derrida on race against an Irigarayan background will increase the legibility of certain aspects of his work. Turning to Derrida's discussions of race will revisit questions about the ethical import of deconstruction that I raised in chapter 2. When read against the background of Irigaray's exposure of the text's reach to politics, economics, and so on, the ethical and political import of Derrida's work registers more clearly. Just as reading Irigaray as Derrida's *supplément* revisited much of the same terrain uncovered by my reading of Derrida in chapters 2 and 3, turning to Derrida as Irigaray's *supplément* involves revisiting much of the terrain covered in this chapter. I will argue that what has gone by several names in this essay—the specular economy/economy of sameness/economy of the "proper"—encodes race in the West (and those places marked by its dominance).

5

Derrida as *Supplément:* Deconstruction and Race on Philosophy's Terrain

Introduction

The trajectory of this project as a whole, the reader will recall, doubles whitefeminism's assignation of race and gender to opposite sides of an impermeable boundary. To engage with questions of race and deconstruction through Derrida's work is to enter the race/gender divide from the other side. This means that woman will disappear from view for a time. The element around which race circulates in Derrida's work carries masculine markings. At the center of the text of metaphysics and its inscription of race lies the figure of man. I use this terminology to set the subject of the text of metaphysics and its specular economy slightly apart from his reflections in other contexts, such as the human sciences (cultural anthropology, psychology, or sociology), philosophy or theology, or even man in his everyday existence. All of these varied and variable subjects rest on the philosopheme of man; that is, on the notion of particular kind of being (human) whose properties and proper end distinguish it from other kinds of being. Man is linked to others of his kind in a variety of ways by the property and proper that they share. I shall reserve the term "metaphysical humanism" to refer to this subject and his context, the text of metaphysics and its specular economy. I appropriate this term because of its links to philosophy and its debates over the content, meaning and shape of the human being. In this chapter, I will show that, despite various attempts to break with metaphysical humanism, the continental tradition remains subject to it. While continental philosophy exhibits particularly legible symptoms of metaphysical humanism's dominance, here I will show that metaphysical humanism also functions in political contexts. Metaphysical humanism links philosophy to politics as specular reflections of each other and of the text of metaphysics and its man.

In calling the subject of metaphysical humanism "man," I follow not only Derrida's usage but also a tradition that the previous chapter suggests runs deep in the culture inscribed by the text of metaphysics. In English, as in other western languages, "man" can mean both generic human being and male human being. When read against Irigaray's exposure of the depth of sexual (in)difference, this conflation of the masculine and the generic registers as more than a linguistic accident or error. Its roots lie in our cultural grammar and its specular economies (sexual, monetary, linguistic). Thus, to follow man through the discourse of race, as this chapter proposes to do, is to reimmerse this project in sexual (in)difference, at least for a time. The fact that following race to its end means leaving behind sexual difference suggests that whitefeminism did not create the divide between race and gender; the divide appears to run to the depths of our cultural discourse. This situation affirms the need to travel the other side of the race/gender divide to its end if that divide is to be overcome.

To follow race's career through Derrida's work is to follow the lines of force that constituted whitefeminism's dealings with race to their end in several senses. Following race to the point where it opens onto sexual difference traces the divide to its end in the sense of limit; that is, where the division between race and sexual difference begins to crumble. In this chapter I will also carry white solipsism to its end; that is, to its (nonoriginary) origin where whiteness becomes legible as a racial mark. In doing so, I will excavate structures within the text of western metaphysics that fund and found white solipsism. White solipsism's end, it will turn out, is also a site from which sexual difference and race can go elsewhere.

As I noted at the end of chapter 4, this chapter will also revisit questions of deconstruction's relationship to ethics and politics. A number of scholars have written on deconstruction and ethics; most notably Robert Bernasconi, Simon Critchley, John Caputo, Charles Scott, and Mark Taylor.[1] All are unwilling to concede to the common view that opposes deconstruction to ethics. All suggest that Derrida's work reinscribes questions of ethics within a larger context. All read deconstruction and ethics through an intertextual network that links Derrida to Heidegger and Levinas, among others.[2] I am sympathetic to much that these philosophers have to say. Like them, I see deconstruction's relationship to ethics in terms of its interest in and enabling of the emergence of alterity. This chapter's investigation into a particular figure of alterity, race, provides productive counterpoints to Critchley's and Bernasconi's work, in particular. Like them, I will argue that Derrida's work with race recontextualizes ethics and politics in relation to philosophy. Rather than evolving out of philosophy or ethics, politics turns out to lie at the end of philosophy, in many senses. The content of my reading of Derrida on race hopes to expand on their accounts, in specific ways. Critchley pays relatively brief attention to Derrida's work on race, focusing instead on the ethical in general.[3] Derrida's work on race is, for Critchley, symptomatic of the *possibility* of ethics in deconstruction, but he does not mine it for philosophical insights intrinsic to that possibility. In contrast, I find Derrida's work on race a crucial site for exploring the relationship between philosophy, ethics, and politics. In this, I align myself with Robert Bernasconi, who has also recently drawn on Derrida's work on apartheid to elucidate the relationship between philosophy, politics, and ethics in deconstruction.[4] The opening sections of this chapter follow the same itinerary through Derrida's texts on race that Bernasconi's reading pursues. I offer a more detailed reading that yields conclusions that complement Bernasconi's insights. I also follow race toward its proximity to sexual difference; a move that neither Critchley nor Bernasconi undertake.

"The Ends of Man": Metaphysical Humanism and Its Limits

Political dimensions to Derrida's work that bear on race's place appear in an essay entitled "The Ends of Man," a lecture given at an international colloquium on philosophical anthropology in 1968 and then revised for publication in 1972.[5] At first glance, the title seems to support those who would dismiss deconstruction as antiethical on the grounds that it proclaims the death of the subject. Feminist scholars have been particularly skeptical of Derrida on this account.[6] Careful reading of "The Ends of Man" does uncover a challenge to metaphysical humanism, but that challenge does not originate with Derrida. In taking metaphysical humanism to its limits, Derrida does something other than proclaim the demise—timely or untimely—of the ethical subject. Rather than undermining critiques of racism, as its reputation as antiethical might lead one to expect, Derrida's deconstruction of the West's notion of the subject situates racism and antiracism in a larger context. Derrida's readings refigure assumptions about philosophy's relationship to politics and humanism's relationship to racism.

Questions of the relationship between philosophy and politics, specifically with regard to man's place are central to "Ends." Derrida begins by connecting the occasion for this essay's production to major political issues of the day. Saying only that he finds these circumstances to be part of the problematic of such a colloquium, he locates his contribution along a horizon of particular political events: the opening of the

Vietnam peace talks, the assassination of the Reverend Martin Luther King, Jr., and the Paris student uprisings. Derrida states that he made his appearance at this colloquium conditional upon being allowed to express his sympathy with those protesting the Vietnam War. Of course, permission was granted, from which Derrida concludes several things. On the one hand, it indicated that the American philosophers hosting the meeting were not necessarily allied with what their government deemed their country's national interest. On the other hand, he writes,

> That a declaration of opposition to some official policy is authorized, and authorized by the authorities, also means, precisely to that extent, that the declaration does not upset the given order, is not *bothersome*. ("Ends," 114)

As Bernasconi notes, these events are not mentioned again in the text. The essay picks up on these themes mainly in its investigation of various philosophers' paradoxical affirmations of what they set out to reject. Bernasconi turns to Derrida's work on apartheid in order to develop what appears only obliquely in "The Ends of Man." In my view, however, significant connections between these comments about politics and the content of "The Ends of Man" can be discerned between the lines. This situation of freedom of expression and its limits reflect the form of democracy (with stress on both "form" and "democracy"), Derrida says. The very possibility of an international colloquium on philosophical anthropology rests on this same political ground.

This colloquium is a microcosm of western thinking and activity. As part of the western social fabric, the colloquium is shaped by western discourse and shares that discourse's concerns and values. The very occurrence of such a colloquium assumes some common ground that can bring differences in nationality, political, and philosophical views into relationship with one another. Both this assumption and the common ground itself witness to the colloquium's immersion in western discourse and its strategies for self-preservation. The presumably universal concepts and discourses of "man" and "philosophy" reflected in the title of the colloquium constitute its common ground. Holding a colloquium on philosophical anthropology presupposes and performs the "we" of humanism. The colloquium enacts the assumption that "we philosophers" constitute a collectivity that transcends the boundaries of nation, politics and specific cultures. Its topic posits a subject, man, who grounds this transcendence. "We philosophers" are a microcosm of "we men." All men may not read Husserl and Heidegger, but the larger "we" should recognize themselves in philosophy's man. Indeed, the philosopher's task is to render legible human existence in, by, and through philosophy's man. But to what degree are such assumptions justified? To what degree does the colloquium also bear witness to their limits?

Derrida suggests that this interest in the universality of man may be an effect of a silent awareness of his nonuniversality. Derrida notes that a colloquium on philosophical anthropology is quite literally unthinkable in many places in the world; it would make no more sense in such places to hold such a colloquium than it would to prohibit it. Derrida suggests that the "anxious and busy multiplication of colloquia in the West" signals a sensing of a "mute, growing and menacing pressure, on the enclosure of Western collocution" and an attempt to master or to "interiorize this difference" by establishing man's universality in international discourse—at least at the site of the colloquium ("Ends," 113).

As was the case in *Dissemination*, philosophy turns out to be symptomatic of larger issues, pressures and contexts. This particular philosophical scene opens onto a hall of mirrors in which diverse areas of western culture appear as reflections of one another. Philosophy reflects politics and politics reflects philosophy. Both, in turn, reflect the context of metaphysics and its limits. Man constitutes the centrifugal figure in this scene. His proper and property are the currencies that fund the specular economy and ground man's claim to universality. However, Derrida's reading also suggests that signs of fissures in this economy also mark man's place. Man links philosophy, politics, and the text of metaphysics, but man's fissures also run from one context to the other.

Having been asked to address the question "Where is France, with regard to man?" Derrida launches into a complex exploration of Sartre, Hegel, Husserl, and Heidegger on philosophical anthropology. His reading uncovers a persistent metaphysical humanism in their work that circumscribes all attempts to break with it. The marks of metaphysics' mastery of man and of fissures in that mastery appear through Derrida's reading of these philosophers. This play between mastery and resistance replays the dynamics of intertextuality uncovered by *Dissemination*. What goes on around man is not entirely subject to these philosophers' authorial intentions. Man's inscription of and in their texts is not, properly speaking, under their control. It occurs within an intertextual context that links these philosophers to each other, to their readers, and to the text of metaphysics and its limits.

Each of the philosophers Derrida discusses intended to overcome metaphysical humanism in its various forms, yet each of them were plagued by readings of their work that missed this point. What occurs around the question of humanism in the history of interpretation of Heidegger's work, especially in France, is paradigmatic. That Heidegger, *the* questioner of metaphysics par excellence—and especially of metaphysical humanism—should require interrogation on this subject is particularly noteworthy.[7] Given Heidegger's own history with Nazism, that such an interrogation should occur in an arena figured by racism is also noteworthy.

Derrida's *solicitation* of the question of Heidegger's humanism begins with a translation problem. Heidegger's *Dasein* was translated into French as *le realité humaine* (human reality). Sartre picked up that translation, which set the context for French interpretations of *Sein und Zeit* for some time to come (up to the time of "The Ends of Man," at least). In many ways, Derrida notes, this is a "monstrous translation" ("Ends," 115). Heidegger selected *Dasein* as the name for the subject of the existential analytic of *Sein und Zeit* in order to break with metaphysical humanism. *Dasein* (literally "there-being") "is not simply the man of metaphysics," Derrida writes ("Ends," 124). But what makes such a "monstrous translation" possible? Is that translation, in fact, *simply* monstrous?

Much in Heidegger's thinking in *Sein und Zeit* (and in his later work, starting with the "Letter on Humanism") resists metaphysical humanism, yet Derrida's double reading produces a *relève* of man in Heidegger's thought. *Relève,* the French translation of *Aufhebung* (Hegelian sublation) aptly describes man's place in Heidegger's work as disclosed by Derrida's reading. Heidegger's negation of humanism purifies man and raises him to a higher form. This sublated man fails to break free of the text of metaphysics and its economy of propriation. Derrida writes: "The value of proximity, that is, of presence in general, therefore decides the essential orientation of this analytic of Dasein" in *Sein und Zeit* and beyond ("Ends," 127). Heidegger delimits metaphysical humanism in the name of the thinking of Being and of the truth of Being. However, insofar as thinking Being names man's essence, that project perpetuates a central motif of metaphysical humanism.

The first layer of man's *relève* takes place at the very beginning of *Sein und Zeit,* Derrida argues, where Heidegger locates the necessary starting point for an inquiry into the meaning of Being. It appears in the form of the innocuous "we"—the "we" who always already have

the meaning of Being available to us in some way. We are the beings
that ask the question of Being. We are the beings to whom the question
of Being belongs—even when we forget to ask it. *Dasein* names this
site that we are and, Heidegger insists, that is all that *Dasein* names.
A site seems to fall considerably short of metaphysical humanism, but
it still fails to break metaphysics' hold over man. "The proper of man,
his *Eigenheit*, his 'authenticity,' is to be related to the meaning of Being;
he is to hear and to question (*fragen*) it in ek-sistence, to stand straight
in the proximity of its light" ("Ends," 133).[8]

   To be sure, the proximity of Being and *Dasein* (or Being and
thinking / dwelling) is not identical to a substantialist metaphysical humanism. As Derrida puts it, "The proper of man, here, is not an essential attribute, the predicate of a substance, a characteristic among others, however fundamental, of a being, object or subject, called man"
("Ends," 133). However, Heidegger reinstates the discursive structure
of man—of that universal humanity inscribed in the economy of propriation. *Dasein* is man's proper in that *Dasein* grounds man's *telos* and
belongs to him. Man, in turn, grounds the "we" of philosophical anthropology. These vestiges of humanism "have authorized all the anthropologistic deformations in the reading of *Sein und Zeit*, notably in
France" ("Ends," 127).

   While Heidegger's attempt to break with metaphysical humanism
did not fully succeed, on Derrida's reading, man may be coming to an
end after Heidegger.

> Is not this security of the near what is trembling today, that is, the
> co-belonging and co-propriety of the name of man and the name of
> Being, such as this co-propriety inhabits, and is inhabited by, the lan-
> guage of the West, such as it is buried in its *oikonomia*, such as it is
> inscribed and forgotten according to the history of metaphysics, and
> such as it is awakened also by the destruction of ontotheology?
> ("Ends," 133)

The preceding chapters have kept a complex notion of "end" or telos
in play, both in relation to their account of the end of philosophy or
metaphysics and in relation to the end of woman. My account in this
chapter of Derrida's reading and writing of the end of metaphysical
humanism similarly draws on the full network of the term's connotations as goal, limit, and essence.[9] Derrida identifies contemporary politics as symptomatic of man's end in each of these senses:

> This trembling is played out in the violent relationship of the whole
> of the West to its other, whether a "linguistic" relationship . . . or

> ethnological, economic, political, military, relationships, etc. Which
> does not mean, moreover, that military or economic violence is not
> in structural solidarity with "linguistic" violence. ("Ends," 134–35)

Recalling the political horizon that marked the lecture's opening
underlines Derrida's point. Each of the political events Derrida mentions constitutes a site where man meets his end, often violently. Vietnam certainly constitutes such a site. U.S. involvement in Southeast
Asia was only the latest step in the West's expansion of its (geographical and ideological) territory over the course of several centuries.[10] Colonialism and imperialism are funded by man's assumed universality
and its limits. As universal, man can and should be everywhere. That
he must colonize in order to fulfill that telos assumes that there are
places where man's proper place is occupied by something other than
man; perhaps a kind of being who resembles man but lacks his proper
constitution. In colonizing, man takes over not-man's property. An investigation into the history of colonialization would surely reveal the
"violent relationship of the whole of the West to its other." Economic
violence, military violence, ethnic violence do indeed show themselves
to be "in structural solidarity with 'linguistic' violence."

One does not have to go abroad to find a site where man's limits
come into view, as another of the political events that mark Derrida's
text suggests. The context within which the assassination of Martin
Luther King occurred marks such a site. Like the war in Vietnam, western imperialism and colonialism set the stage for King's assassination.
The importation of Africans to North America to serve as slaves exhibits all the marks of man and his ends. The slave economy rested on
construing Africans as not-men, as chattel to whom *being* man's property is proper. Such assignation was not met without resistance, as the
history of slave rebellions (public and private, large and small, violent
and nonviolent) and abolition movements illustrates. Like these resistance movements, the Civil Rights movement (which constitutes the
immediate background to King's assassination) exacerbated tremors in
the context of western metaphysics. This movement asserted African
Americans' claim to status as man, as subject of the law, *homo politicus,*
and so on. Against this background, King's assassination registers as
an attempt to still the trembling in the text and the culture it inscribes.
The fact that King was killed while in Memphis, Tennessee, to support
city sanitation workers striking for better pay and working conditions—workers who carried placards saying, I AM A *MAN*—takes on
particular significance against this background.[11] The scene of King's
assassination and its larger context renders legible the lines from lin-

guistic violence to economic, ethnic, physical, and emotional violence, to which Derrida alludes.

I have followed and expanded upon Derrida's oblique indications of man's connection to race's place in the text of metaphysics and its specular economy. My reading of "The Ends of Man" and its political contexts suggests that race constitutes man's end as limit; that is, the boundary separating man from not-man. The full scope of man's relationship to race, especially in political scenes where race is at issue, has not yet appeared. I turn next to a site where race appears at the forefront of Derrida's work. Reading what goes on around Derrida's writings on apartheid South Africa will draw a clearer picture of man's place (and therefore metaphysical humanism's place) in racisms and antiracisms. It will turn out that race's place has everything to do with the multivalent senses of the end of man. Exploring this terrain will reveal man as the site of contestation between racisms and antiracisms. By "site of contestation" I mean that man cannot be located solely on one side of the battle. On one hand, he (and the discursive network surrounding him) grounds apartheid. Linguistic violence will show its collusion with political, economic, and military violences—all of which revolve around the status of man, his proper(ties) and race. On the other hand, man also funds apartheid's resistors. Man's status as the battleground is not accidental to this philosopheme's function in western discourse; it is, rather, intrinsic to its end (as essence and goal).

Race's Place in the Specular Economy: Apartheid

To read Derrida on apartheid is to immerse oneself in a complex intertextual context. What Derrida has to say about apartheid also exceeds the boundaries of his authorial intentions. That Derrida turns his attention to apartheid is not solely his own doing. Derrida's essays on apartheid arise from contexts that are not, properly speaking, entirely his own. "Le dernier mot du racisme" (translated as "Racism's Last Word" in 1986), published in France in 1983, introduces a catalog to accompany a touring art exhibition on apartheid. The exhibition's originators designed it as witness to and a perpetual reminder of the horrors inflicted by this unjust regime. The exhibition was to remain on tour around the world until such time as apartheid came to an end. Derrida's second essay on apartheid, "The Laws of Reflection: Nelson Mandela, in Admiration," constitutes the first essay in a festschrift of sorts in honor of Mandela coedited by Derrida and Mustafa Tlili. This essay inaugurated an exchange between Derrida and two then–graduate students, Anne McClintock and Rob Nixon. McClintock and Nixon take Derrida to task on two counts. They find him hopelessly naive about apartheid's intransigence, especially in the face of the South African government's talent for public relations. They reproach Derrida for being duped by the government's ability to reclothe apartheid in discursive apparel that makes it more palatable to European and American eyes.

Derrida responds to their rebuke in a third essay entitled "But beyond . . . (Open Letter to Anne McClintock and Rob Nixon)."[12] His response to their rebuke accepts and exploits this intertextual context in reading and writing doubly. At one level, the essay reads as an attempt to rein in misreadings of the first essay and its contexts. Thus, it constitutes a reassertion of authorial authority. At the same time, Derrida uses his interlocutors' rebuke to put himself and his first essay in question. His double reading allows the common territory of concerns that he and his interlocutors share to emerge. The reading I offer below of Derrida on apartheid shares the conditions of intertextuality. It draws not just on Derrida's essays, but McClintock and Nixon's as well. What I read in these essays is shaped as much by the readings of Derrida I have offered up to this point (especially "The Ends of Man") as by what might seem to reside inside these essays themselves.

South Africa and its system of apartheid emerged from a European context and were sustained by that context. South Africa is quite literally a creation of European colonialization. Apartheid South Africa (its territorial boundaries, governmental structures, legal systems, etc.) rests on the British colony that preceded it.[13] After the departure of the British, the Afrikaaners (also of European ancestry and white skinned) took over South Africa's governance. In 1948, they established the system of apartheid thereby instituting the South Africa that Derrida describes as "the last word on racism."[14] As a European creation, "South Africa" came into being through and was sustained by the discursive system that made it possible in the first place.

> The history of *apartheid* (its "discourse" and its "reality," the totality of its *text*) would have been impossible, unthinkable without the European concept and the European history of the state, without the European discourse on race—its scientific pseudoconcept and its religious roots, its modernity and its archaisms—without Judeo-Christian ideology, and so forth. ("Beyond," 364)

Derrida makes his case through a double reading of South African political rhetoric as exhibited in South Africa's former constitution and as described in detail from other sources by McClintock and Nixon.

Ontotheology, man, and the economy of propriation shape the logic of this rhetoric. The Afrikaaners' sense of divine sanction for their presence at the helm of South Africa and for its system of apartheid is clearly legible. South Africa is a divine mission established and sustained by a Christian government and an educational system designed to nurture proper citizens. To its core, South Africa represents the form of democracy Derrida cites in "The Ends of Man." In fact, South Africa is a series of specular reflections of/on the political institutions that make up the form of democracy. Apartheid is put in place by South Africa's constitutional democracy; the democracy's complex legal and political system sustains it. As the creation of the nation-state, apartheid is the creation of man as *homo politicus*—that being whose essence is tied up with the creation, enactment, and enforcement of the backbone of the nation-state, the law.[15] Thus, apartheid is itself a specular reflection of western politics and ultimately the text of western metaphysics.

The strategies apartheid regimes used to contain and control black South Africans also register as specular reflections on constitutional democracy's political structures. Apartheid was institutionalized in geographical forms rooted in the concept of the nation-state. Black South Africans were collected and divided into Bantustans, "homelands" supposedly organized along indigenous ethnic and tribal lines.[16] South Africa's indigenous people were not really citizens of South Africa, but of the Bantustans. Each "homeland" ostensibly had its own local government that bore responsibility for education, public works, and the provision of other public goods (see "No Names," 344–45). Yet, because the governments of the Bantustans had no real political or economic power, public works were virtually nonexistent. In South Africa as in the United States under Jim Crow, separate but equal on paper translated to privilege for whites and abysmal conditions for blacks.[17]

Apartheid's political structures reflect the text of metaphysics and its specular economy. The Bantustan system relegated black South Africans to a (non)place that is neither inside or outside South Africa and its larger contexts—the "form" of "democracy" and the text of metaphysics. The Bantustans are simultaneously inside and outside South Africa. As creations of the South African constitutional democracy, they lie within its constitutional boundaries. As excluded from South Africa, they constitute sites of that democracy's limits. The Bantustans reveal South Africa as merely the form of democracy. The Bantustans also refuse a fixed location either inside or outside the form of democracy. As reflections of / on the nation-state, Bantustans share the form of democracy; thus, they reside within the text of metaphysics that funds it. Lacking the powers of the nation-state, however, means Bantustans lack the proper(ties) of nation-states. Insofar as they figure as lack, they reside outside the context's political structures. Thus, the distinction between inside and outside founders where black South Africans reside.

Black South Africans, like their homelands, similarly trouble metaphysical humanism and its politics. Through the Bantustans, black South Africans register as pseudocitizens of pseudostates; that is, as pseudomen. However, the laws that regulate their lives originate not with the Bantustans but with the South African legislature, which excludes black South Africans from its body. As subject *to* laws but not *of* the law, black South Africans constitute a specular reflection of *homo politicus*. Insofar as they resemble *homo politicus* but lack his proper(ties), they mark a point of fissure in man's unity with his proper.

When read against the context of "The Ends of Man," apartheid South Africa constitutes a site where man comes to his end in many senses. As the product of colonialization, South Africa represents a site where man fulfills his telos of universality by extending his reach into the "dark continent." In separating the colonized from the colonizers, race constitutes man's end in the sense of boundary or limit. Setting black South Africans apart from man's proper(ties) establishes a site where man ceases to function. In his absence, any limits that might check violence or violation are also removed, as Derrida points out in his use of a quotation from an Amnesty International report: "As long as apartheid lasts, there can be no structure conforming to the generally recognized norms of human rights and able to guarantee their application" ("Last Word," 337). Removing limits to violence and violation effectively licenses acts of violence and violation. Could the lines from linguistic violence to ethnic and military violence be any more clearly drawn?

So far, reading Derrida on apartheid confirms the subtle indications of metaphysical humanism's role in racisms that I drew out from "The Ends of Man." South Africa constitutes a site where man's universality trembles. However, insofar as man's forced withdrawal from the scene enables and even licenses violence, reading Derrida on apartheid also appears to confirm suspicions that deconstructing the subject spells the demise of ethics. Rather than exacerbate man's trembling, it would seem that antiracism should work on shoring up man and expanding his reach. This threatens to set up an opposition between antiracism's

needs (with regard to man) and feminism's needs (as I have described
them up to this point), against which my project would founder. In
shoring up man, antiracism would necessarily, if unintentionally, perpetuate sexual indifference thus simply deepening the divide between
race and woman. Insofar as man is circumscribed by whiteness, then
shoring up man threatens to erase race from the scene once and for
all.

My reading of Derrida's discussion of antiracist movements uncovers something other than a shoring up of metaphysical humanism.
While these movements do lay claim to man's universality, that claim
registers as more than a simple expansion of his boundaries. Antiracisms take off from the site where man meets his end. Race as the boundary that constituted man's end as limit is fissured from the start by
man's end as goal or aim. Insofar as man aims toward universality,
boundaries set up to prevent that aim's realization will be difficult to
maintain. Race has already shown marks of its instability as a boundary. Black South Africa, as neither properly inside nor properly outside
apartheid South Africa, constitutes a fissure in South Africa and its
larger contexts. Black South Africans as man's specular reflections also
constitute a fissure in apartheid as a metaphysical humanism. Through
that fissure, movements that resist apartheid are able to emerge. Those
movements challenge apartheid on the basis of man's claim to universality; thus, they draw on metaphysical humanism as their resource.
This strategy does indeed run the risk of erasing race and of perpetuating sexual (in)difference. Following Derrida's analysis of movements
of resistance to apartheid as figured by Nelson Mandela will elicit the
specific dynamics in question.[18]

Admiring Mandela

Derrida's essay in honor of Nelson Mandela is a reading of Mandela's
autobiography, *The Struggle Is My Life*.[19] In reading Mandela as the figure of antiapartheid movements, Derrida takes Mandela's title at its
word. Mandela's struggle is his people's struggle; his people's struggle
is Mandela's struggle. Derrida's Mandela names both the particular
experiences of the man Nelson Mandela and the larger collectivity of
people in whose place "Mandela" stands. The title of Derrida's essay,
"The Laws of Reflection: Nelson Mandela, in Admiration," sets the
stage for what is to follow. The essay reads the figure of Mandela in
terms of reflection and speculation. What is admirable about Mandela
is what Mandela admires, Derrida writes. Mandela admires man's

promise of universality, a promise truncated by apartheid. With that admiration, Mandela sets in motion a series of specular reflections on and of man that dislodge him from his fixed place in the racial economy of apartheid. Derrida's reading of Mandela calls to mind Irigaray's strategy of *mimetisme;* Derrida's Mandela takes the position assigned to him by apartheid and its larger context and turns it on its head. Like Irigaray, Derrida's Mandela uses the mirrors of the specular economy to set fire to its dominance by sameness. In Mandela's hands, the concept of universal man becomes a mirror held up to South Africa's face. When reflected in that mirror, race as man's end emerges. Race figures man's end as limit and as goal. In constituting the boundary separating black South Africans from the goods associated with man, the limits of man's universality appear. His universality is circumscribed by race; that is, access to man's goods is reserved for men with white skin and European pedigree. Universal man, then, is first revealed as an instance of false neutrality. Universal man appears to bear no racial marks, but when held up to Mandela's mirror, his racial markings as white become visible. At the same time, Mandela's mirroring challenges race's pertinence and permanence as a boundary separating black South Africans from man and his proper(ties). Mandela challenges man's end as limit in the name of man's end as goal. Insofar as man aims toward universality, Mandela claims, then his end will not be fully realized until the boundary of race comes down.

Man's whiteness meets its end as limit in Mandela's blackness. Mandela uses his own (non)place as man's reflection to bring down race as a barrier. He wields the mirrors of the specular economy to speculate on man's proper as subject of the law. Derrida describes Mandela as a "man of the law" by vocation in two senses (calling and profession). Mandela's status as black lawyer is symptomatic of black South Africans status vis-à-vis man and his proper. South African law imposed several restrictions on black lawyers' ability to practice their profession. Black lawyers had to get permission to occupy office space and a waiver to practice law. Like the Bantustan system, these restrictions located black lawyers in a (non)place that is neither inside nor outside the practice of law. As required, Mandela requested permission to practice law and to occupy office space. The apartheid regime denied him both, putting Mandela in the ironic position of having to break the law in order to practice it. He occupied office space illegally for some time, but his practice was limited to giving legal advice; he could not take on cases. Mandela is also rendered subject *to* the law but not *of* the law in another way. South African law circumscribed black South

Africans' right to protest, effectively rendering protestors outlaws. As an antiapartheid activist, Mandela appears in court from time to time, but only as subject *to* the law prohibiting protest; as outlaw, not as a man of the law (see e.g., "Laws of Reflection," 15–42).

These strategies effectively contain Mandela for a while but, in granting him even limited access to the law, they provide the fissure that allows Mandela to break through this cracked container. Mandela uses his position as (non)lawyer to speculate with the relation to the law assigned to blacks under apartheid. Mandela turns the reflection of South African law back on the origin it claims for itself revealing its shortcomings in that light. He confronts South Africa with the logic of constitutional democracy. Universal man as *homo politicus* and as subject of the law constitutes a centrifugal structure of this political system. In exhibiting race as man's limit within this context, Mandela exhibits apartheid South Africa as the form of democracy. Mandela does not stop there, however. His appeal to constitutional law is grounded in the positing of an even higher law, the law of conscience inscribed on human hearts. Here, Mandela acts as man of the law by calling as well as by training. Mandela's appeal to both laws constitutes a claim to the status of man to whom law is proper. Man as subject *of* and *to* these two laws plays "outside" and "inside" against each other. In grounding black South Africans' claim to man and his proper(ties) in the law of conscience, Mandela resists the state's law (which is external to man) in the name of man's internal law (the law of conscience). In calling South Africa to grant legal recognition to black South Africans' claims on man, Mandela calls South Africa to externalize the law of conscience by becoming its reflection.

In asserting black South Africans' claim to man, Mandela mounts resistance to apartheid's exclusion of blacks in the name of the very same structure that founded and funded apartheid's exclusions.[20] Mandela reflects man in asserting his claim to be a proper subject *of* the law.[21] In so doing, apartheid and its larger context is ungrounded. Space is created for the emergence of a new South Africa. The new South Africa, like Mandela, is a specular reflection of the West's political systems. Mandela's invocation of a new South Africa goes beyond holding South Africa true to its European foundation. He calls South Africa beyond that heritage in two ways. Mandela's vision of a "*revolutionary democracy* in which none will be held in slavery or servitude, and in which poverty, want, and insecurity shall be no more" goes beyond what European/American democracies have realized.[22] Second, Mandela claims roots for the society he envisions that are older than European political ideals. He cites indigenous African political formations that preexisted European colonialization as sites where this vision was realized.

> [Mandela's] reflection lets us see, in the most singular geopolitical conjunction, in this extreme concentration of all human history that are the places or the stakes today called, for example, "South Africa," or "Israel," the promise of what has not yet ever been seen or heard, in a law that has not yet presented itself in the West, at the Western border, except briefly, before immediately disappearing. ("Laws of Reflection," 38)

In disrupting the West's claim to being the sole source of South Africa's democratic aspirations, Mandela overturns assumptions about what lies at the heart of the specular political economy. The new South Africa's democratic ideal is not simply the *faithful* reflection of an ideal of European origin (vs. its perverse reflection in the old South Africa). Insofar as the ideal of democracy in South Africa can trace its roots back to indigenous political formations that predated the era of European colonialization, then assumptions about the relationship between the ideal of democracy and its realization and the relationship between Europe (as origin) and Africa (as copy) are subverted.[23] The (European) ideal, then, can be read as a specular reflection of (the earlier African) reality.

Taking Stock: Derrida on Apartheid

The account I have offered so far of Derrida's work on and with race refutes assumptions that his work is antiethical or apolitical. It also carries my project several steps closer to its end, subverting the race / gender divide that affects whitefeminist theology and theory. My excavation of that divide in chapter 1 led me to ask, What enables whiteness to masquerade as neutrality within whitefeminist theology and theory? What prevents it from emerging as a necessary point of interrogation? I suggested then that answering those questions would entail exploring race's place in the text of metaphysics and its specular economy. Although this inquiry is not yet complete, answers to these questions are beginning to appear.

Whitefeminism exhibits symptoms of white solipsism because whitefeminism constitutes a specular reflection of the text of western metaphysics and its inscription of race. Symptoms of this can be read off of the history of essentialism and its heirs in whitefeminist theology and theory. The essential woman who figured prominently in white solipsism's career in feminist theology closely resembled the liberal humanist subject, I argued. Like metaphysical humanism's man, she was constituted by unity with her proper(ties). As purposeful, she aimed toward realizing her telos as active agent. Though whitefeminists explicitly denied her universality, it reasserted itself within whitefeminist theological texts. These symptoms of whitefeminism's perpetuation of metaphysical humanism are not incidental to its dealings with race. Reading Derrida on apartheid shows that, though man purports to be universal and therefore racially neutral, he has actually been constituted in and by exclusion of those deemed his racial others. Man as reflected in and by Mandela's mirrors is neither universal nor racially neutral; he is, rather, of European origin and white skinned. His claim on universality disguises his whiteness as neutrality up to the point where man encounters his racial others. The conflation of universality with whiteness also shapes the stance man takes toward his racial others. They can be recognized as man only insofar as they resemble him. The same dynamics appear in whitefeminism's history with racial difference, a legacy of its inscription by man. Woman's whiteness only became legible when white women's raced others began to confront whitefeminism. Those raced others are recognizable only insofar as they resemble whitefeminism's woman. Race can, at best, color in the already established outlines. Without the presence of the mirror of the raced other, whiteness remains invisible.

Whitefeminist theory, however, has been engaged in moving beyond the very essentialism that troubled whitefeminist theology's dealings with race. Insofar as breaking with essentialism means breaking with metaphysical humanism, then Derrida's work with race would confirm such moves as rightly directed. At the same time, however, Derrida's analysis of philosophy's inability to break with metaphysical humanism in "The Ends of Man" would caution whitefeminist theory against being too sanguine about its ability to make the break. Insofar as whitefeminism's woman traces her roots back to man, it should not be surprising that the specific contours of whitefeminism's failure reflect man's shadow. That antiessentialism and multiplicity both fail to deal with race adequately registers now as a failure to complete the break with metaphysical humanism. That race constitutes the site where these failures become legible suggests that sexual difference alone cannot carry feminism beyond metaphysical humanism's orbit.

Reading Derrida on apartheid uncovers the roots of white solipsism in whitefeminist theology and theory, but does this site provide any guidance in determining what is required to move beyond white solipsism? I sounded two cautionary notes as I entered this terrain. It appeared that resistance to racism in any meaningful sense (i.e., bringing its violences and violations to a close) required shoring up rather than deconstructing metaphysical humanism. Insofar as Derrida's work aimed toward taking apart metaphysical humanism's subject, then it would indeed seem to close itself off from ethics. On the other hand, if antiracism necessarily involved shoring up humanism, then antiracism and feminism would be working at cross purposes. If antiracism involved simply expanding universal man's reach to include his racial others, then its success would render race impertinent. Antiracism's success, then, would come at the cost of erasing both racial and sexual difference.

Bernasconi argues that Derrida's work on apartheid calls attention to humanism's limits as a tool against racism. At the same time, Bernasconi says, deconstruction is "called by the other of metaphysical humanism" ("Politics beyond Humanism," 118). My reading of Derrida on apartheid, like Bernasconi's, certainly challenges any simple link between metaphysical humanism and antiracism. Man is the site of contestation between racism and antiracism. On one hand, man grounds the logic of racism on which apartheid was constructed and maintained. Apartheid would have been impossible without the notion of man and his proper (*homo politicus,* subject of the law, one who owns property). Apartheid worked by denying black South Africans' status as true men in both obvious and subtle ways. On the other hand, man and his proper also funded movements of resistance to apartheid. Man's end (as goal), to be universal, enables Mandela to call the South African government up short. Metaphysical humanism enables racism *and* antiracism; it grounds antiethics as much as it grounds ethics. This contradictory stance is not unique to metaphysical humanism's career in South Africa; it is, rather, essential to man. In other words, it constitutes the end of man. Does not man's double life in South Africa, Derrida asks, reflect "a domestic war that the West carried on with itself, in its own name? An internal contradiction which would not put up with either a radical otherness or a true dissymmetry" ("Laws of Reflection," 16).

Both humanism and the possibility of its deconstruction emerge from this situation, as do ethics and antiethics, racism and antiracism. This situation troubles any easy equation of humanism with ethics and antiracism. In fact, the project of deconstructing man lines up with ethics and against racism. That project, as it has appeared so far, neither inaugurates nor accomplishes the death of the subject any more than deconstruction inaugurated or accomplished the death of God. Just as God turned out to be afflicted by his opposites (difference, deferral, absence), so man has turned out to be afflicted by not-man. In exploring and exacerbating the fissured border between man and his (raced) other, Derrida excavates the conditions surrounding man and his contexts that can open man up to and for his (raced) other. Rather than disabling political engagement, exposing the foundation of *homo politicus* in undecidability calls for political involvement. Indeed, it confirms Derrida's claim in "The Ends of Man" that philosophy, as the preeminent discourse on man's end, is always already political.

In a certain sense, then, the deconstruction of humanism occurs in the name of man's end as goal (being universal) by exposing man's end as limit. Rather than proclaiming the death of the subject, Derrida takes man to his end—an end that, from its beginning, was always already unfulfilled and unfulfillable. The project of deconstructing metaphysical humanism, at least as carried out to this point, seems no more able to break with metaphysical humanism than any of the philosophers discussed in "The Ends of Man." As Bernasconi points out, Derrida recognizes that metaphysical humanism's purchase on ethics and politics makes it "the price to be paid in the ethicopolitical denunciation of biologism, racism, naturalism, etc."[24] Insofar as this is the case, no matter how ethical or political its effects might be, Derrida's work would seem to be ultimately antithetical to my project. Metaphysical humanism not only risks neutralizing racial difference and erasing sexual difference, it also seems designed to keep the two issues apart. Following the implications of Derrida's work on apartheid appears to widen rather than narrow the divide between race and woman. Insofar as Derrida's reading of apartheid remains within man's (fissured) bounds without raising the issue of sexual difference, this scene perpetuates sexual (in)difference.

Indeed symptoms of this site's perpetuation of sexual (in)difference are not difficult to find. Nothing within Derrida's writings on apartheid considers the possibility that South African women might have distinctive stakes in man's fissures. Winnie Mandela, the only woman who appears in these texts, registers only as Mandela's faithful partner in the struggle. She keeps her troth to Mandela by acting in his stead when he is in prison and by waiting faithfully for his release. Her agenda is his agenda and his agenda is the people's agenda. South African women are, by implication, included in antiracism as "black," but not as "women."[25] Derrida's analysis inverts one of whitefeminism's standard gestures toward African American women. As Elizabeth Spelman argues, whitefeminists ostensibly welcome African American women into feminism's fold as women, as though "African American" and "woman" were separable components of their subjectivities.[26] What claims to gesture toward inclusion actually excludes African American women and perpetuates white privilege.

In addition, insofar as Derrida's analysis of apartheid remains bound to man, it offers no protection against race's ultimate submersion and erasure. Race figures only as a boundary to be overcome. Mandela's reflection reveals man's circumscription by whiteness/blackness as man's end as limit. His speculation with man's proper comes through the fissures in that limit marked by blackness's liminal status in relation to man and his contexts. Race as the boundary between whiteness and blackness constitutes a boundary to be torn down. What productive future, if any, lies ahead for race and man *after* Mandela's speculation runs its course? As man becomes more truly universal, race would seem to become not only less pertinent but less legible. Calling man to fulfill his inherent promise of universality may gain black South Africans' access to man's goods, but only insofar as they can rightfully claim to resemble him. Access to man comes at the cost of racial distinctiveness.

When read in the context of what Derrida describes as "a domestic war that the West carried on with itself, in its own name," then, Derrida's analysis of apartheid exposes the roots of the disease, but stops short of curing it. What will it take for what Derrida calls "radical otherness or a true dissymmetry" to disrupt and reshape the text of metaphysics and its contexts? It seems that man, at least as deployed so far, is not up to the task. Man seems constitutively unable to ground a form of subjectivity where race and sexual difference can remain legible and productive. The specular economy, as Irigaray reminds us repeatedly, is an economy based on sameness. Her work revealed the standard of sameness as masculine; Derrida's work reveals that same standard as Eurocentric and white. The sexual and racial economies funded by the specular economy grant value to those who most closely resemble its standard. Irigaray argued that this intolerance of alterity meant that there was no place for woman as such to speak. Because the position of the subject of discourse is indelibly marked as male when a woman opens her mouth to speak, she assumes a male position when she takes the position of subject. Reading Derrida on apartheid suggests that the same dynamics apply to raced subjects. Thus, access to *status* of the subject is not the issue; rather, the very *constitution* of the subject needs to be refigured for sexual difference and race difference to speak or be heard at all, much less together. This suggests that the deconstruction of metaphysical humanism needs to go deeper and farther if it is to prove useful to my project. The end of metaphysical humanism—in the sense of limit and goal, if not its (im)possible death—has yet to be uncovered. If that end lies in a multiply figured subject, then following metaphysical humanism to its end would help both race and woman resist erasure.

Attention to race occupies Derrida's attention in another setting that this chapter has already visited; the work of Martin Heidegger. Following race through this terrain is to continue in the tracks of metaphysical humanism's career, a career that Heidegger wanted very much to bring to a close. Taking up this setting also brings race and man closer to the scene of their end as originary goal and limit. Thus, it is to take up again the question of the end of man. His end lies where race and sexual difference intersect. His end bears the possibility of metaphysical humanism's closure; a closure that is also an opening that carries race difference and sexual difference beyond the race/gender divide—not as erased in indifference, but as significant structures of a differing subjectivity. Following man to his end through Heidegger's work uncovers a skeletal structure from which racial difference and sexual difference emerge and where they meet. Although Derrida fails to follow through on this potential, this skeletal structure, when combined with Irigaray's woman as *supplément,* provides a fragile (non)foundation for thinking race and sexual difference together in and around multiple subjectivities. The final chapter in this essay will explore the fruits of that supplementation.

Geschlecht II: Vestiges of Humanism in the Hand

Returning to Derrida's reading of Heidegger means visiting a site where deconstruction has been denounced as antiethical with particular vehemence. As this chapter has already shown, Derrida works closely with and through Heidegger's thinking. Controversies over evidence of Heidegger's complicity with Nazism during his brief tenure as rector of a German university have tarred deconstruction with the same brush. That Derrida uses Heidegger's work is often cited as evidence of a lurking immorality in deconstruction.[27] Bernasconi and Critchley both offer sound critical exposés of the scene of this dismissal. Dismissing deconstruction as worthy of attention gives its critics an alibi for bypassing the arduous task of reading Derrida and Heidegger. Bernasconi argues, for example, that these dismissals miss the way both thinkers require that ethics be rethought; a claim that preceding sections of this chapter would support. Deconstruction's critics also fail to take note of Derrida's own investigations into what in Heidegger's thought might have enabled his complicity with Nazism.

"*Geschlecht II*: Heidegger's Hand" seeks out the roots of Heidegger's complicity with National Socialism in his philosophy.[28] It also can be read as a resumption of the critical investigation begun in "The Ends of Man" into Heidegger's *rélève* of humanism and its complicity with racism. *Geschlecht II*'s inquiry occurs on familiar terrain and through familiar strategies. Here, as in *Dissemination*, boundaries between the inside and outside of texts and the relationships of author and text come into question. Like "The Ends of Man," following *Geschlecht II* through Heidegger's work also exhibits philosophy as a political site.

Derrida's *solicitation* of Plato in "Plato's Pharmacy" got its impetus from problems involved in translating *pharmakon*. Derrida's *solicitation* of Heidegger in this essay takes off from problems of translation centered around the term *Geschlecht*. As was the case with *pharmakon*, linguistic asymmetries turn out to be symptomatic of something much more significant. *Geschlecht* is a complex German word that has no neat equivalent in English (though the French *genre* approximates its multiple references). This one word gathers together several references including body, sex, race, genre, gender, lineage, family, and generation. *Geschlecht* speaks and writes all of these meanings simultaneously.[29] Thus, *Geschlecht* brings together the issues that both ground man and call into question his universality. The notions of race / lineage / genre / gender link "human race" (*Menschengeschlecht*) as a whole with its divisibility into specific genres. Derrida's exploration of what circulates around *Geschlecht* in Heidegger's work traces this linkage and its effects. *Geschlecht II* focuses on two genres embedded in *Geschlecht*, the distinction between human and animal being and the division of human beings into nationalities. When (human) race and nationality converge, as Derrida argues they do in Heidegger's texts, the distinction between human being and animal can become a carrier of racism. Derrida argues that the discursive conditions for Heidegger's involvement with Nazism lie in the conflation of these two categories; a conflation that *Geschlecht* makes possible.

According to Derrida, Heidegger explained his involvement with National Socialism as an outgrowth of his desire to support the development of the German nation.[30] He reportedly thought he could participate in Germany's self-development program without supporting Nazi racist ideology. Whether Heidegger is being honest here or not ultimately does not matter to Derrida's analysis. His reading of Heidegger on *Geschlecht* shows that Heidegger was unable to maintain that separation. Derrida's analysis of *Geschlecht* exposes the discursive conditions that maintain the mutual inextricability of nationalism and racism. Insofar as *Geschlecht* circumscribes Heidegger's attempt to think *Dasein* and its heirs, *Geschlecht* encloses his thinking in ethnocentrism. The root of Heidegger's ethnocentrism lies in a more basic form of humanism that *Geschlecht* also carries, the distinction between two genres: man and animal.

Apes constitute the site where man and animal diverge in Heidegger's work, and hands constitute the line of demarcation separating the two genres. Humans are hand-ed, in a very specific sense, while apes are not, Heidegger asserts. Apes can only grasp, while the human hand "reaches and extends, receives and welcomes . . . keeps [and] . . . carries."[31] Heidegger cites no evidence to back up this assertion; why should he? The distinction between man and animal, as old as the text of metaphysics itself, registers as an innocuous statement of fact. This distinction, however, turns out to be central to Heidegger's project and to its relationship to humanism. Handedness bears directly on Heidegger's thinking of Being and the being who thinks Being. "Only a being who can speak, that is, think, can have the hand and can be handy in achieving works of handicraft," Heidegger writes.[32] Heidegger links handicraft in its ordinary senses with the thinking of being. He describes woodworking as bringing out the essence of the wood with which man dwells. Handiwork, though, also names the thinking of Being in general. Thinking Being requires the openness of the hand that can receive the gift, give the gift, a hand that can dwell and be the dwelling. Handedness, then, is coextensive with *Dasein*, the essence of not-other-than-man.[33]

Citing handedness as the line separating ape from man takes on a sinister cast when read against the background of racism's history.[34] Antiblack racism in the United States has used this distinction to great effect. Rhetoric associating black people with apes saturates various vestiges of American racism. In its more refined forms, this distinction funded and founded pseudoscientific arguments for white superiority. In its cruder forms, figures of African Americans as apes or monkeys are commonly found in racist propaganda. The arsenal of racist insults uses that figure as its stock in trade.[35]

Adding *Geschlecht II* to this inquiry after race's place in metaphysical humanism and its larger context, the text of metaphysics and its specular economy, carries man's complicity with racism to its roots. Metaphysical humanism's role in apartheid South Africa is not a case of metaphysical humanism gone awry, nor is it an aberration in man's recent history. As different as South Africa, the United States, and Nazi Germany are from one another, and as distinctive as their racisms may be at certain levels, they are all linked together here in and through man and his end. The founding gesture of metaphysical humanism sets man off from other kinds of being. This distinction is made on the basis of man's end as essence. Thus, in appropriating primatological figures to denigrate raced others, racisms speculate with metaphysical humanism's funds. South African racism, U.S. racisms, and Nazi racism all represent specular reflections of man. Racism's origins lie at the very heart of man.

But what about antiracism? Man also funds antiracism, according to my reading of Derrida on apartheid. Can its resources also be traced back to man's end through *Geschlecht*? I also promised that following man to his end in Derrida's reading of Heidegger would carry the divide between race and gender to its end. Uncovering antiracism's resources at man's end and carrying my promise to its end require passing through *Geschlecht* once more from a different angle. *Geschlecht II*'s predecessor, "*Geschlecht*: Sexual Difference, Ontological Difference," provides that angle of entry and intersection.[36]

Geschlecht I: Genre Differences, Ontological Difference

Like *Geschlecht II,* "*Geschlecht*: Sexual Difference, Ontological Difference" continues Derrida's investigation into Heidegger's humanism. This essay focuses on *Dasein*'s relationship to sexual difference as delineated by Heidegger in a course given at Marburg while *Sein und Zeit* was making the rounds of philosophical discussion. Heidegger's lectures map his discomfort with the direction taken by readings of *Sein und Zeit* on the question of *Dasein*'s relationship to metaphysical humanism. The "anthropologistic deformations" that "The Ends of Man" investigated in France were already occurring in Germany by 1928. In the Marburg lectures, Heidegger tries to get readers of *Sein und Zeit* back on course by disengaging *Dasein* from metaphysical humanism. Heidegger insists, first of all, that *Dasein* precedes the concept of man presupposed by anthropology, ethics, or politics. *Dasein* is more primordial than the notion of a human subject who acts for the good, who engages in political activity, whose culture can be an object of study. *Dasein* is more primordial than the man to whom a proper or properties can belong. *Dasein* is, then, neutral with regard to all such designations and assignations.

Heidegger builds his case for *Dasein*'s primordial neutrality by erecting a fence around *Dasein* that closes it off to sexual difference. Derrida finds two aspects of this strategy particularly noteworthy. Heidegger uses *Geschlecht* as his term for sexual difference; a peculiar choice, says Derrida, given that more specific terms are available in German for this distinction. That Heidegger selects sexual difference as the terrain for erecting *Dasein*'s neutrality is significant, in Derrida's view. Could it be that Heidegger finds himself drawn to sexual difference because, despite its associations with ontic anthropologisms, sexual difference originates at *Dasein*'s (ontological) level? If sexual difference were merely an ontic distinction; that is, if it were simply a matter of distinguishing man from woman on the basis of secondary attributes layered atop a neutral subject, Heidegger's resistance to sexual difference should have simply neutralizing effects. But Derrida's reading of these lectures uncovers something much more complex than a neutering of sexual difference.

Heidegger withdraws *Dasein* from encapsulation within sexual difference *as construed by our current sexual economy;* that is, Heidegger insists that *Dasein* is more primordial than the division between two differends, man and woman. While this strategy separates *Dasein* from the man/woman distinction, it maintains *Dasein*'s proximity to a sexual differing conceived otherwise.

> Should one indeed conclude that sexual difference doesn't depend so simply on whatever the analytic [of *Dasein*] can and should neutralise, metaphysics, ethics, and especially anthropology, or indeed any other domain of ontic knowing, for example biology or zoology? Should one suspect that sexual difference cannot be reduced to an ethical or anthropological theme? (*GI*, 70–71)

More primordial than the division into man and woman is a dispersibility or dissemination, which constitutes one of *Dasein*'s ownmost possibilities. That dispersion grounds *Dasein* as spatial, temporal, and embodied. These structures rest on and reflect *Dasein* as worlded, as always already thrown (*geworfen*), and always already being-with (*Mitsein*). As spatial and temporal, *Dasein* occurs as interval—between birth and death, between other *Daseins* and other genres of occupants of its world. As temporal, *Dasein* is dispersed into the between as the now and then, the now and what-is-to-come, as life and (its own) death. *Dasein* as embodied is implicated in dispersal. *Dasein*'s dispersal into the "between" registers in, on, and through its body. *Dasein* as *Mitsein* also works through *Dasein* as embodied. *Mitsein* makes grouping *Daseins* according to *Geschlecht* possible.

In terms of sexual difference, then, the current sexual economy's division into man and woman presupposes *Dasein* as dispersed. It makes use of *Dasein* as *Mitsein* and *Dasein* as embodied. The binary division between man and woman—whether at the level of sex, gender, or sexual difference—is grounded and ungrounded (at least potentially) in *Dasein*'s dispersibility. *Dasein*'s dispersibility disrupts any attempt to fix those categories absolutely. Whitefeminist theorists have given Derrida's argument in *Geschlecht I* mixed reviews.[37] Kelly Oliver and Elizabeth Grosz applaud Derrida for finding an opening for multiple sexual differences, but they worry that he risks erasing the specificity of what they seem to see as the originary sexual difference, that between male and female.[38] They are particularly worried that Derrida risks erasing awareness of the female body's foundational role as the marker of sexual difference. Grosz argues that embodiment as either male or female constitutes the bedrock of those cultural structures in and through which human beings become sexual subjects. I share their concern that moving too quickly to a vague and abstract multiplicity can bypass the project of thinking carefully through the particular vectors at work in constituting current sexual subjectivities. Certainly, embodiment represents a particularly powerful vector in the current sexual economy. However, I am troubled by their turn to the body as foundation, as though it can be isolated from other vectors—like race, for example, in the current sexual regime—at work in producing and defining sexual subjectivities. African American feminists would certainly resist any assertion that being female is the only aspect of embodiment at work in African American women's development into sexual subjects (or objects) of whatever sort. If that is true for African American sexual subjects, then it is also true for white sexual subjects within this sexual economy.

Rather than closing off attention to particular vectors of power at work in the current sexual and racial economy, I see Derrida's work as offering a site for taking them to their end and beyond. Derrida only explores the consequences of *Dasein*'s dispersibility for sexual difference, but Heidegger's "peculiar choice" of *Geschlecht* as the term for sexual difference calls for reading *Dasein*'s dispersibility in terms of race, as well, I would argue. Radial difference—whether asserted at the level of nature, culture, or metaphysical humanism—is grounded and ungrounded by *Dasein* as dispersible *Mitsein*. If sexual difference resides at *Dasein*'s level, and if *Geschlecht* is its bearer, then perhaps race, too, resides at that level. Let be me clear here. I am *not* claiming that "black" and "white" or "man" and "woman" are ontological categories. Rather, I am claiming that these current divisions are funded by *Dasein*'s dispersibility as borne by *Geschlecht*. Humanity has not always divided itself into races and into sexes / genders (at least not in the same way it has recently come to do).[39] Current racial and sexual divisions need not necessarily have the last word. While dispersibility funds current racial and sexual economies, it also prevents their closure. In so doing, dispersibility holds open a fissure through which other economies might emerge.

Grosz and Oliver are right to warn against moving too quickly to an abstract multiplicity. Exploiting and enlarging the fissure opened up in current sexual and racial economies requires paying careful attention to the history of particular configurations of subjectivities funded by dispersibility, especially our own. At the same time, uncovering man's end in *Geschlecht*'s dispersibility aids my project considerably. Insofar as *Geschlecht* carries sexual difference and racial difference / ethnic difference together *simultaneously*, following man to his end in dispersion breaks through the divide between race and gender. Dispersibility reconfigures the end of man in all its senses (as limit, essence and goal). Dispersibility constitutes man's end as limit of his unity with his proper(ties) and with others of his kind. Man realizes his proper through dispersing his proper(ties) in the variety of genres that constitute him; thus dispersion reconfigures man's end as goal. Man is bound to others of his kind not by sameness but by dispersibility and differentiation. This bond would need to be calculated in terms other than one-plus-one-plus-one, where each unit can stand in for the other. What brings about this recalculation of man's end as limit and goal is not alien to man, but is, in fact, man's end as essence. If *Dasein*, "there-being," is man's essence and if dispersibility is *Dasein*'s essence, then dispersibility constitutes man's essence, as well. Since dispersion constitutes man's end, the name "man" no longer seems to suit it.

Conclusion/Opening

Following the divide to its end has cleared the ground for whitefeminism to think race and sexual difference together. This chapter explains whitefeminism's white solipsism, but has it brought about a cure for white solipsism? Can locating an ontological site where woman and race converge guarantee that whitefeminism will acknowledge the role race already plays in its work? Can it guarantee, moreover, that whitefeminism will move on to more productive engagement with thinking race and woman together? Can it assure us that whitefeminism can enter these waters without risk? The answer is, of course, no. The dangers of succumbing to a false neutrality attend even this site where the race/gender divide meets its end. Access to *Dasein*'s differential structure comes through repeating the neutralizing gestures with which metaphysical humanism dismisses differences. Heidegger's defense of *Dasein* aims toward neutralizing it with regard to those very differences. Insofar as Heidegger succeeds, man, like God, remains alive.[40] Insofar as he fails, fissures in man's disputable claim to neutrality open singular man onto multiple subjectivities. Man constitutes a site of contestation where differencing and neutralizing both circulate as possibilities.

Staving off neutralization in favor of differentiating patterns is not a project accomplished once and for all. *Geschlecht* is a nonfoundational foundation. What it grounds will always be at risk. Whitefeminism can easily embrace putting man at risk, but has often balked at putting woman at risk as well. But if feminism is to follow its telos of becoming a platform for women in all their diversity, then woman must be put at risk. In other words, whitefeminism shares philosophy's predicament as described by Derrida in "The Ends of Man." Like philosophy, whitefeminism's end as goal aims toward universality. Like philosophy's man, race also marks whitefeminism's end as limit insofar as it constitutes the boundary between woman and not-woman. Whitefeminism's end (as goal) calls whitefeminism to investigate race as its end (as limit). Taking up this investigation involves putting woman's end in both senses at risk (limit and goal). To take this step is not, however, to throw woman to the dogs at the bottom of the nihilistic pit. It is, rather, to follow her into and through an abyssal chain of significations and positions that reading race and woman together begin to reveal. The previous chapters have prepared ground that can support whitefeminism's move into productive engagement with such thinking. The next and final chapter will excavate the ground more clearly and indicate directions for thinking beyond the race/gender divide.

6

Through the Looking Glass:
Subverting the Race/Gender Divide

The previous chapters have followed the divide between race and gender to its end from both sides of the divide. I started from the side of woman and followed her to her end in sexual difference. Following sexual difference to its end in Irigaray's multiple woman uncovered sites where race could register, but left whiteness in the position of mastery. Thus, traversing the race/gender divide from the side of woman left white solipsism relatively undisturbed. The ability of whiteness to disguise itself as neutral remained unexplained. This limit to womans' efficacy as a route for disturbing racism confirmed the need to reenter the divide from race's side. Using Derrida as Irigaray's *supplément*, I explored race's place within the context of metaphysics and its specular economy. Inquiry into race in Derrida's work found it located at the end of man in many senses. Against the screen of blackness, whiteness became visible as the mark of man's end as limit. Investigating raced politics uncovered man as a site of contestation between racism and anti-racism, with both able to trace their origins to man. The end of man as goal (to be universal) threatened to bring racial and sexual difference to their ends as well. Engaging with man on this terrain risked neutralizing racial as well as sexual difference and continued to perpetuate the divide between them. Going deeper into the race/gender divide, however, uncovered its end in man's end in yet another sense. Following Derrida through his two essays on *Geschlecht* in Heidegger's work followed man to his end in dispersibility. Insofar as they are funded and founded by man's essential dispersibility, current racial and sexual economies meet their end (which is also their beginning) in *Geschlecht*. *Geschlecht* figures an infinite number of possible dispersions of *Daseins*, thus potentially funding and founding other possible racial and sexual economies. Man's end, then, both grounds and ungrounds racial and sexual (in)difference.

Reading race and woman through Irigaray and Derrida has been helpful in clearing the ground that sustained and nourished the race/

gender divide. Let me trace more clearly the shape of this terrain—and its limits—uncovered by the supplemental readings I have offered in the previous chapters. I will begin by reading woman as *supplément* to race, then race as *supplément* to woman. Derrida's work with race grounded it in metaphysical humanism. Race constitutes man's end in sense of goal and limit, thus, race constitutes a site where man trembles. But what of woman's relationship to man's end? Sarah Kofman, in her contribution to a colloquium at Cerisy on "The Ends of Man" in 1980, comments on the fact that sexual difference makes no appearance in the original staging of "Ends" in 1968, but notes its refusal to be overlooked when "Ends" appears on a new stage twelve years later. Kofman connects sexual difference's appearance to "Ends" as further highlighting the problem of man's universality.[1] No doubt, sexual difference's insistent presence reflects the emergence of the second wave of feminism between "Ends'" two stagings. The reading of Derrida and Irigaray that I offered in chapters 2–4 above, read now in light of chapter 5, affirm but nuance Kofman's point. These earlier chapters register now as describing woman, too, as man's end in the sense of goal and limit. Like man's raced other, man's sexed other marks his end in several senses. Man's proper(ty) is available neither to her nor to man's raced other. Both his sexed other and his raced other serve as negative mirrors for man reflecting him back to himself as he would like to be seen. In reflecting him back to himself, sexual difference and racial difference ground and unground man.

Race and woman are both caught within a specular economy of sameness. Man's raced others, like man's sexed others, function as property to be appropriated and resources to be used (up). Irigaray develops this analysis from woman's side; apartheid exhibits race's inscription within similar dynamics. Denying black South Africans access to man's proper(ty) rendered them exploitable resources available for appropriation by the apartheid regime. Slavery's history in the United States also fits this paradigm. Denying Africans access to man's goods was essential to exploiting them as slave labor.

Race and woman, then, stand in supplemental relationship to one another and to the specular economy that figures them. Each is called to the scene by lack, by desire for plenitude and fullness. As sites of lack, race and woman reassure man of his assumed plenitude and fullness. As figures of man's boundaries, sites that lie just beyond his reach, they fissure his plenitude and fullness. Both race and woman circulate around and through much of the same terrain within the specular economy, but neither can stand in for the other as full and total replacement.

That it is possible to investigate either *supplément* and not encounter its double suggests the distance between them maintained by the specular economy.

Whitefeminism's dealings with race reflect the shape of this terrain. As the history of whitefeminist theology and theory I offered in chapter 1 showed, the roots of whitefeminism's woman lie in man. Whitefeminism's white solipsism can now be read as a reflection of metaphysical humanism's dealings with race. If race and woman are supplements to each other as well as to man, then interrogating one will not necessarily involve interrogating the other. Whichever supplement is left unchallenged goes underground but continues its silent and invisible inscription of the text or context in question. Certainly whitefeminism's double erasure of raced woman—its failure to sustain attention to African American women, its failure to attend to whiteness as a racial mark—confirms this reality. At the same time, this exploration of race's place within the specular economy suggests that signs of fissure in the boundary between race and woman should also mark whitefeminist thought. Indeed, symptoms of such fissures uncovered in chapter 1 now register as such. Whitefeminism has erected itself in and through the exclusion of its raced others and its own race, and yet race leaves its (in)visible mark or trace on whitefeminism's woman at every turn. Like man in South Africa, whitefeminism's woman is affected by what it excludes. In that sense, then, whitefeminism is as much a product of the specular economy's dealings with race as it is of its dealings with gender.

Beyond the Race/Gender Divide?

The question now becomes what to do with(in) this context? Is it possible to break the specular economy's hold over whitefeminism's dealings with race? What might lie on the other side of the race/gender divide? Is it possible, now, on this terrain opened up by the preceding chapters, for whitefeminism to begin more productive engagements with race and woman? What form might these engagements take? Where might they take root? I suggested that *Dasein*'s dispersibility, especially in combination with Irigaray's figure of woman as multiple, could provide a (non)foundation for figuring race and woman together. What sort of a (non)foundation might it be? What would raced woman erected on such a (non)foundation look like? What kind of feminist theory and theology could such an ungrounded ground support?

Uncovering a differing and deferring subject at the base of the race /
gender divide when explored from both sides confirms, chastens, and
supplements whitefeminism's move toward woman as multiple. It
confirms whitefeminism's insight that going in this direction can disrupt metaphysical humanism. It chastens whitefeminism's confidence
that approaching multiplicity through sexual difference is sufficient to
disrupt race's double erasure. It supplements whitefeminism's turn toward multiplicity in doubling sexual difference and deferral with racial
difference and deferral. I would argue, however, that building on this
(non)foundational foundation requires first going backward into history rather than forward into the future. Rather than leaving race to
trace itself invisibly through whitefeminist texts, whitefeminists need
to attend to the way race and woman always already intertwine
through our own subjectivities and history. Since whitefeminism appears to be the product of the history of race, it needs to investigate
the conditions of its own production.

No doubt, such inquiries could take multiple forms, but I want to
devote the rest of this chapter to indicating specific directions opened
up by this essay for investigations into whitefeminism's stake in the
dual history of race and gender.[2] To begin with, this essay suggests
that deconstructive strategies are particularly suitable to the task whitefeminist theory and theology face. Whitefeminist thought has taken its
bearings from metaphysical humanism; thus, it could take its cues from
the approach to interrogating race as metaphysical humanism's end
that the previous chapter uncovered. There, whiteness showed up as
a racial mark indicating man's end as limit when man was reflected
against the screen of blackness. Reading race and woman together
through African American feminist theory and womanist theology
would provide such a screen against which whitefeminism's woman's
whiteness can become visible. Taking on such a project is not to start
afresh on new ground free from racist taint. To the contrary, this strategy begins as a gesture of appropriation. As I noted in chapter 1, African American feminists have criticized whitefeminists for taking up
black women's work in order to learn something about whitefeminism.
Though this strategy begins with the appropriative gesture, I envision
it as taking that gesture to its end in carrying whitefeminism toward
its end in multiple senses. To read for raced women as black and white
is to read doubly. It is to speculate with woman and race in order to
exploit fissures in the divide between them. I would hope that making
visible whiteness's centrality to what has counted as feminist will exhaust white solipsism's invisible mastery over whitefeminist scholar-

ship. Exhausting white solipsism's invisibility through following raced
women through African American feminist theory and womanist theology moves toward realizing feminism's (im)possible telos of providing a platform for resistance to the multiple oppressions women face.

Two sites have figured prominently in the terrain uncovered by the
previous chapters. The discussion of race's relationship to the text of
metaphysics in chapter 5 circulated around two of man's properties,
law and handedness. The discussion of woman in relationship to the
text of metaphysics in chapters 2–4 circulated around the nexus formed
by woman, God, and desire. Both sites proved to be routes to a differing and deferring subject that could ground more productive dealings with race and woman on the other side of the race/gender divide.
That this (un)grounding ground came to light in and through these
sites recommends them as potentially fruitful places to delve into reading race and woman together. In this final chapter, I will conduct heuristic forays into these sites that illustrate their potential for funding
analyses of race and woman together. These forays are exploratory,
not exhaustive. They indicate potential, but stop short of fully realizing
it. I will focus on a limited number of theorists and a limited number
of literary texts here. Work by scholars in African American feminist
literature that bear on these issues ranges far more widely than the
following pages can acknowledge. Nor will the particular contestations
that I uncover exhaust the meaning of these figures of raced women.

Taking on these heuristic explorations involves double reading in a
number of senses. To take up these topics doubles back through terrain
covered by previous chapters, but with several differences. First, the
previous chapters left uninvestigated race's place in the domestic economy of psychoanalysis and woman's place within the political and literary economies. These topics remained closed because they were not
accessible solely through one point of entry into the race/gender divide. Having arrived at the site where the figures of race and woman
converge and diverge, it is possible to take up these inquiries. To do
so requires returning to the work of African American feminist scholars, an area of research left behind in chapter 1. In the beginning of
this essay, their work indicated the breadth and depth of the problems
with whitefeminism's dealings with race. I return to African American
feminist scholars in a different vein now: as productive *suppléments* to
Derrida and Irigaray. It is my hope that the insights these thinkers offer
can now register more fully against the background provided by the
readings I have offered of Irigaray and Derrida. When read as *suppléments* to the readings of race and woman that I have offered so far, the

work of African American feminist scholars will reveal woman as man's double. Like man, she serves as a site where gender and race are asserted and contested. On the one hand, woman proves to be, like man, a site bounded by race. African American feminist writing, however, contests those boundaries and the content of woman that they protect. Ultimately, their work points woman beyond the constraints of the current racial and sexual economies.

Handedness, Literacy, and Literature: Contesting Woman and Race

African American feminists have lodged their strongest critique of appropriative gestures against whitefeminists' use of African American feminist fiction. At the same time, the importance of the development of African American literary traditions in the long struggle against white racism makes African American feminist literature a particularly fruitful potential site for developing more productive strategies for reading race and woman together. Henry Louis Gates, Jr., has argued that literacy and literariness served as an important site for resisting the boundary established between blackness and the concept of man; African American feminist scholars make a similar argument for black women's literature and the concept of woman. The fact that the literary tradition would take on this role accrues significance in light of Derrida's reading of Heidegger on handedness. Gates argues that the development of African American literature beginning in the seventeenth century occurs against the backdrop of fights over African Americans' claim to man and his proper, being literate and literary (defined in this context as being able to write "the King's English" and having a literary tradition). Heidegger's hand (that, among other things, writes) reappears as the mark distinguishing "human" from "subhuman." Gates argues that "the written word, as early as 1700, signified the presence of a common humanity with the European."[3] Gates's analysis further suggests that writing serves as the stamp of man's presence because it stands in for his other properties. Writing provides iterable signs that reason was here. It records history, which is the outworking of reason. Without memory and the mind that lay behind it, there would be no history and "without history, there could exist no 'humanity,'" according to this view (*Figures*, 21).[4] South Carolina registered its fear of slave literacy by passing a law in 1740 that forbade teaching slaves to write (*Figures*, 17).[5] African Americans used literacy and their developing literary tradition to stake their claim to status as human. Gates offers evidence that the (white) public registered this gesture in the same terms. The publication of slave narratives in the United States "separated the African from the Afro-American, the slave from the ex-slave, titled property from fledgling human being" (*Figures*, 4). Abolitionists cited the slave narratives as evidence of African Americans' mental capabilities (i.e., they can compose accounts of their lives, ergo they are "men").

While the narrative of African American women's literary traditions remains itself a matter of contestation, different versions of that narrative all read African American women's literature as a response to the historical context of white racist misogyny. Barbara Christian's *Black Women Novelists* (1980) constituted the first book-length account of black women's fiction to be written.[6] Christian locates the roots of black women's fiction in a practice of resistance. Beginning with Harriet Jacobs's autobiographical narrative, *Incidents in the Life of a Slave Girl*, black women wrote in order to contest and resist racist and sexist portrayals of black women (and men), Christian argues.[7] Later authors shift to a concern with writing black women's experience more generally. Later still, black women writers focus on self-expression (Zora Neale Hurston is case in point). A further shift occurs in black women's fiction in the 1970s, which now turns a critical eye toward the black community itself. Both Hazel Carby and Hortense Spillers are somewhat critical of Christian's teleological narrative. Carby finds that Christian's account rests on an essentialist view of black women as authors and encloses black feminist fiction in a canon. In contrast, Carby argues for holding open "black woman" and "black feminist criticism" as signs to be interrogated because their meaning varies with historical context (Carby, 15–18). Hortense Spillers is troubled by Christian's enclosure of black women's writing in a narrative of progress and self-revelation.[8] In contrast, Spillers proposes a nonlinear narrative that links black women writers to one another by threads running in a variety of directions.

All three (along with Valerie Smith, Deborah McDowell, and Claudia Tate) see African American women's literary traditions as emerging out of a historical context figured by the dual trajectories of race and gender. The historical context against which African American women's writing needs to be read, according to African American literary theorists, is rooted in slavery. African American feminist theorists find the concepts of black woman and white woman at the nexus of these two trajectories. Hazel Carby argues that female slaves and white mistresses represent two different "ideologies of womanhood," to cite the subtitle for her second chapter. What historians call "the cult of true womanhood" endowed the white mistress with the marks of the "true woman": "piety, purity, submissiveness and domesticity" (Carby, 23). She was to be pure, delicate, asexual, obedient, and passive. By contrast, black women were expected to be strong and sexually active—indeed uncontrollably so. Both identities were believed to be legible on women's bodies. White mistresses should look delicate and frail; black women should look strong. The previous chapter uncovered man as a site of contestation in the West's discourse on race; African American feminist theory suggests that woman plays a similar role where these trajectories (race and gender) meet.

Like man, race constitutes woman's end as limit and as goal. Historian Evelyn Brooks Higginbotham's description of the case of *State of Missouri v. Celia* exhibits these discourses coming together with race serving to mark woman's end.[9] The case involved a slave woman who killed her master while trying to fight off his attempt to rape her. The verdict rested on the validity of her claims to status as subject and as a woman. The jury had to decide whether she was a self (and therefore entitled to defend herself) and whether she constituted a woman (who, by definition, could be raped). The jury decided that slave women fit neither category. Her status as property of her master negated any claims to selfhood or womanhood.[10] He could do with her(?) what he wanted; she(?) had no right to resist. Racism's role in defining the woman that lies at the heart of the "cult of true womanhood," usually disguised, becomes visible here. The fact that the name of woman is mortgaged to whiteness appears via race's appearance as the boundary separating (white) woman from (black) not-woman.

African American feminist literary critics and theorists argue that the writings of black women work with, around, through, and against these ideologies of womanhood.[11] Following their readings of African American women's writing through this scene shows that woman serves as a site of contestation in at least three ways: African American women's writing contests stereotypes of black women, white women's ownership of the title to woman, and the content and contour of that woman. This multivalent speculation with woman is particularly visible in African American feminists' readings of Harriet Jacobs's *Incidents in the Life of a Slave Girl*. In this early slave narrative, Jacobs relates the story of her experiences as a slave and her eventual escape from bondage. Escaped slaves were encouraged by abolitionists to write down or dictate narratives of their experiences. These narratives were to provide ammunition for abolition activists by confronting their readers with the inhumane conditions slaves endured. Jacobs's story of her own enslavement and eventual escape fits the bill. Jacobs adopts the genre of sentimental fiction, a genre popular in white women's writing of the nineteenth century, to tell her story. In relating the events of her heroine's life, Jacobs appropriates and bends the genre to fit the story she has to tell. In sentimental fiction, the heroine is primarily the passive object of events. She survives dire circumstances partly through her own pluck, but primarily through receiving timely help from others. The heroine's sexual purity is often threatened. If she loses her chastity, she dies shortly afterward. If she manages to preserve it, her reward for perseverance comes in the form of reunion with her beloved. The plots often culminate with the heroine, after some further struggle, finding domestic bliss in his arms. Thus, the heroine of sentimental fiction closely resembles the "true (white) woman" worshipped by the cult of domesticity.

African American feminist literary critics' interpretations of Jacobs's *Incidents* articulate a complex relationship between the narrative and the genre of sentimental fiction. This complexity centers on the relationship between Linda Brent, the heroine of Jacobs's narrative, and the conventions surrounding heroines of sentimental fiction. Valerie Smith notes that Jacobs/Brent survives and escapes the brutal conditions of slavery with assistance from others.[12] In this respect, Jacobs/Brent remains within the passive contours of this genre's typical heroine. However, relating the events of her life in slavery requires Jacobs to tread carefully in and around genre conventions. Sexual exploitation occupies center stage in Jacobs's/Brent's narrative. Her master clearly has designs on her. To escape him, Jacobs/Brent offers herself to another white man, a friend of her master's, as his lover.

In writing the loss of her sexual purity, Jacobs/Brent breaks with the conventions surrounding the heroine of sentimental fiction. Claudia Tate argues that, at this point, Jacobs switches genres from sentimental fiction to the novel of seduction, but with woman as the free agent.[13] Jacobs portrays this aspect of her life with great solicitude for her white female audience's sensibilities. As Minrose C. Gwin notes, sexual exploitation was an aspect of slavery that white Victorian sensibilities found particularly onerous. Jacobs enlists her readers' sympathy by describing her desire at the time to retain her purity. Rather than a scandalous exercise in wantonness, Jacobs's/Brent's decision to take a lover becomes a choice for the lesser of two evils.[14] Tate reads Jacobs's taking of a lover—and her *admission* of that decision—as acts of "radical, revolutionary autonomy for a woman to record in a public document, irrespective of her social status" (109). This theme of autonomy is carried through in the narrative's conclusion. The narrative breaks with the genre of sentimental fiction by ending not with marriage but with Brent's solitary freedom.

When read as *supplément* to the reading of Irigaray and Derrida I provided in the previous chapters, Jacobs's Brent registers as speculation with woman as defined within the conventions of sentimental fiction. Through appropriating the sentimental heroine as vehicle for her self-representation, Jacobs asserts a claim on woman. The strength of this claim is highlighted by the contrast between the heroine and her mistress, Mrs. Flint. Through her portrayal of Mrs. Flint, Jacobs challenges white women's claim on woman. As Gwin notes, Jacobs's portrayal of Flint reads as an ironic parody of the ideal of true (white) womanhood. Though ostensibly a Christian woman, Mrs. Flint spares no cruelty when it comes to her slave. Mrs. Flint actively pursues Jacobs with hostile and violent intent. Where is the woman celebrated by the cult of true womanhood as a passive gentle, civilizing influence?

Through her portrayals of her heroine and her antiheroine, Jacobs challenges race as the border separating blackness from the figure of woman. A fissure in that border appears: it is Linda Brent, not Mrs. Flint, who most closely resembles the true woman.[15] However, rather than *conform* to this woman, Jacobs uses the character of Linda Brent to contest the ideologies of both white and black womanhood. Jacobs/Brent contests the stereotype of African American women as sexually voracious. The exercise of her sexuality becomes a deliberately chosen survival strategy rather than an expression of uncontrollable sexuality. In its appeal to white women's sympathies, Jacobs's/Brent's strategy also contests white women's exclusive claim on sexual purity. Jacobs/Brent tells her white female readers, like you, I wanted to remain pure; race and class privilege make it possible for you to do so, but not me. Through the fissures enacted in these ideologies of womanhood, an alternative to these constructions of raced women begins to appear. Jacobs/Brent uses her location on the figure of woman's other side to contest the *content* of the ideal woman. Tate's reading highlights Jacobs's/Brent's assertion of agency *through* sexuality. In resisting bifurcation of sexuality from agency, Jacobs/Brent also contests the association of sexuality with passivity. She actively resists abusive conditions and refuses the bonds of domesticity. This speculation with woman breaks her traditional boundaries not in *spite* of Jacobs's/Brent's race, but in and through it.

Such speculation with woman is not without risk. According to Frances Smith Foster, slave narratives' depiction of black women's survival

of abusive situations was often read as further evidence of their emotional and spiritual inferiority.[16] Similarly, Claudia Tate notes that African American women's use of the genre of sentimental fiction is often
read as reinforcing bourgeois ideologies about womanhood, marriage,
and family.[17] She argues that reading these novels against their historical context allows them to be read as novels of liberation. Tate notes
that being able to marry is a civil right that comes with status as citizen.
Although most former slave states had passed laws recognizing slave
marriages as legal, a national guarantee of African Americans' right to
marry came in 1866 with the passage of the Thirteenth Amendment to
the constitution. Significantly, it predates the Fifteenth Amendment,
which granted black men suffrage. Tate writes, "For black people, vot-
ing and marrying were the signs of the race's ascent to manhood and
womanhood. To vote and to marry, then were two civil responsibilities
that nineteenth century black people elected to perform; they were twin
indexes for measuring how black people collectively valued their civil
liberties" (103). Moreover, marriage as portrayed by African American
writers like Frances Harper, for example, is not traditional white patriarchal marriage, but a companionate marriage. The husband and wife
in *Iola Leroy*, for example, are portrayed as partners working together
for racial uplift. Historian Glenda Gilmore's book, *Gender and Jim Crow:
Women and the Politics of White Supremacy in North Carolina, 1896–1920*,
follows the history of several prominent African American families.[18]
Gilmore's account makes it clear that their marriages were not confined
to the traditional model. These marriages can be read as contesting
both the boundaries between woman and blackness and the very content of woman (as man's property) itself.

Two Halves of a Split Subject: Woman, Race and Psychoanalysis

Given psychoanalysis's prominence as the discourse where desire,
woman, and God meet, exploring this site requires first taking on the
question of race's relationship to psychoanalysis. Can psychoanalytic
theory be of any help in diagnosing and analyzing, perhaps even disrupting, race's place in relation to woman in the specular economy?
That is, can raced woman be read in and through psychoanalysis? If
so, to what effect? Whitefeminist scholars are just now beginning to
interrogate the place of whiteness in psychoanalytic theory.[19] Hortense
Spillers has tested psychoanalysis on African American contexts in a
series of articles. What Spillers accomplishes in this terrain makes her
a particularly important *supplément* at this point in my project.

Spillers's skepticism about psychoanalysis as a tool for theorizing about African American subject positions is clearly marked. In an essay entitled " 'The Permanent Obliquity of an In(pha)llibly Straight': In the Time of the Daughters and the Fathers," she asks whether psychoanalysis will work in contexts that "do not replicate moments of its own historical origins and involvements" (129).[20] Spillers tests psychoanalysis's adaptability, in this essay, by applying it to narratives of father/daughter incest within African American fiction. Spillers concludes that psychoanalysis illuminates African American texts and contexts "only by accident" (148). The accident of cultural imperialism that brings Africa into contact with Europe through its progeny, America, provides the bridge that allows psychoanalysis to cross.

In "Mama's Baby, Papa's Maybe: An American Grammar Book," Spillers uses psychoanalysis to read the effects of that accident in producing slaves and their African-American descendants.[21] As Spillers reads it, the slave trade begins in acts of robbing native Africans of all that makes up their subjectivity: body, will, soul, cultural context, familial context, and even gendered identity. African bodies are severed from their wills and their desires in being captured and turned into (in)human cargo. Spillers's analysis of the terrors and horrors of the slave ships gives new meaning to the term "Middle Passage." The slaves-to-be are suspended in an oceanic void that cuts them off from their former identities as it bears them toward an unknown future. In Freudian terms, the ocean figures as the (non)place of (non)identity, an apt description of this (non)site. The Middle Passage aimed to wipe the slate clean, to eradicate any traces of native identity, humanity, and will in order to produce blank bodies and souls with broken wills ready to be imprinted with an identity not their own. Sexual (in)difference serves as a grid through which this robbery occurs, Spillers argues. The slave trade turns African bodies into captive bodies through erasing the difference between African male bodies and female bodies. Spillers notes that few traces of sexual differentiation mark the accounts of the slave trade; ledger books do not count men and women separately, nor do the traders' narratives of life aboard the ships report distinctive activity on the part of female cargo. Traces of sexual differentiation appear primarily in allocations of space. Calculations of the amount of cargo a ship can hold rest on allotting smaller spaces to women and children. The sexual economy described in and by psychoanalysis is graphically *re*presented here.

The erasures enacted in the Middle Passage are repeated again and again within the slave economy. As a captive people, Spillers argues, imported Africans (and their descendants) were denied access to the terms of family and therefore of subjectivity, sexuality, and gender. The economy of slavery rested on the disruption of kinship systems among slaves. Slave marriages were not recognized as legal; they were sustained, if at all, through gestures of paternalistic benevolence that could be reversed at any time. Slave fathers had no claim on their offspring, nor did slave mothers. Slaves, then, could not properly be husbands or wives, fathers or mothers, daughters or sons. Their exclusion from these sites, rites, and rights amounts to excluding them from status as women or men. Spillers calls the slave women "females" because, she argues, they are not a different *kind* of woman; they were not really women at all (480).[22]

Spillers's work uncovers a set of mirrors that situate white women and African American females as "twin actants on a common psychic landscape" (474). Within slavocracy and what has replaced it, white women and black females are bound together as doubles of each other. In chapters 2–4 above, psychoanalysis served as a door into the hall of mirrors that constituted the specular economy. Traversing that hall of mirrors uncovered woman at the heart of the specular economy; she is the currency that keeps the sexual, familial, linguistic, and philosophical economies going. Only (in)visibly white women enter the domestic circle where they move from daughter to wife to mother (all positions marked by the phallus), Spiller argues. African American females are repeatedly denied access to woman; they are, by definition, caught in the defective mirror image of that circle. The legacy of slavery is seen in the stereotypes of the African American (non)family articulated, for example, in the notorious Moynihan report. Spillers, like other African American feminist theorists, criticizes the myth that black mothers are matriarchs.[23] Within white racist misogyny, black mothers do not constitute a legitimate route for the transmission of cultural inheritance. To describe black mothers as "matriarchs" is a misnomer that identifies African American mothers as the defective doubles of white mothers. The presence of the father in the stereotypical white family contains white mothers within patriarchal boundaries. The father's absence in the stereotype of the black family releases black mothers from their proper constraints thereby marking the black family as pathological.[24] The black father's absence registers as a lack that the black mother cannot fill.

Spillers further argues that black and white women constitute two halves of a split sexual subject. As my analysis in chapters 3–4 showed, (white) woman's desire is not her own, in several senses, within the current sexual economy. Her desire is his desire, in many ways. Her desire to be the object of his desire serves to get his desire going. The question or possibility of her *jouissance* has no place within the phallocratic sexual economy. In contrast, Spillers argues, African American women are constituted as nothing but desire, nothing but sexuality. This is not to say that black women's *jouissance* counts in this economy; quite the contrary.[25] White men's sexual exploitation of slave women was justified by the very definition of "black woman."

The division of sexual subjectivity between white women and black women sets up a relationship of hostility between black women and white women within the context of slavocracy. According to Hazel Carby, white men were supposedly unable to resist black women's allegedly uncontrollable sexuality. Thus, the very presence of black slave women threatened the "conjugal sanctity of the white mistress" (Carby, 27). Considerable evidence exists that documents jealousy between mistresses and slaves and the harsh treatment that resulted from it.[26] Spillers points to the relationship between Linda Brent and her mistress, Mrs. Flint, in Jacobs's *Incidents* as one example. Once Mrs. Flint became aware of Mr. Flint's interest in Brent/Jacobs, she began to make frequent nocturnal visits to Linda's bedside. Mrs. Flint's actions on these visits ranged from simply staring at Brent/Jacobs, to interrogating her about Mr. Flint, to planting suggestions in her head, to touching her. Spillers reads in Mrs. Flint's behavior a desire to appropriate the slave woman's body in order to become the object of Mr. Flint's desire. The black woman's body, Spillers argues, becomes an object that, "in an amazing stroke of pansexual potential—might be invaded/raided by another *woman* or man" ("Mama's Baby," 474).[27]

Taking Whitefeminism through the Looking Glass

These heuristic forays have begun to indicate what exploration of these sites through the figures of raced women (as black and white) could produce. I have focused on African American feminist literary theory, but other African American feminist scholars (including womanist theologians and ethicists) also situate their work against the historical background of racism and resistance to it. From bell hooks and Angela Davis, to Hazel Carby and Patricia Hill Collins, to Katie Cannon, Delores Williams, Marcia Riggs, and Cheryl Townsend Gilkes, neither theorizing or theologizing take place apart from the historical background that produced raced women. The exploratory forays I have taken in this chapter suggest that the history of colonization that produces and shapes African American women's history produces and shapes white-feminism's history, too. The cult of true womanhood is not the product of gendered ideology alone, but of a raced ideology as well. The woman idealized by the cult of domesticity is articulated in and through her alter ego, the slave woman. Mistress and slave are specular reflections of each other constructed in and through a racial and sexual economy that is both Eurocentric and phallocentric. These women's different values are determined by what they contain and what they produce. The sexual and racial economy issues in an economy of reproduction as well as production. These economies are, in turn, specular reflections of the context of metaphysics.

These insights gleaned from African American feminist theory confirms the move made by some whitefeminist theorists and theologians to acknowledge the effects of this history on women. As I noted in chapter 1, Judith Butler and Drucilla Cornell thematize the effects of this split subject on relations between black women and white women. In *Bodies that Matter*, Butler reads Nella Larsen's *Passing* in light of these dynamics, as Cornell (in *Transformations*) reads relationships between coworkers during a labor dispute. Theologians Wendy Farley and Mary McClintock Fulkerson both acknowledge the effects of the cult of domesticity on women. However, I would argue that the importance of this history reaches even deeper—to the very heart of whitefeminist theory and theology. These fields of inquiry are also products of this history, and they exhibit signs and symptoms of it. The linchpin that keeps whitefeminism bound to this history in unproductive ways is, I would argue, the concept of woman upon which it rests. The subject of whitefeminist theorizing and theologizing in the second wave of feminism remains indebted to the "true woman" of the nineteenth century. This woman was erected in and through her opposite, the slave-woman. Thus, whitefeminism's exclusionary gestures arise from its woman's end, which is her beginning.

Given this legacy's tenacious hold on whitefeminism, I would argue that whitefeminist theorizing and theologizing on the basis of either women's multiplicity or embodiment needs to look back into its history before aiming toward the future. Projecting into the future as though racism no longer poses a problem will simply leave the race/gender divide in place. To examine this context is to enter a complex scene, for both black and white women. As Carby and Spillers both argue, race and woman converge in a number of different ways at any given historical point. If, for example, whitefeminist theories of the body are to begin to acknowledge the difference race makes for women, then the effects of race's history on women's bodies must be taken into account. Spillers articulates ways that black women's bodies were (literally) inscribed as captive bodies/raced bodies ("Mama's Baby"). Historian Glenda Gilmore argues that white supremacy was erected in and through the bodies of women, white and black. Two tools of white supremacist activism support Gilmore's claim. Lynching was justified by the need to protect white women's bodies from invasion by black men. Antimiscegenation laws marked white women's bodies as off limits to black men even as they left untouched white men's access to black women's bodies. What effects did this history have on white women's bodies? Can its legacies be read in the cultural demands placed on white women's bodies?

Whitefeminist Theology as a Route toward Whitefeminism's End

Whitefeminist theology has a distinctive role to play in this project of carrying whitefeminism to its end. In these final pages, I want to sketch the outlines of that role and the place deconstruction occupies in it. Whitefeminist theology, like whitefeminist theory, needs to investigate symptoms of its own inscription by the history of raced woman. Using deconstruction to take whitefeminist theology to its end would involve first engaging further in double readings of feminist and womanist theology together within their larger contexts. Taking off from Spillers's insight that black and white women represent two sides of a split subject, I would propose reading whitefeminist and womanist theological texts together in order to render visible their two subjects in relation to each other. Such readings would need to situate these subjects within the history of raced woman, especially as that history has been borne out through the theological tradition. Fully exploring this context would involve carrying a reading of race and woman into explorations of the theological tradition. Modern Christian theology grew up in a culture where these discourses of race and woman were coming into their own. To what degree do the texts of the theological tradition reflect this discursive context?[28] Engaging in this work goes beyond the current American context that has dominated my current project to investigating the European roots of discourse about race and woman. Deconstructive readings of the tradition would locate signs and symptoms of such inscription and of resistance to it.

Whitefeminist theology's subject, however, is distinctive from whitefeminism's subject in general. Whitefeminist theology construes its subjects as theological subjects; that is, as subjects in relation to a divine other. This distinctive feature adds dimension to whitefeminist theology's contribution to bringing whitefeminism to its end. This essay has uncovered evidence that God the Father, as the center of the text of western metaphysics and its specular economy, is implicated in the history of racial and sexual (in)difference. The most substantial development of this claim with regard to ontotheology came in my exploration of the terrain of sexual (in)difference. However, if ontotheology and metaphysical humanism are two sides of the same coin, then one should not have to dig too deeply to uncover ontotheological roots to racism, as well. Indeed, symptoms of those roots can be glimpsed in chapter 5.[29] Whitefeminist theology has actively challenged God the Father's ownership over theological discourse, primarily at the level of images, metaphors, and models for the divine. Such challenges appear to have had little effect on whitefeminist theology's white solipsism. Just as man is proving difficult to shake, so God the Father's mastery, we might suspect, will be difficult to escape. As I argued in chapter 2 above, God the Father plays the role of guarantor of truth and of man's mastery over his proper(ties)—including the texts he authors. Despite whitefeminist theology's questioning of God the Father, there are indications that he continues to mark whitefeminist theology's texts. Sheila Davaney argues that God serves as a guarantor for woman's truth in feminist theological texts (see Davaney, 38–44). Taking whitefeminist theology toward its end, then, would also involve examining whitefeminist theology for signs of inscription by the God/man duo in female disguise and for signs of a thinking of divine alterity that exceeds such inscriptions.

Whitefeminist theology's role in taking whitefeminism toward its end, as I have described it so far, is deconstructive in the strategies it would employ. However, if metaphysical humanism and ontotheology are both at work in sexual and racial (in)difference, then moving toward sexual/racial difference would have a stake in a thinking that arises out of the deconstruction of this two-sided coin. Thus, whitefeminist theology would be a particularly appropriate site for engaging the resources that Irigaray and Derrida have to offer. I argued in chapter 2 that Derrida's work exposes deep connections between sexual (in)difference and God the Father's mastery. I also noted that woman figures as a fissure in that mastery in Derrida's work. Derrida's more recent work includes more sustained discussions of religion. As I noted in chapter 2, some of Derrida's readers have seen connections between his thinking of *différance* and negative theology. Derrida has taken up that question in texts collected in (and commented upon by other scholars) *Derrida and Negative Theology.* I have argued elsewhere that his work on negative theology is haunted by the figure of sexual difference.[30] Both Derrida and Irigaray make room for a thinking of divine alterity that exceeds ontotheology, and both connect that alterity to sexual difference. Derrida invokes the figure of the *khora* as the unthought transcendental and maternal ground of philosophy.[31] In her later work, Irigaray turns toward evoking the figure of the "sensible transcendental" that grounds and ungrounds the philosophical tradition. Irigaray's readings of Heidegger and Nietzsche, for example, expose certain elements (air, in Heidegger's case; water, in Nietzsche's) as the forgotten context of their work.[32] These elements are transcendent (in that they serve as ground) but also sensible (in that they are material). Her evocations of these sensible transcendentals fund a thinking of both a transcendent/immanent alterity and sexual difference together. The fact that these figures are associated with nature, and nature, in turn, with woman is not coincidental. In exposing these (non)foundations, Irigaray uncovers (or un"earth"s) a mat(t)ernal figure at the base of the philosophical tradition. Irigaray imagines that these feminine figures could fund relations between women, between women and men, and between both *genres* and divinity that resist sameness in favor of multiplicity.[33]

Of course, as this essay has shown, charting one's course solely through sexual difference will not ensure that one engages with race in any productive way. For this reason, connections between God the Father's mastery and racial (in)difference also need to be pursued. Irigaray, as one might expect from my critique of her work in chapter 4, offers few if any resources for such thinking, but Derrida offers several. *Of Grammatology* involves an analysis of Rousseau which attends to his ethnocentrism. *Of Spirit* returns to the question of Heidegger's racism in connection with his appropriation of the highly charged term *Geist* (spirit). *Geist*'s theological associations form part of the context that *Of Spirit* problematizes.

At the same time, as was the case with this essay, to claim that Derrida and Irigaray offer resources for a project involving sexual and racial (in)difference is not to offer their work as unproblematic panaceas for all that ails us. As I argued in chapter 4, Irigaray's differing woman disappears from Irigaray's screen when she proposes replacing male imagery for the divine with female imagery. Indeed, in these contexts Irigaray maintains the connection between metaphysical humanism and ontotheology. The gender of God and the subject may be different, but the structural unity of the divine/human pair remains the same.

Derrida's later work, much of which deals with religion, continues to open toward sexual difference, but these openings occur within landscapes dominated by masculine figures. In "Circumfession," his autobiographical contribution to Geoffrey Bennington's *Jacques Derrida*, Derrida positions himself as a contemporary Augustine. *The Gift of Death*, an inquiry into the network connecting responsibility, secrecy, and sacrifice, features the story of the near sacrifice of Isaac.[34] Derrida's restagings of these dramas, which are foundational to patriarchal religious traditions, are hardly simple repetitions. Derrida plays the Augustinian position, for example, in a variety of ways to diverse and complex effects. Significantly, female figures often mark the points where these restagings break the boundaries of traditional religion. Can the cracks marked by these female figures be held open, or will the patriarchal onto-theo-logic that surrounds them reseal them?[35] Insofar as these cracks provide glimpses into an (im)possible future, is it a future that is compatible with a feminism moving toward its own (im)possible telos on the other side of the race/gender divide? Will using these cracks as footholds for religious reflection require the employment of other resources to prevent the divide between race and gender from regaining its (in)visible hold?

Conclusion/Opening

What would the work briefly outlined here produce? In what sense would following its paths provide a cure for whitefeminism's exclusionary tendencies? Let me use the figure of the end once more to describe what I can see. On the one hand, the paths I have outlined stay true to feminism's end as origin and goal. Feminism aimed to provide a platform from which *all* women could resist and overcome the variety of oppressions they face. Insofar as deconstruction provides resources and strategies for undercutting barriers to this goal, it remedies the problems that have prevented whitefeminism from fully participating in the realization of this aim. At the same time, deconstruction poisons that aim insofar as it rests on woman as a ground for sameness. To follow this path will not yield an inclusive feminist theology or theory of woman whose content all women share in common. Instead this path attempts to think women differently by passing through the disrupted gestures and discourse of whitefeminism. To follow this deconstructive course is not to pave over the fissures that ground the race/gender divide; it is, rather, to deepen the fissures in this ground (the context of metaphysics and its reflections) so that other racial and sexual economies might emerge. It is to strive to keep woman open as a site of contestation on which and through which theorizing and theologizing differences between women can take place. Such a strategy is not without risk, and there are no guarantees that it will succeed. In "The Ends of Man," Derrida warns of the "force and efficiency of the system that regularly change[s] transgressions into 'false exits' " (135). The history of racism and antiracism in the United States illustrates Derrida's claim. From the vantage point of most late-twentieth-century Americans, slavery and the Jim Crow laws that replaced it read as transgressions against African Americans. Transgressions *of* the Jim Crow laws by Martin Luther King, Jr., Rosa Parks, and others, become not-transgressions in subsequent whitewashed historical accounts because hindsight shows the laws to be erroneous once man's territory extends certain properties to African Americans. On the other hand, attempts to dismantle racism turn into false exits as those who have historically benefited from the system find ever more creative ways to turn modifications to their ends. The end of the institution of slavery sends the system scrambling for new ways to keep former slaves from gaining full access to the goods associated with status as man (the Jim Crow laws). Jim Crow laws are struck down, and the right to vote is extended to African Americans, but problems of economic inequity, to use just one example, remain. Affirmative action programs are instituted as a means to fight discrimination in the workplace, and white workers turn antidiscrimination rhetoric on its head and claim *they* are. the real victims of discrimination. Whites may now recognize their brothers and sisters in black skins, but only as long as that difference is *no more* than skin deep. Similarly, the history of race's double erasure within whitefeminist theory and theology as I described it in chapter 1 bears the marks of the system's "force and efficiency."

Moreover, to propose a contested woman as a ground for theorizing and theologizing may seem indeed to ask feminism to swallow a glass of hemlock. To uncover woman as site of contestation is not to finally uncover a stable ground beyond the reach of white solipsism or racism. As site of contestation, woman can provide a platform for resisting limitations, but also remains vulnerable to their reassertion at the point of excess. Given her history, woman as site of contestation is particularly vulnerable to recapitulation by the economy of sameness. This essay has shown, however, that feminism has always been (un)-grounded by a contested woman. The task feminism faces involves recognizing and negotiating the terms of the contest in ways that promote coalitions among those who would gather under its flag.

One final note: I do not envision theorizing and theologizing on the other side of the race/gender divide as a merely textual therapy that bears at best a tangential relationship to the realities of the multiple oppressions that are so determinative of women's lives. Such a reading of the relationship between theory, theology and practice assumes a split between language and reality that, I have argued, both Derrida and Irigaray challenge. Irigaray describes the political stake of her work as having to do with "the fact that women's 'liberation' requires transforming the economic realm, and thus necessarily transforming culture and its operative agency, language" (*The Sex Which Is Not One*, 155). The discourse of the specular economy (or the text of metaphysics) is the ether in which all western institutions—the family, the economy in its strict sense, the political sphere, the church, the academy— are embedded and spoken. I have argued that whitefeminism's own inscription by this discourse sets a hegemonic trajectory for its dealings with differences among women that runs counter to feminism's stated aims. This hegemony is not limited to ways whitefeminists theologize or theorize but carries over into whitefeminists' attempts to embody solidarity with African American women. As Derrida notes in "The Ends of Man," the relationship between "linguistic" violence and what we usually think of as violence (economic and sexual exploitation, rape, political, military, and economic violences) is complicated and difficult to trace. Nonetheless, as I noted earlier, he insists (as does Irigaray) that these violences are in "structural solidarity" with one another ("The Ends of Man," 135). The lines from the deconstruction of the context of metaphysics in books to the deconstruction of the political, economic, and psychological systemic violence that this context makes possible (and which perpetuate it) will probably also be difficult to trace. Certainly enacting disruptions in practicing women differently on the political scene will be difficult.[36] However, I hope I have shown that to attempt attacks against women's oppression *without* attending to the systemic violence at work in the discourse that inscribes the institutions and individuals we hold responsible for oppression—*and ourselves*—is to risk following false exits that either leave the system in place or reinstate it on new ground.

Notes

Introduction

1. For example, Angela Davis's *Women, Race and Class* (New York: Random House) was published in 1981. Pauli Murray's "Black Theology and Feminist Theology" appeared in *Black Theology: A Documentary History*, edited by Gayraud S. Wilmore and James H. Cone (Maryknoll, N.Y.: Orbis Books) in 1979. Katie G. Cannon's *Black Womanist Ethics* (American Academy of Religion Academy Series, no. 60 [Atlanta: Scholars Press]) was published in 1988 and was followed shortly by Jacquelyn Grant's *White Women's Christ and Black Women's Jesus: Feminist Christology and Womanist Response* (American Academy of Religion Academy Series, no. 64 [Atlanta: Scholars Press, 1989]).

2. Kimberly Christensen, " 'With Whom Do You Believe Your Lot Is Cast?': White Feminists and Racism," *Signs* 22, no. 3 (spring 1997): 617–48.

3. In a published dialogue with Marianne Hirsch and Nancy K. Miller, Gallop identified black feminist literary critics as having replaced French theorists (esp. Jacques Lacan) as those whose approval she most desires (Gallop, Hirsch, and Miller, "Criticizing Feminist Criticism," in *Conflicts in Feminism*, edited by Marianne Hirsch and Evelyn Fox Keller [New York: Routledge, 1990]). Deborah McDowell, the token target of Gallop's transference, provides a trenchant analysis of this very troubling scene. See McDowell's "Transferences: Black Feminist Thinking: The 'Practice' of 'Theory,' " in *The Changing Same: Black Women's Literature, Criticism, and Theory* (Bloomington: Indiana University Press, 1995): 156–75, esp. 172–75.

4. Elizabeth Abel, Barbara Christian, and Helene Moglen, eds., *Female Subjects in Black and White: Race, Psychoanalysis, Feminism* (Berkeley and Los Angeles: University of California Press, 1997).

5. Ann DuCille,"The Occult of True Black Womanhood: Critical Demeanor and Black Feminist Studies," *Signs* 19, no. 3 (spring 1994): 591–629 (reprinted in Abel et al., 21–56).

6. A word here about my choice of terminology. I use "whitefeminism" in order to highlight the fact that what counts as "feminist" is always already racially marked (I make this argument in chap. 1 below). I have tried to reserve the term "feminist" to name what might lie on the other side of what I will call the race/gender divide—including the occasional present glimpses of such a future. The slippage it maintains between an (im)possible future and feminism's present difficulties is unavoidable and very much in keeping with my argument. As I will argue in chap. 6, there are no guarantees that can secure

the realization of the promise marked by "feminism." The risk of slippage will always attend it. I also retain the term because of its connection to African American feminism where, as I shall also argue in chap. 6, such a future—for both white and black women—is more regularly invoked.

7. Tina Chanter, *Ethics of Eros: Irigaray's Rewriting of the Philosophers* (New York: Routledge, 1995), 132.

8. My use of the term "gender" here evokes the distinction between sex and gender that, until very recently, dominated Anglophone feminism. I will argue in chap. 1 below that the divide this project interrogates runs deeper than this distinction; thus, using "gender" in the divide's name is somewhat problematic. I chose this term for its breadth rather than its depth, however. As the essay proceeds, it will become clear that this divide separates man and race as well as woman and race. Since "gender" includes both categories, it seems best suited to my purposes. I ask my readers to refrain from locating the race/gender divide using preestablished maps like sex/gender in order to allow its full depth and breadth to unfold along with my argument.

9. Heidegger's *Sein und Zeit* (translated as *Being and Time*, translated by John Macquarrie and Edward Robinson [New York: Harper & Row, 1962]) centers around this task. For an exposition of this problematic in the entirety of Heidegger's corpus, see David Farrell Krell's "General Introduction: The Question of 'Being'" in Martin Heidegger, *Martin Heidegger: Basic Writings*, edited and with an introduction by David Farrell Krell (New York: Harper & Row, 1977), 3–35.

10. I put "deconstruction" in quotation marks here to mark a gap, for different reasons, between these thinkers and what goes under this name. "Deconstruction" names an American academic phenomenon that traces itself back to Derrida's early work but has taken on a life of its own. Derrida marks the distance between his own work and what deconstruction often connotes in a number of places. See Rodolphe Gasché's discussion of Derrida's stance toward deconstruction in *The Tain of the Mirror: Derrida and the Philosophy of Reflection* (Cambridge, Mass.: Harvard University Press, 1986), 118–20. Irigaray's relationship to deconstruction is even less immediate. In associating her with it here, I indicate the way I read her work in relation to Derrida's work (see chap. 4 below).

11. For a discussion of the relationship between *destruktion* and *deconstruction*, see Robert Bernasconi, "Seeing Double: *Destruktion* and Deconstruction" in *Dialogue and Deconstruction: The Gadamer-Derrida Encounter*, edited by Diane P. Michelfelder and Richard E. Palmer (Albany: State University of New York Press, 1989): 233–50. See also Peggy Kamuf's introduction to *A Derrida Reader: Between the Blinds* (New York: Columbia University Press, 1991), xviii.

12. For more on double reading, see Bernasconi, "Seeing Double," 245–47.

13. See Harold Coward and Toby Foshay, eds., *Derrida and Negative Theology* (Albany: State University of New York Press, 1992).

14. Paula M. Cooey, *Religious Imagination and the Body: A Feminist Analysis* (New York: Oxford University Press, 1994), 19–25.

15. I call woman, race, and God *figures* in order to be able to exploit this term's association with both the visual arts and economics. *Figure* brings to mind art concerned with representing the human form, yet it is also associated

with accounting. Both sets of associations will be important to my analysis of these figures in what follows. I place "woman," "race," and "God" in quotation marks in order to separate them from certain assumptions that attend them. As I will note later in the text, these terms' proper location is under debate in many circles. (Is woman primarily a product of biology or of culture? Does race have any biological foundation or is it simply a social construction? Is God real or merely a figment of human imagination?) The parameters of these questions will be problematized as my argument progresses. I anticipate this by alerting readers to resist immediately locating the referents of woman, race, and God using the maps assumed by the questions listed above. As figures, these terms begin as sketchy outlines that will accrue connotations, depth, and contour as the argument progresses.

16. For an interesting, though ultimately disappointing (in my view), account of feminist political experimentation funded by Irigaray's work in an Italian context, see the Milan Women's Bookstore Collective, *Sexual Difference: A Theory of Social-Symbolic Practice*, Theories of representation and difference series, edited by Teresa de Lauretis (Bloomington: Indiana University Press, 1990). (Translated from *Non credere di avere dei diritte: La generazione della libertà femminile nell'idea e nelle vicende di un gruppo di donne*, by Patricia Cicogna and Teresa de Lauretis). See also Luisa Muraro's discussion of the Milan Collective. Muraro, "Female Genealogies," in *Engaging with Irigaray*, edited by Carolyn Burke et al. (New York: Columbia University Press, 1994), 317–33.

17. See, e.g., Chandra Talpade Mohanty's "Under Western Eyes: Feminist Scholarship and Colonial Discourses" in *Boundary 2* 12, no. 3, 13 , no. 1 (spring/ fall), 1984; excerpted and reprinted in *The Post-Colonial Studies Reader*, edited by Bill Ashcroft, Gareth Griffiths and Helen Tiffin (New York: Routledge Press, 1995), 259–63 and Teresa de Lauretis, *The Practice of Love: Lesbian Sexuality and Perverse Desire* (Bloomington: Indiana University Press, 1994).

18. Evelyn Brooks Higginbotham, "African-American Women's History and the Metalanguage of Race," *Signs* 17, no. 2 (1992): 251–74, esp. 255; quoted by Evelynn Hammonds in "Black (W)holes and the Geometry of Black Female Sexuality," *differences: A Journal of Feminist Cultural Studies* 6, nos. 2–3 (1994): 126–45, esp. 127. See also DuCille, 591–629.

Chapter 1

1. An earlier version of this discussion of feminist theology has been published as "Questioning 'Woman' in Feminist/Womanist Theology: Irigaray, Ruether, and Daly," in *Transfigurations: Feminist Theology and the French Feminists*, edited by C. W. Maggie Kim, Susan M. St. Ville, and Susan M. Simonaitis (Minneapolis: Fortress Press, 1993).

2. See Delores S. Williams, "The Color of Feminism," *Christianity and Crisis* 45 (29 April 1985): 164–65, and "The Color of Feminism: Or Speaking the Black Woman's Tongue," *Journal of Religious Thought* 42, no. 1 (spring/summer 1986): 42-58. For similar arguments, see also Jacquelyn Grant, *White Women's Christ and Black Women's Jesus: Feminist Christology and Womanist Response*, American Academy of Religion Academy Series, no. 64 (Atlanta: Scholars Press, 1989). See also Marcia Riggs's comments (among others) in Cheryl Sanders et al., "Roundtable Discussion: Racism in the Women's Movement," *Journal of Femi-*

nist Studies in Religion 4, no. 1 (Spring 1988): 93–114. Riggs points out that white women and black women are subject to different means of social control. White women are controlled through privilege and black women through being demeaned. Katie Cannon's argument on the distinctiveness of the Christian social ethic of black women rests on a similar assessment of differences in experience but is not limited to that position (see Katie G. Cannon, *Black Womanist Ethics*, American Academy of Religion Academy Series, no. 60 [Atlanta: Scholars Press, 1988]). Cheryl Sanders argues that differences in experiences fund a different agenda (see Cheryl J. Sanders, "Womanist Theology/Feminist Theology: A Dialogue," *Daughters of Sarah* 15 [March–April 1989]: 6–7.) For other criticisms of whitefeminist thought and practice, see Barbara Smith's introduction to *Home Girls: A Black Feminist Anthology*, edited by Barbara Smith (New York: Kitchen Table: Women of Color Press, 1983), xix–lvi, and, in the same collection, Bernice Johnson Reagon, "Coalition Politics: Turning the Century" (*Home Girls*, 356–68). See also *This Bridge Called My Back: Writings by Radical Women of Color*, edited by Cherrie Moraga and Gloria Anzaldua (New York: Kitchen Table: Women of Color Press, 1983).

3. Pauli Murray also makes this criticism of whitefeminist theology in "Black Theology and Feminist Theology," in *Black Theology: A Documentary History*, edited by G. S. Wilmore and J. H. Cone (Maryknoll, N.Y.: Orbis Books), 398–417. For the disturbing details of the history of relations between white and black women activists, see Paula Giddings, *When and Where I Enter: The Impact of Black Women on Race and Sex in America* (New York: William Morrow, 1984; reprint, New York: Bantam Books, 1985). This history forms the backdrop of more theoretical works, including Angela Y. Davis's *Women, Race, and Class* (New York: Random House, 1981), bell hooks's *Ain't I a Woman: Black Women and Feminism* (Boston: South End Press, 1981), and Hazel V. Carby's *Reconstructing Womanhood: The Emergence of the Afro-American Woman Novelist* (New York: Oxford University Press, 1987). This history sets the context of Katie Cannon's work in *Black Womanist Ethics*, as well.

4. Rosemary Ruether faces this history head on (as I will discuss later) in *New Woman/New Earth: Sexist Ideologies and Human Liberation* (New York: Seabury Press, 1975). Susan Brooks Thistlethwaite's *Sex, Race, and God: Christian Feminisms in Black and White* (New York: Crossroad, 1989) is the only other work by a whitefeminist theologian that I am aware of that deals in substantive ways with this troubled history. However, both Ruether and Thistlethwaite locate the blame for the racism of the suffragette movement on the shoulders of patriarchy; Thistlethwaite specifically blames the suffragettes' dependence on classic liberalism. I do not mean to suggest that Thistlethwaite is wrong to implicate liberal humanism in white women's racism. As this chapter will show, I am sympathetic to this claim. I do, however, want to point out a pervasive pattern of different assessments in black and white feminist writing that reflects in part a reluctance on the part of whitefeminists to admit to racism.

5. Some whitefeminist theologians take the further step of attempting to thematize differences in experience. Probably the two whitefeminist theologians who attempt to work at this intersection in the most thoroughgoing way are Sharon Welch (*A Feminist Ethic of Risk* [Minneapolis: Fortress Press, 1990]) and Thistlethwaite. Both deal with issues of difference in terms of different experi-

ences. Thistlethwaite's book attends to differences in agenda between white and black women, which she grounds in differences in experiences. I will refer to both works as my argument proceeds.

6. In *Metaphorical Theology: Models of God in Religious Language* (Philadelphia: Fortress Press, 1982) and again in *Models of God: Theology for an Ecological, Nuclear Age* (Philadelphia: Fortress Press, 1987), Sallie McFague argues that ecological theology is a priority for First Worlders given the degree of responsibility they hold for exploitation. Sharon Welch and Mary McClintock Fulkerson also mine their particular social locations in productive ways. I provide a more thorough discussion of their work below.

7. Emelie M. Townes, "A Black Feminist Critique of Feminist Theology," in *Wesleyan Theology Today. A Bicentennial Theological Consultation,* edited by Theodore Runyon (Nashville: Kingswood Books, 1985), 189–91.

8. The Combahee River Collective also issues a similar call (see "The Combahee River Collective Statement," in Barbara Smith's *Home Girls,* 281). In a similar vein, Renita Weems argues that white women need to renounce race privilege before work toward solidarity can begin (see Sanders et al., "Roundtable Discussion," 106.

9. Feminists working out of neopagan goddess traditions often label themselves *thealogians* to mark their break with a discipline traditionally centered on a male deity. Feminist theologians working within Jewish or Christian traditions tend to retain the traditional spelling even though they challenge their field's dominance by male images of deity.

10. Mary Daly, *Beyond God the Father: Toward a Philosophy of Women's Liberation* (Boston: Beacon Press, 1973); *The Church and the Second Sex* (New York: Harper & Row, 1968).

11. Mary Daly, *Gyn/Ecology: The Metaethics of Radical Feminism* (Boston: Beacon Press, 1978); *Pure Lust: Elemental Feminist Philosophy* (Boston: Beacon Press, 1984). Subsequent citations of *Pure Lust* will appear as *PL* in the text.

12. Audre Lorde, "An Open Letter to Mary Daly," in Moraga and Anzaldua, 94-97.

13. See *PL* for a full elaboration of her critique of this "horizontal violence" (70–72) and for descriptions of what women would be like beyond the reaches of patriarchy (80, 143–45).

14. Here again, my criticism overlaps one offered by Jacquelyn Grant, who reads Daly as completely refusing to admit that white women can be racist (Grant, 170–72).

15. Quoted by Paula Giddings in *When and Where I Enter,* 66. Giddings's source for this quotation is Roslyn Terborg Penn, *Afro-Americans in the Struggle for Woman Suffrage* (Ph.D. diss., Howard University, 1977; University Microfilms International, Ann Arbor, Mich.), 82.

16. Laurel Schneider's article, "From New Being to Meta-Being: A Critical Analysis of Paul Tillich's Influence on Mary Daly" (*Soundings* 75:2 [summer/fall 1992]: 421–39) warns against problems with such charges (see esp. n. 17). Although she offers no specific evidence, Teresa de Lauretis also finds such charges problematic when leveled against Anglophone feminists like Daly (Teresa de Lauretis, "The Essence of the Triangle or, Taking the Risk of Essentialism Seriously: Feminist Theory in Italy, the U.S., and Britain," *differences: A*

Journal of Feminist Cultural Studies 1 [summer 1989]: 3–37), which I discuss later in this chapter.

17. In *Gyn/Ecology*, Daly describes women as "token torturers" in the practices of suttee, genital mutilation, and foot-binding. Women are often the agents of these practices, but only because they want to do what men find pleasing. Thus, men are the *real* agents, in Daly's eyes, because they determine women's desirability (see *Gyn/Ecology*, chaps. 3, 4, 5).

18. Of course, Daly's appropriation of philosophy is neither wholesale nor uncritical, by any means. She distinguishes feminist fundamental ontology from traditional fundamental ontology on various grounds. My argument here is that this recapitulation of our philosophical heritage keeps in play too much that is problematic for women.

19. See, e.g., the introduction to *PL*, esp. 2.

20. See, e.g., 26–27, 87, and 176 of *PL*. Jacquelyn Grant also finds this utopian vision exclusionary as does Sheila Davaney. Grant argues that black women are invited to participate in Be-friending, but only as women, not as blacks (Grant, 170–72). They are invited, i.e., to participate only insofar as they are the same as what Daly clearly intends to be True Women. As Davaney notes, the women whose experiences count in Daly's world are only those women who experience biophilic consciousness (Sheila Davaney, "The Limits of the Appeal to Women's Experience," in *Shaping New Vision: Gender and Values in American Culture*, edited by Clarissa W. Atkinson, Constance H. Buchanan, and Margaret R. Miles, Harvard University Women's Studies in Religion Series, no. 5 [Ann Arbor, Mich.: UMI Research Press, 1987], 39–41).

21. Thistlethwaite also falls into this same pattern. She argues that plantation mistresses treated slave women so badly because they saw them as a buffer between the mistresses and their husbands; i.e., slave mistresses were primarily victims of the system (Thistlethwaite, 30). She continues this pattern throughout her book, as I will note.

22. Rosemary Radford Ruether, *Sexism and God-Talk: Toward A Feminist Theology* (Boston: Beacon Press, 1983). Hereafter, this book will be cited as *S&GT*.

23. Rosemary Radford Ruether, *Women-Church: Theology and Practice of Feminist Liturgical Communities* (San Francisco: Harper & Row, 1985). Hereafter, this book will be cited as *WC*.

24. The baptism rite includes a rite of confession of ways in which the individual has been a victimizer or has benefited from acceding to oppression (*WC*, 129). Ruether's rite of reconciliation includes a rite of repentance from horizontal violences between middle-class white women and poor women of color (*WC*, 133–35.). Also, two rituals for the Easter season are directed toward the intersection of oppressions. Her Ash Wednesday liturgy includes a section on sins against racial minorities (*WC*, 247). Ruether suggests a stations of the cross liturgy that consists of a walk through Washington, D.C., that stops at places that symbolize issues of injustice in our world today (*WC*, 119).

25. Amba (Mercy) Oduyoye, "Reflections from a Third World Woman's Perspective: Women's Experience and Liberation Theology," *Irruption of the Third World Challenge to Theology*, Papers of the Fifth International Conference of the Ecumenical Association of Third World Theologians, 17–29, August 1981, New

Delhi, edited by Virginia Fabella and Sergio Torres (New York: Orbis Books, 1983), quoted in *WC*, 56.

26. My criticism overlaps in some ways with one offered by Sheila Davaney but also remains distinct from it at this point. Davaney criticizes feminist theology's tendency to appeal to an existing commonality that all women share. She argues that such commonalities have yet to be constructed. Davaney proposes that, instead of assuming their existence and acting on that assumption, we should rather seek out similarities and differences in our experiences and build coalitions where these experiences coincide (Davaney, 46). This pragmatic goal sounds helpful, on the surface. However, I would argue that it fails to attend to the depth of the rift between white and black women. In particular, it fails to acknowledge that the root of that rift is not just different (but equal?) experiences, but white women's racism.

27. Davaney describes the connection of women's vision with truth in feminist theology as a classically modern ontological/epistemological claim (Davaney, 40–48). The difference between our readings lies in our proposals for carrying feminist theology beyond recapitulations of traditional notions of subjectivity. Davaney suggests that feminist theology relinquish such notions and the claims for truth that they ground in favor of relative and pragmatic truth claims. What is true is not what corresponds to what really is, she suggests, but to what furthers the causes of women. The subsequent chapters of this essay will argue that feminist theology's recapitulation of traditional notions of subjectivity and truth occurs against a highly complex background. Moving to a pragmatic standard of truth would not constitute an intervention that could alter this background.

28. Thistlethwaite offers what *amounts* to an excuse for feminist theology on those grounds. She excuses the nineteenth-century suffragettes' racism on the grounds that they based their agenda in classic liberal humanism (Thistlethwaite, 32–33). She excuses Daly's racism, in particular, on the co-optation of her work by the male philosophical tradition through Tillich and Heidegger (Thistlethwaite, 46–47).

29. Mary McClintock Fulkerson and Rebecca Chopp each offer a complementary critique of the impact of vestiges of liberal humanism in whitefeminist theology. Both see feminist theology's dependence on a liberal humanist subject as one piece of its larger embeddedness in liberal discourse (and its understanding of truth) in general. Fulkerson develops a complex and sophisticated schema to replace liberal humanism that can better account for women's diverse positions in various Christian communities and practices. See Mary McClintock Fulkerson, *Changing the Subject: Women's Discourses and Feminist Theology* (Philadelphia: Fortress Press, 1994), which I discuss below; for Rebecca Chopp, see *The Power to Speak: Feminism, Language, God* (New York: Crossroad, 1989).

30. I cite here only a few of the most significant discussions, several of which will come under consideration in this essay. Elizabeth V. Spelman, *Inessential Woman: Problems of Exclusion in Feminist Thought* (Boston: Beacon Press, 1988; referred to below as *IW*); Judith Butler's *Gender Trouble: Feminism and the Subversion of Identity* (New York: Routledge, 1990); Drucilla Cornell, *Beyond Accom-*

modation: Ethical Feminism, Deconstruction and the Law (New York: Routledge, 1991); Rosi Braidotti, *Patterns of Dissonance* (New York: Routledge, 1991); Diana Fuss, *Essentially Speaking: Feminism, Nature, and Difference* (New York: Routledge, 1989); Denise Riley, *"Am I That Name?": Feminism and the Category of "Women" in History* (Minneapolis: University of Minnesota Press, 1990).

31. I refer here, of course, to Davis's *Women, Race and Class* and hooks's *Ain't I a Woman.*

32. Patricia Hill Collins, *Black Feminist Thought: Knowledge, Consciousness, and The Politics of Empowerment* (London: Harper Collins Academic Press, 1990).

33. See esp. chap. 4 of Collins's book.

34. Valerie Smith, "Split Affinities: The Case of Interracial Rape," in *Conflicts in Feminism,* edited by Marianne Hirsch and Evelyn Fox (New York: Routledge, 1990), 271–87. See also Patricia Williams, "Mirrors and Windows: An Essay on Empty Signs, Pregnant Meanings, and Women's Power," in *The Alchemy of Race and Rights: Diary of a Law School Professor* (Cambridge, Mass.: Harvard University Press, 1991), 166–78.

35. Williams, *Alchemy of Race,* 174. Sexual stereotyping also significantly affects black men in American culture. Valerie Smith notes that, when Charles Stuart claimed that the man who killed his wife in their parked car was black, Boston police bought his story hook, line, and sinker and made life rather miserable for black men in that neighborhood. It took them some time to begin to suspect Stuart himself (276). In an 11 March 1997 broadcast, National Public Radio's *Morning Edition* reported that the NAACP was raising questions about possible racial bias in the military's handling of recent accusations of sexual misconduct at training facilities. According to the report, four women recanted their original charges of sexual assault against a supervising officer, saying that they were coerced into making the charges in order to protect themselves from being prosecuted for having consensual sex with a superior officer. Although the races of the parties in question were not clearly identified, the story led listeners to assume that one or more of the enlistees was white while the falsely accused officer was black. This scene's resemblance to the numerous scenes that led to lynchings (where white women sometimes lied about sexual misconduct in order to protect their perceived virtue) is disturbingly apparent.

36. Teresa de Lauretis, "Upping the Anti (*sic*) in Feminist Theory," in Hirsch and Fox, *Conflicts in Feminism,* 255–70. See also de Lauretis, "The Essence of the Triangle," 3–37. Gayatri Chakravorty Spivak concurs with this view of the tenor of the debate. See Spivak with Ellen Rooney, "In a Word: Interview," *differences* 1 (summer 1989): 124–56; esp. 129.

37. Evelynn Hammonds makes a similar critique of race's lack of effect on queer theory. Queer theorists, she argues, pay token attention, at best, to, e.g., black lesbians. Articles by and about black lesbians and gay men are included in the lesbian / gay studies reader, but none of the other contributors takes account of them. This occurs despite explicit intentions to the contrary stated in the reasons for adopting the term "queer theory" as outlined by Teresa de Lauretis in *differences*' first issue on queer theory (vol. 3, no. 2 [1991]). See Hammonds, "Black (W)holes," 126–45.

38. I must note one problem I find with Spelman's account. She argues that black women are not always deemed inferior to black men in racist culture.

This assertion seems problematic to me, on its face, given claims made by African American scholars. Katie Cannon, e.g., points out that apportionment formulas after Reconstruction counted freed black men as equivalent to three-fifths of a white man. Freed black women had no value at all (Cannon, 31). I also think of Nanny's description of black women as "de mule[s] uh de world" in Zora Neale Hurston's *Their Eyes Were Watching God* ([Philadelphia: Lippincott, 1937; reprint, Urbana: University of Illinois Press, 1981], 29). Cannon and others have argued that the most demeaning and worst paying jobs are traditionally allotted to women of color. This claim comes too close to the problematic way concerns about the terrible statistics on the quantity and quality of life for young black men are described on occasion. Much is made of the risks they face, while risks faced by young black women are ignored. I would be inclined to argue that our racist society values neither black men nor black women, but the ways in which society exhibits that lack of value differs in each case. I think this argument would parallel the one made by Marcia Riggs and others that the means of social control exercised against white women differs from that exercised against black women (see Sanders et al., "Roundtable Discussion," 100).

39. Spelman cites several examples of this in feminist theorists' references to nineteenth-century American history (*IW*, 119–22) and Aristotle's view of the polis (37–56).

40. Such a criticism is implicit in Hazel V. Carby's location of her theoretical perspective in terms of race, gender, and class (16–17; see n. 3 above). Sheila Briggs makes this criticism of feminist theory and theology. See Sheila Briggs, "The Politics of Identity and the Politics of Interpretation," *Union Seminary Quarterly Review* 143 (1989): 163–80, and "What Feminist Theology Is Saying about Race and Class," Antoinette Brown Lecture, Vanderbilt Divinity School (19 March 1990). Audre Lorde also makes this criticism of feminist theory in general as well as of Mary Daly's work in particular (Moraga and Anzaldua, 94–97).

41. Spelman's book has been mostly well received by African American feminist theorists. Evelyn Brooks Higginbotham speaks positively of it in "African-American Women's History and the Metalanguage of Race," 255. bell hooks is appreciative of her work, with some reservations: she would have liked Spelman to have given more explicit credit (other than in footnotes) to those African American feminist theorists whose work informed her own and to have considered what black women say about *gender*, not just about race (bell hooks, *Yearnings: Race, Gender and Cultural Politics* [Boston: South End Press, 1990], 21).

42. See, e.g., Elizabeth Grosz's *Volatile Bodies: Toward a Corporeal Feminism* (Bloomington: Indiana University Press, 1994), 213, nn. 20, 21; Tina Chanter's *Ethics of Eros*, 268, n. 9, and 274, n. 14; Drucilla Cornell's *Transformations: Recollective Imagination and Sexual Difference* (London: Routledge, 1993), 204, n. 2 and 223, n. 31; and Rosi Braidotti's *Patterns of Dissonance*, 170. All of these theorists cite Spelman approvingly. All of their projects are directed toward enabling the thinking of differences between women, and yet only Cornell devotes significant time to the discussion of race. Grosz opens with promising comments about the significance of raced bodies, but race drops quickly out of the picture.

None of these theorists acknowledges that Spelman's larger point that race writes feminist's texts—implicitly, if not explicitly—might apply to their current texts, as well.

43. De Lauretis, "The Essence of the Triangle," 3–13.

44. The phrase "taking the risk of essentialism" comes from the subtitle of de Lauretis's "The Essence of the Triangle." Leslie Wahl Rabine argues that essentialism is an unstable yet unavoidable dimension of feminist discourse. She further claims that assertion of an essence has a different effect if the one doing the asserting is marginalized—i.e., if one is a woman (see Leslie Wahl Rabine, "Essentialism and Its Contexts: Saint-Simonian and Post-Structuralist Feminists," *differences* 1 [summer 1989]: 105–23). While I am sympathetic to the first assertion, the latter claim shows Rabine's failure to grapple seriously with African American feminists' criticisms of whitefeminist thinking. Marginality alone is not sufficient to defuse the exclusionary effects of essentialism. In this chapter I have shown that the concept of an essential woman—whether intentionally asserted or simply assumed—sets up a new center that locates other women at other margins.

45. Spivak and Rooney, 126–33.

46. Rosi Braidotti and Drucilla Cornell are two primary examples of practitioners of this strategy (see below).

47. Wendy Farley makes a similar point in her most recent book, *Eros for the Other: Retaining Truth in a Pluralistic World* (University Park: Pennsylvania State Press, 1996). She argues that neither essentialism nor antiessentialism are capable of dealing with women's diversity. Her reasons for making this claim differ somewhat from mine, as does her constructive proposal for dealing with woman. I discuss her constructive proposal later in this chapter and will return to it in the last chapter.

48. For discussions of this historical shift, see Moira Gatens, "A Critique of the Sex/Gender Distinction" in *A Reader in Feminist Knowledge*, edited by Sneja Gunew (London: Routledge, 1991), and Tina Chanter, "Tracking Essentialism with the Help of a Sex/Gender Map," *Ethics of Eros*, 21–46.

49. See Moira Gatens's *Imaginary Bodies: Ethics, Power, and Corporeality* (London: Routledge, 1996) for a particularly potent discussion of this point.

50. Rosi Braidotti, *The Nomadic Subject: Embodiment and Sexual Difference in Contemporary Feminist Theory* (New York: Columbia University Press, 1994).

51. Rosi Braidotti, "The Politics of Ontological Difference," in *Between Feminism and Psychoanalysis*, edited by Teresa Brennan (New York: Routledge, 1989), 100; emphasis mine.

52. See esp. the introduction and chaps. 3 and 4 of *Beyond Accommodation*.

53. For Cornell's most sustained discussion of African American women in her latest book, see Drucilla Cornell, *The Imaginary Domain: Abortion, Pornography, and Sexual Harassment* (New York: Routledge, 1995), chap. 4.

54. Deborah McDowell, "Transferences: Black Feminist Thinking: The 'Practice' of 'Theory,'" in *The Changing Same: Black Women's Literature, Criticism, and Theory* (Bloomington: Indiana University Press, 1995), 156–75. Ann DuCille offers a similar criticism of this tendency in "The Occult of True Black Womanhood: Critical Demeanor and Black Feminist Studies," *Signs* 19, no. 3 (spring 1994): 591–629 (reprinted in Abel et al., *Female Subjects in Black and White: Race,*

Psychoanalysis, Feminism [Berkeley: University of California Press, 1997], 21–56).

55. See Valerie Smith, "Black Feminist Theory and the Representation of the Other" in *Changing Our Own Words: Essays on Criticism, Theory, and Writing by Black Women*, edited by Cheryl Wall (New Brunswick, N.J.: Rutgers University Press, 1989), 38–57.

56. Delores Williams, e.g., names "discourse and work with black women in the churches" as womanist theology's primary audience. See *Sisters in the Wilderness: The Challenge of Womanist God-Talk* (Maryknoll, N.Y.: Orbis Books, 1993), xiv.

57. Time will tell whether (and how) Gatens follows up on this potential, but conversations with her suggest that she is acutely attuned to it and well poised to fulfill it.

58. Amy Hollywood also faults Cooey for extracting Morrison's characters from the complex historical and linguistic context Morrison employs. She is particularly worried by Cooey's immediate appropriation of Pilate Dead (*Song of Solomon*) as figuring a new universal subject that welcomes all, in and through difference. See Amy Hollywood, "Transcending Bodies?" *Religious Studies Review*, 25, no. 1 (January 1999), in press.

59. Judith Butler, *Bodies that Matter: On the Discursive Limits of "Sex"* (New York: Routledge, 1993).

60. In fact, her critics do more to perpetuate the liberal humanist subject than Butler does. Their reading of Butler views her through such a subject. Opening one's closet and choosing a gender-of-the-day assumes a subject fully present to itself, whose actions and intentions are coextensive, and whose identity lies below its surface.

61. Some of Butler's work since *Bodies that Matter* sustains attention to race and its imbrication with gender and sexuality—at least in the case of blackness as a racial mark. Her analysis of the Supreme Court's treatment of cross burning vs. its treatment of pornography is powerful and insightful (Butler, "Burning Acts: Injurious Speech," in *Deconstruction Is/in America: A New Sense of the Political*, edited by Anselm Haverkamp [New York: New York University Press, 1995], 149–80; reprint, Judith Butler, *Excitable Speech: A Politics of the Performative* [New York: Routledge, 1997], 43–69). Butler's *Psychic Life of Power: Theories in Subjection* (Stanford, Calif.: Stanford University Press, 1997) develops carefully articulated theories of subjection that Butler tests against examples drawn from scenes figured by sexuality, race, or gender. However, these three vectors are considered separately, for the most part, and whiteness as a racial mark slips into invisibility once again. Considerable potential remains in Butler's work, however, for thinking these vectors together.

62. Higginbotham, 251–52.

63. hooks, *Yearnings*, esp. chaps. 2, 3, and 7.

64. See Barbara Christian, "The Race for Theory," in *Within the Circle: An Anthology of African American Literary Criticism from the Harlem Renaissance to the Present*, edited by Angelyn Mitchell (Durham, N.C.: Duke University Press, 1994), 348–59.

65. See Deborah McDowell's "Transferences" and Valerie Smith's "Black Feminist Theory," 38–57. Deconstruction's relationship to African American

feminist literary theory is certainly contested, primarily because of deconstruction's role in African American literary theory written by men like Henry Louis Gates, Jr. (see chap. 5, below). The notorious "exchange" between Gates, Houston Baker, and Joyce Joyce staged in the pages of *New Literary History* (18 [1987]) is symptomatic, McDowell argues, of tendencies to align African American feminist work on the side of politics or practice vs. theory. (This instance occurs within African American theoretical debates, but McDowell also shows the same dynamics at work in whitefeminist theory.) On the one hand, McDowell questions why and how African American feminist writing and what counts for theory (i.e., deconstruction) came to be situated on opposite sides at this particular moment in history. Wary of deconstruction, particularly because its announcement of the death of the author comes just as African American women are beginning to count as authors, McDowell also sees some points of commonality between deconstruction and African American feminist theorizing. Valerie Smith sees potential in deconstruction as long as one keeps it contextualized within historical and material conditions, something deconstruction is unlikely to do on its own, in her view. I will return to African American feminist theory in chap. 6 below.

66. See Kelly Oliver, *Reading Kristeva: Unravelling the Double Bind* (Bloomington: Indiana University Press, 1993), 163–68. She also rightly problematizes American feminists' labeling of Kristeva, Irigaray, and Hélène Cixous as "the French feminists." Oliver argues that none of them are, properly speaking, French. Each of them would resist being labeled "feminist" because of what that term means in France; thus, they are not really representative of, much less exhaustive of, French feminism.

67. For this discussion, see chap. 4 below.

68. Jacques Derrida, *Positions*, translated by Alan Bass (Chicago: University of Chicago Press, 1981), 82.

Chapter 2

1. References to whitefeminist theorists' accounts of Derrida will appear throughout this chapter and the next. For African American feminists' views on deconstruction, see chap. 1 above.

2. Huston Smith's "The View from Everywhere: Ontotheology and the Post-Nietzschean Deconstruction of Metaphysics" must rank at the bottom of accounts of deconstruction based on nothing more than hearsay. He reads Derrida's critique of metaphysics as directed toward the end of any "worldview that provides a sense of orientation" (in *Religion, Ontotheology, and Deconstruction*, edited by Henry Ruf [New York: Paragon House, 1989], 43). Ironically, as is often the case in these readings-by-hearsay, some of the arguments he offers as refutations of deconstruction have a strong Derridean ring to them, a ring his truncated reading of Derrida will not allow him to hear.

3. See, e.g., M. Derrol Bryant, "From 'De' to 'Re' or . . . Does the 'Future of Ontotheology' Require the Recovery of the Experience/Sense of Transcendence?" in Ruf, 74; L. Hughes Cox, "The Paradox of the Limit, the Parable of the Raft, and Perennial Philosophy," *Listening* 24 (winter 1989): 23; John Wall, "Deconstruction and the Universe of Theological Discourse, or Who Is Jacques Derrida and What Is He Saying about the Logos?" *Saint Luke's Journal of Theol-*

ogy 28 (September 1985): 251–65; James Olthuis, "A Cold and Comfortless Hermeneutic or a Warm and Trembling Hermeneutic: A Conversation with John D. Caputo," *Christian Scholar's Review* 19 (1990): 346. John Cobb, who finds some positive things to say about deconstruction, also argues that "it objects to any notion that there is a non-linguistic reality" and bases his preference for Whiteheadian process metaphysics in part in its ability to preserve what he deems to be a more accurate understanding of the referential capacity of language ("Two Types of Postmodernism: Deconstruction and Process," *Theology Today* 47 [July 1990]: 156).

4. Raschke, "The Deconstruction of God" in *Deconstruction and Theology*, edited by Thomas J. J. Altizer et al. (New York: Crossroads, 1982). In the preface to this volume, Raschke writes, "It is fitting today that deconstruction should spread throughout the corpus (or 'corpse') of theology, because the theological mind has been responsible for the modern elevation of the linguistic signifier, which Derrida's 'play of difference' exposes as . . . a veiled abyss, a nothingness" (viii). Charles Winquist's reading is more subtle. He seems to read Derrida as uncovering language's limits; its inability to express what exceeds its grasp (see *Epiphanies of Darkness: Deconstruction in Theology* [Philadelphia: Fortress Press, 1986], esp. 108–23). I would also locate Mark C. Taylor on this more subtle side of the spectrum. Taylor's early work stressed inextricability from the chain of reading and writing at the expense of attention to the complex intricacies of intertextuality (see, e.g., *Erring: A Postmodern A/theology* (Chicago: University of Chicago Press, 1984). His more recent work (e.g., *Altarity* [Chicago: University of Chicago Press, 1987] and *Nots* [Chicago: University of Chicago Press, 1993]) adopts strategies of writing through reading that redress the one-sidedness I find in his earlier work.

5. John Olthuis simply refuses the pessimism he reads as emerging from deconstruction. He argues, "Life is more than flux. It is flux with an inner dynamic, a spirit, a direction, a presence: God" (357). Kenneth L. Schmitz also argues that Christianity offers an answer to deconstruction ("From Anarchy to Principles: Deconstruction and the Resources of Christian Philosophy," *Communio: International Catholic Review* 16 [spring 1989]: 69–88).

6. See, e.g., Cox, 20, and Frank Flinn, "Reconstructing the Deconstruction of Ontology" in Ruf, 127–38.

7. In *Derrida on the Mend* (West Lafayette, Ind.: Purdue University Press, 1984), Robert Magliola argues that Derrida's critique is directed at how we *think* about thinking, reality, and language and how those habits of thought transport meaning, not as critiquing thinking *itself*, reality *itself*, language *itself*. Thus, he understands deconstruction's project to be disproving logic and philosophy. "Any philosophy of presence can be disproven" (351). Joseph O'Leary's book, *Questioning Back: The Overcoming of Metaphysics in Christian Tradition* (New York: Winston Press, 1985), which deals with Derrida only as a footnote to Heidegger, also takes the position that Derrida's critique is directed toward traditional metaphysics.

8. See Kevin Hart, *The Trespass of the Sign: Deconstruction, Theology, and Philosophy* (Cambridge: Cambridge University Press, 1989). Hart sees Derrida's critique as reductive. He comments upon "how boldly Derrida has reduced the *whole* of Western thought to metaphysics" (16; emphasis in original). He

also thinks deconstruction applies almost exclusively to philosophy and has consequences for other realms only to the degree that philosophy intersects with them. As I will argue, these thinkers' views of the locus of the problem as strictly intraphilosophical shape the way they see the intersection between deconstruction and theology as well as their view of deconstruction's implications for politics and ethics. Jean-Luc Marion sees deconstruction as useful for exposing idolatries, but ultimately he thinks true (and very traditional) theology can go beyond metaphysics by leaving philosophy behind (see Jean-Luc Marion, *God without Being*, translated by Thomas Carlson [Chicago: University of Chicago Press, 1991]). These book-length examples of positive readings of deconstruction resemble positions put forth as early as 1983. The earliest version of this type of argument was offered by Louis Mackey in "Slouching toward Bethlehem: Deconstructive Strategies in Theology" (*Anglican Theological Review* 65 [July 1983]: 255–72). According to Mackey, Derrida's claim that there was "nothing outside the text" (which he interpreted to mean that signs are purely arbitrary) brought theology back to Martin Luther. It reminded theology that all it has, finally, is faith; and it must simply trust that faith is sufficient. Wall argues that deconstruction teaches theology to give up its dependence on philosophy and look instead to the God who changes lives. Magliola argues that the Christian is "delivered from Derridean anxiety. [He or she] knows through the experience of faith (and sometimes through mystical awareness) that it is entirely *appropriate* for reason to fall short; the Christian knows that . . . his [sic] future can be a thorough frequenting of the Divine" (148; emphasis in original).

9. Magliola, e.g., writes "God is logically knowable by man [sic], but this logical knowing is inadequate—and inadequacy here always means that God cannot be *completely* targeted by logocentrism, He cannot be 'comprehended'; in the sense of circumscribed, 'grasped all the way around' by logic, *even when logic is operating upon divinely revealed truths*" (159; emphasis added). O'Leary distinguishes the God of philosophy from the God of faith (see chap. 2, esp. 67–73). Hart argues that those who would align Derrida solely with secularism vs. religiosity are mistaken. Derrida can neither affirm nor deny God's existence, can neither be theistic nor atheistic. He thinks theology has yet to tap the resources that could emerge from entertaining Derridean thought, and he proposes the mystical tradition of God-talk as providing a way to do so. I agree with Hart's assessment of the current state of affairs in theology. However, Hart's own attempt to engage Derrida's work winds up too close to Magliola's position and *far* too close to the traditional (at least, since Aquinas) understanding of negative theology. While he claims he wants to argue that positive theology and negative theology are *suppléments* to each other, he understands their relationship in a very traditional sense. Negative theology serves as a check that ensures that positive theology is talking "about *God* and not just about human images of God" (104; emphasis in original). This is, I would argue, precisely the version of negative theology from which Derrida wants *clearly* and emphatically to distance himself (see Derrida, "How to Avoid Speaking: Denials" (translated by Ken Frieden, in Coward and Foshay, 73–142); and my own unpublished discussion of this topic in "Divine Speculations in Irigaray

and Derrida," presented to the Society for Phenomenology and Existential Philosophy, 1 October 1994, Philadelphia.)

10. Some of these theologians argue that theology already contains a deconstructive impulse. For Hart, that impulse is located in negative theology and mystical theology; for Magliola it resides in mysticism and, quite improbably, the Council of Nicea; for O'Leary, it resides in the essence of Christianity. Certainly the attempts by mystics to speak of their experience with the sacred exhibits a deconstructive impulse, but no strand of western thinking will be altogether free of metaphysics.

11. This reading of deconstruction provides a backdrop assumed by much contemporary feminist theory (see, e.g., the introductions to the anthologies mentioned in chap. 1 above and *The Thinking Muse Feminism and Modern French Philosophy*, edited by Jeffner Allen and Iris Marion Young [Bloomington: Indiana University Press, 1989]). For very explicit invocations of deconstruction, see the special issue of *Feminist Studies* 14, no. 1 (spring 1988) devoted to deconstruction and feminism, the anthologies *Feminism/Postmodernism* (edited by Linda Nicholson [New York: Routledge, 1989]) and *Feminism as Critique* (edited by Seyla Benhabib and Drucilla Cornell [Minneapolis: University of Minnesota Press, 1987]) as well as Drucilla Cornell's *Beyond Accommodation* and Braidotti's *Patterns of Dissonance*. Linda Kintz's position serves as one example. In her contribution to *The Thinking Muse*, "In-Different Criticism: The Deconstructive 'Parole,' " Kintz argues that Derrida denies the ability of language to refer unambiguously to truth.

12. This is somewhat true even of Derridean feminists. Nancy Holland separates the content of deconstruction from its form. While she remains somewhat suspicious of the content of Derrida's work when it bears on woman, deconstructive strategies, she thinks, can be usefully appropriated by feminists for their purposes (see Nancy Holland, *Is Women's Philosophy Possible?* [Savage, Md.: Rowan & Littlefield, 1990]). While I agree with Holland that deconstructive strategies will be helpful to feminism, I also see some value in the content of Derrida's work with woman, as I will show in chap. 3 below. Elizabeth Grosz's recent defense of Derridean feminism sees Derrida as complicating feminist politics and its understanding of its relationship to patriarchy. In that sense, deconstruction poses certain challenges to feminism (see Elizabeth Grosz, "Ontology and Equivocation" in *Feminist Interpretations of Jacques Derrida*, edited by Nancy J. Holland [University Park: Pennsylvania State University Press, 1997], 73–102). Peggy Kamuf's essay in the same volume articulates a persuasive account of the challenges deconstruction poses to feminist concepts of subjectivity, one to which I will return in chap. 3 (see Peggy Kamuf, "Deconstruction and Feminism: A Repetition," 103–26).

13. Grosz, "Ontology," 84–85. In the introduction to *Is Women's Philosophy Possible?* Nancy Holland provides a thoughtful response to this suspicion on the part of feminists. She notes that these assessments of Derrida's usefulness are sometimes contradictory. "It is too subjective and not subjective enough; it does too much and too little; it destroys old foundations and old authorities but leaves none for our own use" (14). Grosz discusses a number of other objections to Derrida that I will attend to in later chapters.

14. Theologians frequently raise this question. See, e.g., Cox, Wolofsky ("Derrida, Jabès, Levinas: Sign-Theory as Ethical Discourse," *Prooftexts* 2 [September 1982]: 283–302), Olthuis, as well as Joseph Prabhu's contribution to "On Deconstructing Theology: A Symposium on *Erring: A Postmodern A/Theology*" (Edith Wyschogrod et al., *Journal of the American Academy of Religion* 54 [fall 1986]: 541). Other readers follow Sallie McFague's line. They recognize the power of deconstruction to unmask idolatries but think that it cannot provide any secure constructive place to stand. See Cobb and see also Robert S. Gall, "Of/From Theology and Deconstruction," *Journal of the American Academy of Religion* 58 (fall 1990): 413–37. Mark C. Taylor provides a very welcome critique of these claims in *Nots* (see "Not Just Resistance," 73–75). Taylor deplores the lack of consideration given to the ethical implications of Derrida's work, particularly by scholars in religious studies. In his view (as in mine), questions of ethics and religion are tied together in Derrida's work and thus need to be thought through together. I view this study as very much the kind of work called for by Taylor.

15. With only a couple of notable exceptions, theological readings of Derrida by men also see little possibility for an alliance between feminism and deconstruction. Raschke is the most dismissive. On the basis of his reading of Derrida's reading of woman in Nietzsche's texts, Raschke concludes that Derrida "banish[es] woman to nothingness" (in Altizer et al., 28). I will show this reading to be seriously flawed in the next chapter. Hart likewise rejects the idea that deconstruction might be relevant for feminism on the grounds that it renders ethics in general too problematic. Marion never mentions feminism as an issue. Moreover, he seems blind to the fact that his text perpetuates the very economy that Derrida's work with woman equates with phallocentrism. Winquist and Taylor are the notable exceptions. Both recognize one of Derrida's goals as attempting to make a place for the "others" of metaphysics and recognize that woman constitutes one of those "others." Winquist mentions this possible consequence of deconstruction in the introduction to *Epiphanies of Darkness*, but his awareness fails to inform his work in any significant way. Taylor's *Altarity* acknowledges woman as a site of alterity in his readings of Kristeva and Lacan. This attention to woman-as-other is a welcome change from the disturbing picture painted in "Text as Victim" (Taylor's contribution to Altizer et al.'s *Deconstruction and Theology*). In this earlier piece, Taylor's description of interpretation reads like a rape scene in which the text (female) requires (and indeed requests) violation by the interpreter (imaged as male). I am not denying the descriptive power of Taylor's portrayal, nor am I arguing that Taylor originates this view of interpretation. Interpretation can have these connotations in western culture. However, I was disturbed to see these dynamics pass through his text without coming into question—especially when it seems to me that Derrida's work with woman opens the door to questioning them.

16. See *The Power to Speak*, 135, n. 9.

17. McFague, *Models of God*, 23; Welch, 150; Fulkerson, esp. 151–54.

18. See Rodolphe Gasché, *The Tain of the Mirror: Derrida and the Philosophy of Reflection* (Cambridge, Mass.: Harvard University Press, 1986), 278–93, esp. 278, 279. This work will appear hereafter as *Tain*.

19. Derrida, "Living On: Border Lines," translated by J. Hulbert, in *Deconstruction and Criticism*, edited by Harold Bloom et al. (New York: Seabury Press, 1979), 83; cited by Gasché, *Tain*, 279.

20. Derrida, *Of Grammatology*, translated by Gayatri Spivak (Baltimore: Johns Hopkins University Press, 1976), 158.

21. See Geoffrey Bennington, *Jacques Derrida* (Chicago: University of Chicago Press, 1993), 93. For Gasché's discussion of this same point, see "Structural Infinity" in *Inventions of Difference: On Jacques Derrida* (Cambridge, Mass.: Harvard University Press, 1994), esp. 144–45.

22. See, e.g., Irene Harvey, *Derrida and the Economy of Différance* (Bloomington: Indiana University Press, 1986); John Llewelyn's *Derrida on the Threshold of Sense* (New York: St. Martin's Press, 1986); and Gasché's *Inventions of Difference*. Each of these provides narrative reconstructions of Derrida's relationship to philosophy. Though the most difficult of the group to read, Llewelyn provides close readings of Derrida's readings on various figures from continental philosophy, structuralism, and Anglo-American philosophy. Mark C. Taylor's anthology *Deconstruction in Context: Literature and Philosophy* (Chicago: University of Chicago Press, 1986) contextualizes Derrida's work through providing representative essays from philosophers and other theorists on whom Derrida has drawn. Taylor's introduction to this volume provides a very helpful and accessible short narrative of the background of deconstruction. Charles Scott's *The Language of Difference* (Atlantic Highlands, N.J.: Humanities Press International, 1987) thinks in Derridean fashion through Derrida's predecessors (Nietzsche and Heidegger) and contemporaries (Deleuze and Lacan). From the side of literary criticism, Geoffrey Bennington and Christopher Norris (*Derrida* [Cambridge, Mass.: Harvard University Press, 1987]) offer two of the most helpful and accessible approaches to Derrida for nonphilosophers. Bennington's short text, *Jacques Derrida*, writes doubly. The larger portion of each page is devoted to Bennington's topical elucidations of Derrida's work. The margins of each page, written by Derrida, border on autobiography. Derrida keeps a running commentary on Bennington's account of him and counters it with reflections on his past and present. On the question of ethics and deconstruction, see Simon Critchley, *The Ethics of Deconstruction: Derrida and Levinas* (Cambridge, Mass.: Blackwell, 1992) and essays by Robert Bernasconi. Further discussion of these texts will come in chap. 5 below.

23. Both Irene Harvey and John Llewelyn describe Derrida's work as quasi-transcendentalist insofar as it investigates the foundations of philosophy. Both acknowledge that Derrida breaks with the transcendentalist program in uncovering philosophy's founding in difference and deferral.

24. For discussions of each of these (non)concepts and their (non)foundational qualities, see *Tain*, chap. 9, esp. 194–217.

25. This description also fits an important element of Mark Taylor's description of Derrida. Taylor provides a clear and helpful discussion of Derrida in relation to other thinkers of radical alterity (Kierkegaard, Blanchot, Levinas, Bataille) in the introduction to *Deconstruction in Context*, 1–34.

26. In other words, like the *pharmakon* in "Plato's Pharmacy," they are both remedy and poison. Taylor also notes the danger of turning deconstruction

into simply the end of a historical process or turning it into a coherent and therefore comprehended program (contained and restrained behind borders). See the acknowledgements to *Deconstruction in Context*, vii.

27. The same dynamic fits what Gasché describes in the introduction to *Inventions of Difference*. He identifies Richard Rorty and Taylor as two poles of interpretations of Derrida against which he wants to contend. According to Gasché, Rorty isolates the productive side of the Derridean infrastructures while Taylor highlights their disruptive side. In turn, Gasché acknowledges that Taylor insists on Derrida's disruption of philosophy-as-usual in opposition to Gasché's portrayal of Derrida's continuity with the philosophical tradition.

28. One whitefeminist theorist takes note of God's place in connection to woman's place. Mary C. Rawlinson asks questions about Derrida's work on and with the figure of negative theology that, while legitimate, also might find answers in Derrida's own earlier work, as this chapter will argue. See Rawlinson, "Levers, Signatures and Secrets: Derrida's Use of Woman" in *Derrida and Feminism: Recasting the Question of Woman* (edited by Ellen K. Feder, Mary C. Rawlinson, and Emily Zakin [New York: Routledge, 1997]: 69–85, esp. 80–82).

29. Jacques Derrida, *Dissemination*, translated by Barbara Johnson (Chicago: University of Chicago Press, 1981). In notes and citations I will refer to this work as *D*.

30. "The Double Session," one of the essays that I will discuss, plays a prominent role in Gasché's reading of "nothing outside the text." Christopher Norris's introduction to Derrida's work features a discussion of "Plato's Pharmacy," the second essay in *Dissemination* (see "Derrida on Plato: Writing as Poison and Cure," in Norris, chap. 2, 28–62).

31. See "Différance" in Derrida's *Margins of Philosophy*, translated by Alan Bass (Chicago: University of Chicago Press, 1982), esp. 16, n. 19.

32. For an account of this pattern I have described, see G. W. F. Hegel, *Science of Logic*, translated by A. V. Miller (New York: Humanities Press, 1969). For a fuller discussion of Hegel in relation to Derrida, see Taylor's introduction to *Deconstruction in Context*, 1–10.

33. For the details on Derrida's presentation of Hegel, see *D*, 20–47.

34. "If [the dialectic method] is done successfully, if the life of the subject matter (*Stoff*) is ideally reflected as in a mirror (*spiegelt sich ideell wider*), then it may appear as if we had before us a mere a priori construction (*Konstruktion*). . . . With me . . . the ideal (*ideell*) is nothing else than the material world (*Materielle*) transposed (*umgesetzte*) by the human mind, and translated (*übersetzte*) into forms of thought" (Karl Marx, *Capital*, translated by Samuel Moore and Edward Aveling [New York: International Publishers, 1967], 17–19. Marx's text quoted in translation with original German inserted by Derrida; *D*, 32).

35. Derrida describes Hegel as "the last philosopher of the book and the first thinker of writing" (*Of Grammatology*, 26).

36. See esp. Harvey, 77 and 207. While I agree with Harvey that *différance* and metaphysics stand in economic relationship to one another, I think Harvey tends to underplay *différance*'s disruptive effects. While metaphysics and *différance* together do constitute "the play of the world" (to use her phrase; 207),

as it is currently, I think *différance* also holds out the (im)possible possibility of another order.

37. For Derrida's development of this neologism, see "Différance" in *Margins of Philosophy*, 1–27. For helpful elucidations of it, see Gasché, *Tain*, 194–205, and Bennington, 70–84.

38. Some of Derrida's readers see a resemblance between *différance* and the way so-called negative theologies talk about God. See *Derrida and Negative Theology* for essays on this topic by scholars in religious studies and by Derrida. For a helpful discussion of Derrida's stance on this issue, see Bennington, 78–79.

39. An earlier version of this portion of my argument appears in my "Crossing the Boundaries between Deconstruction, Feminism, and Religion," in Holland, *Feminist interpretations*, 193–214.

40. Those readers of Derrida who, like Margaret Whitford, locate him in what she calls "the anti-Platonic tradition which runs from Kant to Derrida, via Hegel, Heidegger, and Nietzsche" miss the complexity of Derrida's engagement with the philosophical tradition as well as the complexity of the tradition's engagement with Plato (see Margaret Whitford, *Luce Irigaray: Philosophy in the Feminine* [London: Routledge, 1991], 105). Whitford is trying to distinguish Irigaray from Derrida in highly problematic ways, as I shall argue in chap. 4 below.

41. *The Post Card: From Socrates to Freud and Beyond* (trans. Alan Bass [Chicago: University of Chicago Press, 1987]), one of Derrida's later books that I will discuss below, takes off from a postcard a friend sent him of an old sketch of Plato and Socrates that in many complex ways blurs distinctions between their identities / their positions in Plato's texts. Derrida's reading of this postcard calls into question any easy answer to questions of derivation and priority between Socrates and Plato.

42. Although Derrida does not explain his use of this term to describe Plato's text, one can extrapolate from his analysis the reason for its use. The term has many resonances from its Greek roots to its current use as a term for a certain kind of word puzzle. In Greek, the prefix *ana* means "between, in the midst of." *Gramme* means "letter, writing" (see entries for both words in *A Greek-English Lexicon of the New Testament and Other Early Christian Literature*, 5th ed. [Chicago: University of Chicago Press, 1979]). One of the marks of the text of metaphysics involves assuming the superiority of speech over writing. As the following pages show, Plato's texts instantiate that assumption *and* undercut it. Thus, running just below the surface of Plato's text, which seems to be the instantiation of the text of metaphysics, runs another layer of writing between the lines (a writing between letters?) that undercuts its mastery. When examined through the strategy of double reading / writing, Plato's texts turn out to be not simply what they seem at first glance, but a kind of puzzle made with words.

43. For a related discussion, see Derrida's comments in the "Roundtable on Translation" in *The Ear of the Other: Otobiography, Transference, Translation*, edited by Christie McDonald, translated by Peggy Kamuf (Lincoln: University of Nebraska Press, 1985), esp. 114–26.

44. "Play" is a loaded word in the field of disputes over the value of Derrida's work for philosophy and for philosophical theology. Some of Derrida's critics read the focal role of "play" (*jeu,* in French) in Derrida's corpus as evidence that his work lacks the seriousness appropriate to philosophical thinking, especially in light of the difficult issues that face our time. Theological appropriations of deconstruction have picked up on the more obvious connotations of play (as the opposite of work, the carefree play of children who need give no thought to their basic needs, as promoting a kind of glee in the face of the abyss that has always undergirded theology, etc.) to the neglect of some of the finer shades of its connotations that Derrida also capitalizes upon in his work with *jeu.* These would include associations with the play of opposites, e.g., light and shadow, in a painting, or polysemic meanings in poetic images, or the play within the structure of a skyscraper that enables it to withstand wind, vibration, storms, earthquakes but also threatens its stability. There is a certain lightness to Derrida's touch that does call forth the more obvious connotations of "play," but they never occur without their more serious siblings, as careful attention to Derrida's writings reveals.

45. Derrida describes his work as working at contextuality in a broad sense in his responses to questions raised by Gerald Graff in "Afterword: Toward an Ethic of Discussion" in *Limited, Inc.* (Urbana: University of Illinois Press, 1988), esp. 136–37 and 147–48.

46. Morny Joy describes Derrida's analysis of *pharmakon* as "indulgences" ("Derrida and Ricoeur: A Case of Mistaken Identity [and Difference]," *Journal of Religion* 68 [October 1988]: 514). I trust that this exegesis of the analysis, its grounds, and what is at stake in it, refutes Joy's trivializing of this aspect of Derrida's argument.

47. Although time does not permit me to deal with this now, this analogy also appears in the famous allegory of the cave later in the *Republic* (bk. 7) in which Plato describes the process of coming to real knowledge. The allegory of the cave constitutes a point at which Derrida and Irigaray overlap, as I note in chap. 4 below.

48. This is one of the founding gestures (again, I am not saying Plato is the first to make it, necessarily) of metaphysics in the sense of the science of being. One can look ahead from this point (or back from the present) to Kant and the distinction between *noumena* and *phenomena,* to Husserl and the call of phenomenology, "to the things themselves," to Heidegger and the call of being. Even at its inception, the object of this science withdraws itself.

49. Neither of Gasché's books take up the issue of Derrida and feminism or the place of sexual difference. However, I would argue that a discussion of Derrida on reflection (which provides Gasché's entré into *Tain*) is incomplete insofar as it misses the gendered and sexual dynamics that attend it. Gasché's response to Jean-Luc Marion's discussion of the implications of Derrida's work for questions about God, like Llewelyn's (and Marion's), makes nothing of God's masculinity (see Gasché's "God, For Example" in *Inventions of Difference,* 150–70). Bennington discusses both in his tour of important topics in receptions of Derrida's work (on God, see 78–79; on Derrida's relationship to feminism, see 205–27), but he does not develop any relationship between the two terms. Llewellyn discusses woman, but only in relation to Derrida's reading of

Nietzsche in *Spurs* (Derrida, *Éperons: Les styles de Nietzsche/Spurs: Nietzsche's Styles*, trans. Barbara Harlow [Chicago: University of Chicago Press, 1978; French/English version, 1979]), which I discuss in chap. 3 below. He connects the play in different meanings of woman-as-truth to the play of the *pharmakon*, but does not discuss the gender dynamics common to both (see "Anasemiology," 83–90, in *Derrida on the Threshold of Sense*). Only Nancy Holland has noticed a conjunction between God and woman, though she takes it in a slightly different direction. See "The Treble Clef/t: Jacques Derrida and the Female Voice" in *Philosophy and Culture: Proceedings of the Twenty-seventh World Congress of Philosophy* 2 (Montreal: Editions Montmorency, 1988): 654–58.

50. See Mary Daly's *Beyond God the Father*, Sallie McFague's work on different models of God (esp. *Models of God*), and Elizabeth A. Johnson's *She Who Is: The Mystery of God in Feminist Theological Discourse* (New York: Crossroad, 1992), to list just a few of the important texts on this issue.

51. This is nowhere more evident than in Jean-Luc Marion's *God without Being*. See my "The (Im)possible Possibility of Theology without God."

52. Alice Jardine's *Gynesis* (Ithaca, N.Y.: Cornell University Press, 1985) raised such questions early on. Kelly Oliver is among the most recent feminists to raise them. See her *Womanizing Nietzsche: Philosophy's Relation to the "Feminine"* (New York: Routledge, 1995), which I will discuss in the next chapter.

53. Stéphane Mallarmé, *La musique et les lettres*, 646–47, as quoted by Derrida in Barbara Johnson's translation (*D*, 235, n. 44).

54. Mallarmé, 872, as quoted by Derrida (*D*, 55).

55. Mallarmé, 875–76, as quoted by Derrida (*D*, 55).

56. I use this awkward and somewhat peculiar phrase in place of something like "heterosexual economy" for several reasons that will become clearer as this argument proceeds. See "Freudian Figures" in chap. 3 below.

Chapter 3

1. See Braidotti, *Patterns*, 102. Gayatri Chakravorty Spivak and Rosi Braidotti are both associated with this critique. See, e.g., Gayatri Chakravorty Spivak, "Displacement and the Discourse of Woman," in *Displacement: Derrida and After*, edited by Mark Krupnick (Bloomington: Indiana University Press, 1983), 169–95, "Feminism and Critical Theory," in *In Other Worlds: Essays in Cultural Politics* (New York: Routledge, 1987), 84–91; and Braidotti, *Patterns*, 98–108. Spivak, of course, has several positive things to say about Derrida as well. Irigaray also accuses Derrida of bypassing the specificity of female embodiment, though in a more nuanced way. See Luce Irigaray, "Le v(i)ol de la lettre" in *Parler n'est jamais neutre* (Paris: Éditions Minuit, 1985), 149–68.

2. "Women in the Beehive: A Seminar with Jacques Derrida," in *Men in Feminism*, edited by Alice Jardine and Paul Smith (New York: Methuen, 1987), 189–200. Derrida's interview with Christie McDonald, "Choreographies," has appeared in a number of places. See *The Ear of the Other*, 163–85; Nancy Holland's *Feminist Interpretations of Jacques Derrida*, 23–42; and its original version in *Diacritics* 12 (summer 1982): 66–76. For an evenhanded and accurate discussion of "Choreographies" and its larger context, see Tina Chanter, *Ethics of Eros*, 231–39.

3. Margaret Whitford provides a prime example of such a reading. She ar-

gues that Irigaray takes what is helpful from Derrida while avoiding his basically nihilistic tendencies (see *Luce Irigaray: Philosophy in the Feminine*). For a much more accurate discussion of Irigaray's relationship to Derrida as Irigaray sees it, see Chanter, chap. 6.

4. On this broad question, I align myself with Elizabeth Grosz, Peggy Kamuf, and Peg Birmingham in Nancy Holland's *Feminist Interpretations of Jacques Derrida*. See also Tina Chanter's "On Not Reading Derrida's Texts: Mistaking Hermeneutics, Misreading Sexual Difference, and Neutralizing Narration" in Feder et al., 87–113.

5. See my article, "Questions of Proximity: 'Woman's Place' in Derrida and Irigaray," *Hypatia* 12, no. 1 (winter 1997): 63–78.

6. See Spivak's introduction to Derrida's *Of Grammatology*, xlvii.

7. This is not to say that Derrida leaves Freud and Nietzsche "unmolested"—or Marx or Mallarmé, for that matter—by deconstruction, as Hart alleges (139). I would argue that the readings Derrida gives of Mallarmé and of Marx in *Dissemination* are deconstructive readings. His reading of Mallarmé, in particular, takes on the canonical view of Mallarmé as an idealist. Derrida's reading suggests that this Mallarmé is a product of literary criticism. The figure of Mallarmé is no more or less deconstructed than the figure of Plato in *Dissemination*. As this section of my argument will show, the same holds true for Nietzsche and Freud in Derrida's readings of them.

8. Other reasons identified by Derrida include the advent of particular sociopolitical challenges in acute forms (e.g., resistance movements of various sorts like the Civil Rights movement, the women's movement, the French student uprisings, etc.); all of which build upon the legacy of the past, as does the philosophical tradition. I will focus attention on the workings of these movements in Derrida's thinking later in this chapter and in chap. 5.

9. Derrida makes this point in "Freud and the Scene of Writing," (*Writing and Difference*, translated by Alan Bass [Chicago: University of Chicago Press, 1978]), 229.

10. Several of the terms that Derrida's work features have Freudian roots and / or resonances. The notion of the *trace*, e.g., has roots in Freud's descriptions of the graphological relationship between the unconscious and consciousness. Whereas in Freud's texts, the undecidability of the trace is continually remastered by a metaphysics of presence, Derrida's appropriation of it exacerbates its undecidability, its productivity, its ability to elude that mastery. He adopts it as descriptive of the inscription of *différance* and other undecidables in the text of western metaphysics.

11. Derrida, *Writing and Difference*, 227–28; emphasis in original.

12. "Positions: Interview with Jean-Louis Houdebine and Guy Scarpetta," in *Positions*, 111, n. 3.

13. Freud met resistance to his views from other psychoanalysts including Melanie Klein and Ernest Jones. The controversy over his views continued in this country in the second wave of feminism in the second half of this century. Many feminists offered critiques of Freud. Current feminist theorists are returning to the scene of the crime, as it were, often through coming into contact with French thought informed by psychoanalytic theory, including that of La-

can, Derrida, and Irigaray (as well as other French writers such as Julia Kristeva, Catherine Clément, and Hélène Cixous).

14. Andrea Nye, in the fifth chapter of her book *Feminist Theory and the Philosophies of Man* (London: Croom Helm, 1988), contrasts the biologism of American psychoanalysis with Lacan's reading of Freud that moves away from "regressive references to anatomy or instinct" (137) to the ways thought and language engineer sexual difference. See also the introductions to *Feminine Sexuality: Jacques Lacan and the école freudienne* (New York: W.W. Norton, 1982) by its editors, Jacqueline Rose (translator of the volume) and Juliet Mitchell. They similarly argue that Lacan engineers a shift in understanding the locus of psychodynamics from biologism to discourse.

15. The significance of Lacan's phallocentrism for feminism is hotly contested within feminist theory. Such scholars as Juliet Mitchell, Jacqueline Rose, and Ellie Ragland-Sullivan who want to appropriate Lacan for feminism argue that his phallocentrism does not render such a partnership problematic. Against those feminist theorists who take the view that phallocentrism simply moves male privilege to another level, they argue that moving the referent of desire away from an anatomical organ to a discursive sign means anatomy really is *not* destiny for women *or* for men. Ragland-Sullivan claims one can only read Lacan's phallocentrism as valorizing male privilege if one equates the phallus with the penis and thus with male human beings (Ellie Ragland-Sullivan, *Jacques Lacan and the Philosophy of Psychoanalysis* [Urbana: University of Illinois Press, 1986], 298–308). I will not take a position on Lacan and *feminism* until I have explored the place of woman in Derrida's double reading of the text of metaphysics. I will discuss these issues further in chap. 4 when Lacan returns to my discussion through Irigaray.

16. I am primarily basing this reading in two of Lacan's essays, "The Meaning of the Phallus" and "The Phallic Phase and the Subjective Import of the Castration Complex" in Mitchell and Rose, 74–86 and 99–122, respectively. For Freud's discussion of femininity, see "Some Psychical Consequences of the Anatomical Differences Between the Sexes," in vol. 19 of *The Standard Edition of the Complete Psychological Works of Sigmund Freud*, 24 vols., edited by James Strachey (London: Hogarth Press, 1953–74). Other works by Freud consulted for this essay are "Female Sexuality," in vol. 21; "The Dissolution of the Oedipus Complex," in vol. 19; "Femininity," in vol. 22; and *Three Essays on the Theory of Sexuality*, in vol. 7.

17. So, e.g., Lacan's group's partition of the debate within psychoanalysis over femininity entails a refutation of the position of Freud's student, Ernest Jones, on the grounds that he gives too much weight to pure anatomy. The Lacanian position argues, to the contrary, that anatomical differences alone are not sufficient to produce effects of such weight. Anatomical figures can set the stage for the Oedipus complex *because* they are read through the screen of the Oedipus myth. See "Castration Complex" in Mitchell and Rose, esp. 109.

18. I mark "resolution" and "with" (and "is" and "has" with regard to the phallus below) to call attention to the problematic status of these achievements. The subject carries traces of the Oedipal drama with him throughout his life; its resolution, if achieved, is always under threat. The resolution of the Oedipus

complex for women is even more problematic. The full extent of those problems awaits further discussion in chap. 4.

19. For reasons that will only become obvious once the discussion of Irigaray is underway, "heterosexuality" is a misnomer for the trajectory of this desire. Irigaray will argue that what counts as feminine in this trajectory is hardly other to what counts as masculine.

20. At least ostensibly this is true. As the next chapter will show, Irigaray challenges this assumption.

21. Mitchell and Rose contend that Lacan's exposure of the split in subjectivity reveals any claim to the superiority of masculinity as illusory. Because of the valorization I note above, I find this reading of the import of Lacan's split subject a little overstated. The split certainly undercuts claims to mastery, but to problematize is not to render illusory.

22. My reading of Lacan on this issue is drawn from Lacan's "God and the *Jouissance* of ~~The~~ Woman" and "A Love Letter," both translated by Jacqueline Rose in Mitchell and Rose, 137–61.

23. Linda Alcoff, "Cultural Feminism versus Post-Structuralism: The Identity Crisis in Feminist Theory," *Signs* 13, no. 3 (spring 1988): 405–36.

24. Lacan writes, "Short of something which says no to the phallic function, man has no chance of enjoying the body of the woman, in other words, of making love" ("God and the *Jouissance* of ~~The~~ Woman" in Mitchell and Rose, 143).

25. Derrida, *The Post Card*, 481, n. 60.

26. Derrida, *The Post Card*, 411–96. In this section, Derrida is engaged in a reading of Lacan's "Seminar on 'The Purloined Letter,' " translated by Jeffrey Mehlman (*French Freud, Yale French Studies* 48 [1972]). Bass leaves the title untranslated because it invokes two readings: *facteur* can mean both "postman" and "factor" (*The Post Card*, 413). Thus, what is under examination here is both the "factor" of truth in Lacanian psychoanalysis *and* "postmen" who attempt to deliver letters to their designated destinations (Dupin in Poe's short story, "The Purloined Letter," tries to return the letter to its author, the queen; Lacan in Derrida's discussion tries to return the "letter" of Freud's texts to their author).

27. For a much more detailed feminist reading of this and other "essays" in *The Post Card*, see Gayatri Chakravorty Spivak's "Love Me, Love My *Ombre, Elle*," *Diacritics* (winter 1984): 19–36.

28. Derrida also makes this accusation against Lacan in "Différance" (in *Margins of Philosophy*, 1–27, esp. 6, n. 5).

29. Before I even discuss the content of this aspect of Derrida's work, it is important to point out that the fact that Derrida attends to this issue *at all* refutes Linda Kintz's claim that he "does not factor gender or color as disruptive or inappropriate threats to the specular dialectic" (Linda Kintz, "In-Different Criticism," 131). As I will argue in the next chapter, gender and color function to disrupt the specular economy in many places in Derrida's work.

30. Jacques Derrida, *Éperons: Les styles de Nietzsche/Spurs: Nietzsche's Styles*, translated by Barbara Harlow (Chicago: University of Chicago Press, 1978; French/English version, 1979). Subsequent references to this work will appear as *SP*. I indicate where I am using my own translation of the French text; other-

wise, the Harlow translation is cited. An earlier version of my reading of *SP* appears in my "Questions of Proximity."

31. See, e.g., Elizabeth A. Meese, *(Ex)tensions: Refiguring Feminist Criticism* (Urbana: University of Illinois Press, 1990), 25 (cited by Chanter, 238); Oliver's *Womanizing Nietzsche;* Alice Jardine's *Gynesis;* Ellen K. Feder and Emily Zakin's "Flirting with the Truth: Derrida's Discourse with 'Woman' and Wenches," in Feder et al., to name a few.

32. "Woman is condemned, debased, scorned as a figure of the power of evil. The category of accusation is therefore produced in the name of truth, of dogmatic metaphysics, of the credulous man who advances truth and the phallus as his proper attributes" (*SP*, 96, my translation).

33. This claim is not what feminist theorists Mary Poovey or Rosi Braidotti take it to be. Poovey reads "woman does not exist" as meaning woman is *only* a social construction. What woman means in any given time / place / situation is, at least in part, socially constructed, but that is not Derrida's point here. His point is that woman has no place in the scheme of being. Poovey implies that, if woman is socially constructed, then woman is easily available to social engineering under feminist control. I would argue that this assumption misreads the tenacity of social constructions. Woman will not easily be moved. Moreover, social constructions build on / are complicit with discursive structures. As Irigaray will argue (and as Derrida's analysis of the play of gender to this point has shown), western discourse has kept woman in the same place for a very long time. That will not easily change—and that is the level where Derrida is working. See Mary Poovey, "Feminism and Deconstruction," *Feminist Studies* 14 (spring 1988): 51–65. Derrida's reading of Nietszche on woman also challenges Braidotti's nihilistic interpretation of "woman does not exist" cited above. Obviously the three positions identified by Derrida in Nietzsche's text each have content. The positions may not be ones Braidotti likes, but Derrida is not granting them authority (at least in the case of the first two). In fact, his work with them *undercuts* their authority. Insofar as they are typical positions granted to woman, exhibiting her elusion of them is a good thing, I would argue.

34. To further counter Braidotti's reading of woman as "empty set," I would argue that woman eluding the "fix" of metaphysics is not the same thing as *being* an empty set.

35. This metaphor gains in status or scope when one recalls that Heidegger is also party to this text. Veiling and unveiling play on the Heideggerian register of truth as *aletheia* and also speak of the withdrawal of the truth of being in the metaphysical epoch. I will draw out this connection in my evaluative comments at the end.

36. *Tombe* also plays between two meanings. As a form of the verb *tomber,* it means "to fall." As noun, *la tombe* means "tomb" (see *SP*, 147, translator's n. 4). So "the veil falls / the veil tomb"; "the erection falls / the erection tomb"; "the signature falls / the signature tomb."

37. Ellen Feder and Emily Zakin, while more appreciative of what Derrida *does* offer, make similar criticisms of *Spurs'* inability to break with masculine desire and to open subjectivity up to women. See their "Flirting with the Truth: Derrida's Discourse with 'Woman' and Wenches" in Feder et al., 21–51.

38. In this sense, I disagree with those who identify Derrida's project in *Spurs* as deconstructing *woman*. I would argue that Derrida is deconstructing *man* in showing that his constitutive desire is unfulfillable.

39. As Gayatri Chakravorty Spivak puts it, in Derrida's landscape, there is no use for the *hysteron* (uterus); much less the clitoris—which she argues marks the point of woman's exceeding of masculine economies because it has no function within reproduction or, I would add, within man's-desire-for-woman as desire for his *own* pleasure ("Displacement and the Discourse of Woman," 82). Spivak's point is well taken; however, simply selecting another anatomical figure that comes from woman's side will not evade phallogocentrism. The economy of reproduction, as it currently stands, is hardly woman friendly, as Spivak notes. The uterus can all too easily be cut off from the rest of woman and marked with the father's name. Two examples come to mind from recent events. A local newscast reported on a protest outside Planned Parenthood by a right-to-life group. The (male) speaker for the group intoned, "Sixteen years ago today, Planned Parenthood applied for a license to kill babies before they're born *inside minor girls* without their parents' consent and *inside women* without the baby's father's consent" (WMC, "Action News Five," 1 July 1992). I found a recent television commercial for a local hospital's maternity facilities equally disturbing. The ad opens with a picture of only the torso of a pregnant woman rubbing her hand over her stomach. The scene then switches to pictures of the fetus as it develops within the mother's womb. The whole fetus appears on camera, but no other features of the mother are displayed. She figures as a faceless, legless incubator singing a lullaby. The clitoris also can get trapped in the phallogocentric economy. Within that economy, it has never served as a mark of woman's appropriate pleasure. Instead, as Irigaray will argue, it figures as defective penis, the pleasures of which the mature woman is supposed to replace with the pleasures of the vagina.

40. Barbara Harlow's translation: "Nietzsche must have *been familiar with* all the *genres*" (*SP*, 29); emphasis added.

41. Harlow's translation with the major differences between my version and hers highlighted: "At once, simultaneously or successively, depending on the position of his body and the situation of his story, *Nietzsche was all of these*. Within himself, outside of himself, Nietzsche *dealt with* so many women" (*SP*, 101). "Dealt with" is an accurate translation of *avait affaire*—perhaps even more accurate than mine—but the double entendre cannot be heard. Similarly, to add the phrase "Nietzsche was all of these" puts the stress on the first part of the couplet in each "He was / He dreaded" and the sexual connotations recede further from view.

42. Here again, the fact that Derrida investigates the terrain of sexuality and desire and finds it inscribed by the text of metaphysics renders invalid one of the ways Hart tries to exempt a renewed theology from deconstruction's critique. Hart argues that a theology chastened by deconstruction could turn to the writings of Christian mystics as a source for a nonmetaphysical theology. He makes this claim on the grounds that the mystics were concerned with *loving* God, not with *knowing* God, and that love is not subject to metaphysics. Clearly what passes for love in the phallogocentric economy is as inscribed

by metaphysics as what passes for knowledge. A certain reading of Christian mystical texts could indeed be useful for a deconstructed theology because of the interplay of the divine, the human, and gender in their work, e.g., but not on the grounds Hart proposes.

43. The question of gift and an economy of the gift arises elsewhere in Derrida's work, including his very recent *Given Time: I. Counterfeit Money*, translated by Peggy Kamuf (Chicago: University of Chicago Press, 1992). A reading of that line of thought in conjunction with this analysis in *Spurs* would be important to follow.

44. This also repeats a motif of *Dissemination*—the motif of the title. Against the mirror of the logic of the hymen, the father's seed disseminates unchecked and out of his control. Here as well, it is instructive that Derrida names this text after the masculine dispersal rather than the feminine.

45. So, e.g., in the first half of *The Post Card*, Derrida addresses repeated letters to an unnamed and differently shaded (but nearly always female) recipient—letters that never arrive and that show no evidence of the sender's receipt of same *from* the unnamed woman / lover / wife / mother / sister his *envois* (literally *sendings/letters*) address. In "Displacement and the Discourse of Woman," Spivak addresses the play of genders in other places in Derrida's corpus, including *Glas*. Spivak discusses the original French version of *Glas* (Paris: Galilée, 1974); "The Law of Genre," (translated by Avital Ronell, *Glyph* 7 [1980]: 202–32); and "Living On: Borderlines" (translated by James Hulbert, in *Deconstruction and Criticism*, edited by Harold Bloom [New York: Seabury Press, 1979]). One aspect of *Glas*'s double-columned text involves the solicitation of Hegel's logic that facilitates the perpetual elusion of its presumed consummation, absolute knowledge (*savoir absolu*, in French, or *sa* for short—a feminine possessive pronoun). The other column traces the "mother" of man's-desire-for-man as figured in Genet's writing. Derrida undertakes a similar strategy in "The Law of Genre" and "Living On: Borderlines." In "The Law of Genre," Derrida and Blanchot play at mother / daughter dynamics, switching places first with mothers and daughters and then with each other. "Living On: Borderlines" also plays with father / daughter relationships.

46. Drucilla Cornell and Rosi Braidotti (with Gayatri Chakravorty Spivak occupying the middle position) indicate the paradigmatic poles of feminist response to the play of woman. Cornell is satisfied with Derrida's work with sexual difference, for the most part. She reads *Spurs* as a utopian choreography of a new dance of sexual difference (see *Beyond Accommodation*, 79–106). Braidotti sees nothing of benefit for feminism in Derrida's dance with woman in part because she sees nothing of women in his writing (but I debate this reading above). Spivak agrees with Braidotti on the absence of consideration of the material aspects of women's oppression, but contradicts Braidotti's interpretation of Derrida's woman. (In "Displacement and the Discourse of Woman," Spivak is disturbed that woman occupies the place of indeterminacy in Derrida's work. However, she does not go along with Braidotti in reading indeterminacy as empty set. Spivak even says a strategic yes to that association in "Feminism and Deconstruction, Again: Negotiating with Unacknowledged Masculinism" [in Brennan, 206–23.]) However, Spivak does identify a limit to

Derrida's play with woman; it remains within what she calls "the itinerary of [man's] desire" ("Displacement," 186). My position comes closest to Spivak's, but I would insist that the object of that desire needs to be specified at all times *because* the object is so specific. Not only is it not (at least on the surface) man's-desire-for-man, but it is man's-desire-for-woman construed in a certain way. Whatever this construal of woman is, I would argue (with Irigaray) that it is not a real alterity. Thus, I think Cornell overreads what Derrida's choreography accomplishes. Real sexual difference requires a different sexual economy than the one currently in place.

47. "Feminism and Deconstruction, Again," in Brennan, 206–24. My critique of Derrida converges with Spivak's in many places, but this is one place where we diverge.

48. My critique will intersect with one offered by other feminist theorists, though with some important differences. Leslie Wahl Rabine claims the play of woman in Derrida's texts "absorb[s] the feminine into a reuniversalizing of the male subject." ("A Feminist Politics of Non-Identity," *Feminist Studies* 14 [spring 1989]: 16). Rabine's formulation does not do sufficient justice to the element of disruption in that subject. Similarly, Spivak contends that Derrida appropriates woman for the purposes of becoming androgynous (Spivak, "Feminism and Critical Theory" in *In Other Worlds*, 76–92). She is referring to places such as in "Women in the Beehive," where Derrida connects his desire to write like a woman with his desire to be able eventually to move gender beyond gender and to move sexuality beyond sexual difference as limited to the current binary system (i.e., outside the reach of metaphysics). I am not sure that "androgyny" (either personal or discursive) is an appropriate name for this desire (nor am I convinced that Derrida wants this only for himself, as Spivak implies) because beyond gender/sexuality as Derrida seems to envision it would be beyond what androgyny conjures up. It would be beyond the space of a neutral subject, I would think, as well as beyond woman and man in any combination. At the same time, I share her suspicion of this goal, though for additional reasons. It is difficult to imagine what lies beyond sexual difference if one is convinced (as I am) by Irigaray's claim that western culture has not yet *seen* sexual difference.

49. For all Derrida's criticisms of Lacan, I find it striking that they wind up in such similar places with regard to woman. Lacan also adopts a strategy that resembles Derrida's renunciation. Early in "God and the *Jouissance* of T̶h̶e̶ Woman," Lacan announces himself as "*the subject supposed to know*" (139; emphasis in original). In announcing himself, I would argue that he doubles that position and thereby installs a moment of undecidability in it that undercuts this claim to mastery even as he asserts it. My reading of this dynamic is supported by what goes on in the rest of the text. Over and over again, Lacan reveals just how ignorant he is about woman and her *jouissance*—deliberately. Thus, one could say his "Love Letter" ("Une lettre d'amour," in *Feminine Sexuality*, 149–61), which follows "God and the *Jouissance* of T̶h̶e̶ Woman," never arrives, like the *envois* of Derrida's *Post Card*. Whether Derrida (or Lacan) is aware of this effect in their texts is beside the point. Their meaning-to-say is not in question here. I am attempting to describe the effects of the play of

gender within texts authorized (and not) by Derrida's signature. The same holds true for the rest of my reading of the play of gender in Derrida's work.

50. At least Lacan mentions the possibility of such, though he claims "women know nothing of it" (see "God and the *Jouissance* of The Woman," 146). Again what this means would require *considerable* unpacking—word by word. This issue will come up again in my discussion of Irigaray.

51. My critique again coincides to a degree with that raised by other feminist theorists. Spivak offers a similar criticism regarding the lack of attention to material conditions of women's oppressions in each of her readings of Derrida on the question of woman. Insofar as the absence of these kinds of references is what Rosi Braidotti has in mind when she argues that the feminine in Derrida has nothing to do with the historical realities of women's lives, I concur with her. On the other hand, I do not think this signifies, as some feminist theorists argue, a basic incompatibility between deconstruction and politics or ethics—especially feminist versions of both, as I argue in the previous chapter. Derrida's analysis of the situation of feminism and women's studies in "Choreographies" and "Women in the Beehive" exhibits significant attention to the political difficulties faced by feminism and women's studies in the current climate.

52. This is not to say that Derrida never runs the risk of appropriating woman's place. Entering into that controversy is not directly pertinent to my project here. Let me simply refer my readers to discussions of Derrida's occasional remarks about wanting to write from woman's place. For Derrida's own comments to this effect, see "At This Very moment, Here I Am" (in *Re-Reading Levinas,* edited by Robert Bernasconi and Simon Critchley [Bloomington: Indiana University Press, 1991], 11–48) and "Choreographies." For discussions of these places, see Oliver, Critchley, and especially Chanter, "On Not Reading Derrida's Texts," in Feder et al., 87–113.

53. On this point, I am in agreement with Tina Chanter and Gayatri Chakravorty Spivak. Spivak learns from Derrida's critique of phallogocentrism and from his repeated warnings against replacing it with hysterocentrism, but she finally has to "go somewhere else with [deconstruction]" ("Displacement and the Discourse of Women," 173). She describes this "somewhere else" as an intervention from the other side of sexual difference, from the side of woman—and she thinks that would be a genuinely different starting point. Tina Chanter similarly argues for a difference between deconstruction deployed from the side of woman and from the side of man ("Antigone's Dilemma," in Bernasconi and Critchley, 131). I find the direction in which Irigaray goes the most helpful.

54. See her "Love Me, Love My *Ombre, Elle.*" Spivak reads this as the positive value in Derrida's use of motifs like invagination, hymen, etc., as marker for the border of metaphysics (see esp. 19–24).

55. See, e.g., Elizabeth Grosz, "Ontology and Equivocation: Derrida's Politics of Sexual Difference" (in Holland, *Feminist Interpretations of Jacques Derrida*), 94–95, and Kelly Oliver's *Womanizing Nietzsche,* 66. Grosz applauds Derrida's interest in multiple sexualities, but she, like Oliver, wants to insist that male and female body marks are irreducible. I find it difficult to distinguish such a claim from a pre-Butlerian biological essentialism.

56. See Kamuf's "Deconstruction and Feminism: A Repetition" (in Holland, *Feminist Interpretations of Derrida*), 103–26.

Chapter 4

1. See, e.g., Whitford, chap. 6; Oliver, *Womanizing Nietzsche*, chap. 4; and Chanter, chap. 6. Oliver reads Irigaray's *Marine Lover of Friedrich Nietzsche* (translated by Gillian C. Gill [New York: Columbia University Press, 1991]) as a critical response to *Spurs* (83–125). Chanter situates several of Irigaray's shorter essays in relation to Derrida's work. Oliver and Chanter both note that Irigaray criticizes Derrida for failing to attend to the place allotted to woman's body and to materiality in western discourse. Peg Birmingham takes on the task of defending Derrida against this criticism as sounded by Irigaray, Susan Bordo and others (see Peg Birmingham, "Toward an Ethic of Desire: Derrida, Fiction and the Law of the Feminine" in Holland, *Feminist Interpretations*, 127–46.

2. Patricia Huntington, "Fragmentation, Race, and Gender: Building Solidarity in the Postmodern Era," in *Existence in Black: An Anthology of Black Existential Philosophy*, edited by Lewis R. Gordon (New York: Routledge, 1997): 185–202.

3. Chris Weedon's assessment exemplifies such readings. Irigaray "produces a radical theory of the female libido based in female sexuality and autoeroticism which celebrates the female body" (Chris Weedon, *Feminist Practice and Poststructuralist Theory* [London: Blackwell, 1987], 56). Andrea Nye argues that Irigaray uncovers the "feminine substance which the words of men have concealed" (151; for the full account, see 148–64). Also, see e.g., Janet Sayers, *Biological Politics: Feminist and Anti-Feminist Perspectives* (New York: Tavistock, 1982), 131–32. Toril Moi, in *Sexual/Textual Politics: Feminist Literary Theory* (London: Routledge, 1988) offers a much more appreciative reading of Irigaray but concludes (I think, wrongly) that Irigaray falls into essentialism against her will (see 127–49).

4. See Elizabeth Grosz, *Sexual Subversions: Three French Feminists* (Winchester, Mass.: Unwin Hyman, 1989) and Margaret Whitford 's *Luce Irigaray: Philosophy in the Feminine*. See also similar accounts of Irigaray's work by Diana Fuss in *Essentially Speaking* (chap. 4) and Rosi Braidotti (*Patterns*, 248–63).

5. Grosz, e.g., describes Irigaray's goal as "the recategorization of women and femininity so that they are now capable of being autonomously defined according to women's and not men's interests" (*Sexual Subversions*, 105). Whitford speaks of Irigaray's goal as promoting a new female subject—one who can master language, to whom truth is proper (*Luce Irigaray*, 41–45, 116–17.). For Whitford, the problem seems to be women's *access* to subjectivity, not the structure of subjectivity itself. Access to subjectivity requires that women have a symbolic set of models with whom they can identify.

6. The argument of the first chapter of Paula Cooey's *Religious Imagination and the Body* takes Irigaray's essentialism as an established fact (19–25). Cooey seems entirely unaware of the large body of literature on this subject that has emerged within Irigarayan scholarship in the fifteen years since these charges were first made.

7. Luce Irigaray, *This Sex Which Is Not One*, translated by Catherine Porter and Carolyn Burke (Ithaca, N.Y.: Cornell University Press, 1985), and *Speculum of the Other Woman*, translated by Gillian C. Gill (Ithaca, N.Y.: Cornell Univer-

sity Press, 1985). Hereafter, references to these works will be cited as *TS* and *S*, respectively. An earlier version of my reading of Irigaray on the problem of essentialism appeared in my "Questioning Woman" in Kim et al.

8. On this, cf. Moi, 100, and Nye, 152–53.

9. At the beginning of this question-and-answer session, Irigaray posits this type of question as the question to which all others return. In this instance, the question is, "*Are* you a *woman?*" She responds, " *'I'* am not *'I'*, I *am* not, I am not *one*. As for *woman*, try and find out. . . . In any case, in this form, that of the concept and of denomination, certainly not" (*TS*, 120). For now, I only want to raise the reader's awareness of the problems these kinds of refusals create for essentialist accounts of Irigaray's work. I will return to explain what is at stake in this refusal later and how to understand it. See also *TS*, 148–49, 155–56.

10. This difference in interpretation points to a larger issue that divides my reading from that offered by Whitford. Whitford adopts her reading in order to distinguish Irigaray from Lacan—especially from the Lacan of Seminar XX ("God and the *Jouissance* of The Woman" and "Love Letter"). She takes great pains to distinguish Irigaray from both Lacan and Derrida (see, e.g., *Luce Irigaray*, 53 and 136–140). Whitford acknowledges that Irigaray adopts some Lacanian and Derridean insights and strategies, but believes that Irigaray escapes what she identifies as their nihilistic (in Derrida's case) and socially conservative (in Lacan's case) tendencies. These tendencies, combined with what Whitford reads as their negative evaluations of feminism, render both men of little help to feminism. This distinction between Irigaray and these two figures rests on very flat-footed readings of both male figures. I argued in the previous chapters that Derrida is not nihilistic, nor is Lacan necessarily socially conservative, nor is their work necessarily antifeminist—whatever their personal politics might be. Moreover, Whitford's work calls for an alternative reading of Irigaray's relationship to Derrida and to Lacan. Indeed, Whitford acknowledges that her own reading may be limited (see esp. *Luce Irigaray*, 212, n. 5). Irigaray, like Lacan and Derrida, takes "woman does not exist" to mean that woman exceeds the order of metaphysics and of being.

11. The terrain covered by the term "general grammar" overlaps that covered by the terms Whitford uses more often, the "cultural symbolic" or "cultural imaginary." I concur with Whitford that by using "symbolic" and "imaginary," Irigaray means to recall what have become technical terms in Lacanian discourse. However, she also intends to exploit other connotations of the terms. I am suggesting that the term "general grammar" resonates similarly with Derridean terminology. I highlight it here as a reminder that Irigaray's work is not confined to the context of psychoanalytic theory.

12. For a full discussion of the relationship between sexual difference and sex/gender, see Chanter, chap. 1.

13. This is the point on which I find myself most in agreement with Whitford. She contends that Irigaray has not received sufficient attention as a *philosopher* and that misreadings of her work reflect this neglect. I have to disagree, however, with Whitford's alignment of Irigaray with "the anti-Platonic tradition which runs from Kant to Derrida, via Hegel, Heidegger, and Nietzsche" (*Luce Irigaray*, 105). This characterization oversimplifies both Irigaray and Der-

rida (and their relationship to Plato) as well as the other philosophers in this list. The readings of Plato provided by Irigaray in *Speculum of the Other Woman* and by Derrida in *Dissemination* (see chap. 2 above) are far more complex and subtle than "anti-Platonic" suggests.

14. It is helpful to keep Derrida's work in mind at this point. As noted above, Irigaray's "general grammar" and Derrida's "text of western metaphysics" are similar sites. I have argued in previous chapters (and will strengthen this point in the next chapter) that the text of western metaphysics is hardly confined to the sphere of philosophy in Derrida's work. Likewise, Irigaray's "cultural grammar" is hardly confined to psychoanalysis *or* philosophy, as I shall argue. Just as Irigaray often gets read as simply a critic of psychoanalytic theory, so Derrida often gets read as simply a critic of philosophy. In both cases, readers tend to separate one area under *solicitation* and view it as an end in itself rather than as a site that is symptomatic of larger issues.

15. Irigaray takes up additional readings of other philosophers using the strategies I will describe here in her more recent work. *Amante marine* (translated as *Marine Lover*) reads Nietzsche, *L'oubli de l'air* reads Heidegger (see *L'oubli de l'air chez Martin Heidegger* [Paris: Éditions Minuit, 1983]). *Éthique de la différence sexuelle* (Paris: Éditions Minuit, 1984), translated as *An Ethics of Sexual Difference* (translated by Carolyn Burke and Gillian C. Gill [Ithaca, N.Y.: Cornell University Press, 1993], revisits some philosophers in *Speculum* (e.g., Descartes and Aristotle) but also adds others (e.g., Spinoza).

16. Chanter's *Ethics of Eros* takes on a reading of Irigaray as a philosopher as its project. In the process, Chanter provides thorough and insightful interpretations and assessments of Irigaray's reading (or, as Chanter aptly calls it, "rewriting") of the philosophers.

17. I have left the title untranslated because it plays on *la mère* (mother) and *la mer* (sea). So, to translate literally, "A Mother/Sea of Glass/Ice."

18. Plotinus's description of the threat that matter poses to being exhibits classical misogynist lines. Also, Plotinus notes that matter has often been represented as poor because it has nothing of its own and its need for form is insatiable. This trope recalls the mythic figure of woman as voracious mouth that also appears in Freud's "Femininity" (see *S*, 115).

19. Irigaray alludes to a resemblance between the unregulated world and the suspicion that attends it in Kant's analysis and the disorder of hysteria and its treatment in Freud's work (*S*, 210–13). Hysteria can be read as both a psychic disfunction and a disruption of the body's proper order, which psychoanalytic treatment seeks to restore.

20. Immanuel Kant, *Prolegomena to Any Future Metaphysics That Will Be Able to Present Itself as a Science*, translated by Peter G. Lucas (Manchester: Manchester University Press, 1953), sec. 287, 42; *Critique of Practical Reason*, translated and edited by Lewis White Beck (Chicago: University of Chicago Press, 1949), sec. 8, 135, 295; both are cited by Irigaray (*S*, 203).

21. Although my concern in this chapter is not to develop an account of how *Irigaray* understands her work in relation to Derrida's, it is worth noting a certain proximity. My reading to this point comes close to certain aspects of what Irigaray says about Derrida herself in "Le v(i)ol de la lettre," as described by Chanter (245–51). Chanter suggests that Irigaray criticizes Derrida for be-

lieving that nothing lies outside the play of *différance*. Irigaray would argue that woman—in all her materialities—rather than nothing is what funds this play.

22. See "Volume-Fluidity" in *S*, 227–240 and "Volume Without Contours," translated by David Macey, in *The Irigaray Reader*, edited and with an introduction by Margaret Whitford (Oxford: Basil Blackwell, 1991), 53–67. For Irigaray's own commentary on the significance of "L'incontournable volume," see Elizabeth Hirsh and Gary A. Olson, " 'Je-Luce Irigaray': A Meeting with Luce Irigaray," translated by Elizabeth Hirsh and Gaeton Brulotte, *Hypatia* 10, no. 2 (spring 1995): 93–114.

23. Berry's claim is based on attending to the order of the essays in *Speculum*. *Speculum* goes backward through the philosophical tradition (from Freud to Plato). Irigaray's own comments on *Speculum* in a recent interview go even farther than Berry's. Irigaray describes the order as involving multiple mirrorings. She acknowledges her inversion of history in starting with Freud and ending with Plato, but she also points out several instances of redoubling in the interior of the book. This combination of comments sets *Speculum* in an interesting relationship to *Dissemination*. Both texts play with beginnings and endings of the larger context they question. See Philippa Berry, "The Burning Glass: Paradoxes of Feminist Revelation in *Speculum*," in Carolyn Burke et al., *Engaging with Irigaray* (New York: Columbia University Press, 1994).

24. To understand Irigaray's use of psychoanalysis, one first has to recall the significant differences between psychoanalytic theory and practice in France and in many Anglophone countries, which I described in my discussion of Lacan in chap. 3. In that discussion, I noted that Andrea Nye describes the difference as a contrast between the biologism of American psychoanalysis and its "regressive references to anatomy or instinct" (137) with Lacan's move to consideration of the ways thought and language engineer sexual difference. She recognizes that, in Lacanian theory, men and women can take up either male or female positions, "which shows how little any physical reality is the determinant" (137). Oddly enough, this reading of the relationship of body, gender, and discursive positions does not carry over to her reading of Irigaray. Other critics of Irigaray make similar misreadings. Morny Joy's complaint that Irigaray does not distinguish carefully enough between what in woman comes from her biological femaleness and what comes from her socially constructed feminine gender reveals not a *problematic* ambiguity in the meaning of *feminine* in French but Joy's failure to recognize the level at which Irigaray is working, that of discourse (see "Equality or Divinity: A False Dichotomy?" 9). If anything, the ambiguity of *feminine* helps Irigaray make the point that discourse inscribes both biological femaleness and socially constructed gender. This also bears directly on understanding why Irigaray's work, as Moi says, "takes as its starting point a basic 'morphology' (Gr. *morphe*, 'form') [of woman]" (Moi, 143). Moi finds Irigaray's reasons for differentiating between "morphology" and "anatomy" rather obscure. I read this as a deliberate move on Irigaray's part to underscore the locus of her work as discourse because we never have access to anatomy *per se*, only anatomy as shaped/formed by *discourse*. This discourse *inscribes/prescribes/proscribes* such distinctions.

25. For this discussion, it is important to recall certain aspects of my discus-

sion of the phallus in Lacan's thought in chap. 3. The phallus is not the same thing as the penis; it is a discursive term, not a biological organ. I argued that the phallus in Lacan's framework is the prime signifier of desire, of law, and of value in culture and language as a whole. The absence of the desired object structures desire and sets it in motion. Desire is always unfulfilled (desire here means not only sexual desire for a potential partner, but a more fundamental desire for fullness or unity in any and all levels of lived existence). The phallus represents that lost object. For a fuller explanation, see my discussion of this dyad in Lacan's work in chap. 3. Surprisingly, feminist theorists who find Lacan helpful for feminism often find Irigaray problematic. I would argue that such findings are based in the caricature of Irigaray's work against which my reading contends. Ellie Ragland-Sullivan finds Irigaray guilty of equating the phallus with the penis and thus with male human beings (273). She reads Irigaray as offering an equally literal reading of women's bodies as a counter strategy. My reading of Irigaray concurs with Elizabeth Grosz's defense of Irigaray against Ragland-Sullivan. Grosz argues, as I argue in this chapter, that Irigaray is neither reading Lacan's phallus nor writing women's bodies literally. She is, rather, both reading and writing at the level of the cultural imaginary (see Elizabeth Grosz, *Jacques Lacan: A Feminist Introduction* [New York: Routledge, 1990], 140–46). Irigaray would, I think, respond to defenses of Lacan with a "yes, but. . . . " Yes, the phallus is not another name for penis. Yes, the name of the Father does not refer directly to literal fathers. Yes, responsibility for the phallocentrism of Lacan's accounts rests finally with that of our culture. Yes, the phallus, as Lacan himself argues according to Grosz (*Jacques Lacan*, 116–26), takes on this role in part because it "is" visible and our culture privileges sight/visibility. Exactly, Irigaray would say, and by contrast, women offer nothing to the eye. Moreover, Irigaray's project confirms that the phallocentrism of our cultural imaginary is implicated in women's oppression. Insofar as this cultural imaginary shapes our lives, its phallocentrism will not be able to maintain neutrality. It will in some way value its biological analogue in opposition to the lack of it:

> The symbolic function of the phallus envelops the penis as the tangible sign of a privileged masculinity, thus in effect naturalizing male dominance. . . . The relationship between phallus and penis is not arbitrary, but socially and politically motivated. The two sexes come to occupy the positive and negative positions not for arbitrary reasons, or with arbitrary effects. It is motivated by the already existing structure of patriarchal power, and its effects guarantee the reproduction of this particular form of social organization and no other. (Grosz, *Jacques Lacan*, 123–24)

26. Moi, Nye, and others criticize Irigaray for not recognizing the historical/material aspects of women's oppression and focusing only on the psychological (see Moi, 147–48; Nye, 153–54). I will have occasion to return to this issue later, but for now, I want to point out that such a criticism at least needs to take into account the agenda of Irigaray's reading of Freud as stated here and as carried out in the essay in *Speculum*.

27. Moi, 141–42; Whitford also addresses the Marxist element in Irigaray's

work, although she does not address Moi's critique (see *Luce Irigaray*, esp. 21 and 56).

28. Irigaray uses both "penis" and "phallus" in this essay without explaining their relationship to one another. This silence is probably responsible for some of the accusations of biologism directed at her by some of her critics. As I argued previously (see chap. 3 above), the phallus is *the* object of desire in our culture in Lacan's framework. Because it is always lacking, something else always comes to stand in for it. Freud's phallocentrism is not simply a fancy name for the penis's centrality to his work. In his analysis of femininity, the penis stands in for the phallus in the castration complex; then, in the woman's maturity, the child stands in for the phallus. While penis and phallus are not simple equivalents, they are not unrelated. It is no coincidence that the object of desire in our androcentric culture would be shaped like a penis nor is it mere coincidence that the penis would take its place in an account of psychosexual development. One could imagine, Irigaray notes, that a male might be construed according to his lack of a womb or lack of fully developed breasts. For such to occur would presuppose a different cultural imaginary. That the penis is the thing of value is due, Irigaray argues, to the phallus's domination of our cultural value system. The value that accrues to the penis also accrues to all things associated with its bearer, as the rest of Irigaray's analysis will argue.

29. This is another strength to Irigaray's arguments. It avoids the chicken/ egg debates over what is to blame for women's oppression: economic forces, women's biology, acculturation (nature vs. nurture), etc. This means that the answer to the subsequent question, "Where do we start to resist?" is "Everywhere!"

30. Anglophone feminists often criticize Irigaray (along with the other so-called French feminists) for not being political enough or for not attending to the material conditions of women's oppression. According to Nye, Irigaray suggests that "women should abandon futile attempts to negotiate in a man's world. They should not attempt to gain political or economic power. Instead, in analysis with feminist therapists, they must discover the repressed female side of sexuality" (Nye, 153) and new ways of living together as women. Likewise, Moi argues that Irigaray refuses to "consider power as anything but a male obsession. For [Irigaray], power is something women are *against*" (Moi, 147–48). To support her claim, Moi cites part of a statement from Irigaray regarding her resistance to being a part of any group within the women's liberation movement. Moi's citation makes it look as though Irigaray takes this stand because she does not want to get her hands dirty. The context of the passage makes it clear that she wants to refuse power as hierarchical authority, the power implicit in defining woman. I think it is clear from the passages I have just cited that Irigaray recognizes that achieving liberation requires engagement with the political realm, and that necessarily means an engagement with power and powers. Her work reminds those who want to focus on the political that it does not exist separate from the general grammar Irigaray analyzes. The history of the politics of women's issues in both France and the United States reveals repeatedly the numerous and varied strategies that politics uses to reduce the threat to the status quo that women's demands pose. (Claire Duchen's book, *Feminism in France: From May '68 to Mitterand* [London: Routledge and

Kegan Paul, 1986] offers an excellent account of those dynamics on the French political scene that is helpful in positioning Irigaray's relationship to feminism in France.) Moi argues that one can easily separate the biological from the social and the material from the discursive. To go after discursive oppression / repression is to necessarily put the biological / social / material oppression aside. It is clear that Irigaray thinks, anyway, that these are all implicated / imbedded in the discursive. Bourgeois marriage, prostitution, etc., reflect / are reflected by discourse. Irigaray describes the political stake of this questioning as follows: "The fact that women's 'liberation' requires transforming the economic realm, and thus necessarily transforming culture and its operative agency, language. Without such an interpretation of a general grammar of culture, the feminine will never take place in history, except as a reservoir of matter and of speculation" (*TS*, 155; see also *TS*, 64, 66–67, 81–82, 125, 127–28, 135, 142, 155, 164–65, 184–85).

31. This quotation (along with several others) directly contradicts Andrea Nye's claim that Irigaray advocates pure separatism as the only way women can get free of the masculine symbolic (see Nye, 149–53). For other instances, see *TS* (32–33 and 127–28). My reading of Irigaray will make it clear that this is not her goal.

32. When I turn to issues of race and class in a moment, I will argue that whitefeminism's own subjection to an economy of sameness—with white women as the standard—helps explain the hegemony at work in the history of relations between black and white women activists in this country.

33. Irigaray writes, "I am a woman. I am a being sexualized as feminine. I am sexualized female. The motivation of my work lies in the impossibility of articulating such a statement; in the fact that its utterance is in some way senseless, inappropriate, indecent. Either because *woman* is never the attribute of the verb *to be* nor *sexualized female* a quality of *being*, or because *am a woman* is not predicated of *I*, or because *I am sexualized* excludes the feminine gender. . . . I can thus speak intelligently as sexualized male (whether I recognize this or not) or as asexualized. Otherwise, I shall succumb to the illogicality that is proverbially attributed to women" (*TS*, 148–49).

34. It is interesting that the incest forbidden here is mother / child, not father / child. A consideration of this issue raises another problem in relation to the Oedipus complex. How would one read Freud on that issue from that vantage point? In a sense, the scene of the daughter's place in the Oedipal context both forbids this incest (the daughter's desire for her father is both aroused and deferred) and applauds it (the daughter *should* turn her desire from her mother toward her father). See also Catherine Clément's account of the Oedipus complex arising from Freud's refusal to believe stories of daughters' seduction by fathers ("Seduction and Guilt," in Catherine Clément and Hélène Cixous, *The Newly Born Woman*, translated by Betsy Wing [Minneapolis: University of Minnesota Press, 1986], 40–59).

35. Other Irigarayan scholars read Irigaray's strategy and style in similar ways. See essays by Carolyn Burke, "Irigaray through the Looking Glass," "Translation Modified: Irigaray in English," and Dianne Chisholm, "Irigaray's Hysteria," in Burke et al., *Engaging Irigaray*, 37–56, 249–61, 263–83, respectively. This relationship of the inside to the outside is crucial for understanding

Irigaray's inscription of the feminine imaginary. If, as I noted earlier, Irigaray's goal were to escape the masculine symbolic (as Nye suggests), it would present two major problems. If psychosis constitutes the outside of the symbolic, to attempt a complete break with the symbolic would be, as some of Irigaray's critics charge, to relegate woman to logical incoherence or to hysteria, if not to psychosis. I trust it is clear from this section of my argument that Irigaray is not after this sort of goal. Second, Nye goes on to argue that, as long as we grant psychoanalysis the last word on patriarchy, women will always and only be relegated to the margins or to the status of Lacan's *pas tout*. Nye seems to interpret the *pas tout* as absolute nothingness, a problematic interpretation according to Catherine Clément (see Clément's *The Lives and Legends of Jacques Lacan*, translated by Arthur Goldhammer [New York: Columbia University Press, 1983], 62). Nye suggests that we simply refuse to grant psychoanalysis this power, and thus we will move out of the shadow of Oedipus. If the issues here were simply competing accounts of subjectivity or of the human psyche (i.e., if this were merely a debate within psychoanalytic theory and its competitors or even within philosophical anthropology), I could grant Nye's point as a possible strategy; however, the issues here run deeper in our cultural tissue. Irigaray is after what *shapes* psychoanalytic discourse. What she finds at work there is this text of western metaphysics / general grammar of western culture; a persistent patterning that structures our institutions, our philosophical tradition, and our economy in the narrow sense and is most easily visible in psychoanalytic theory. If one finds this account convincing, then one has to recognize that this text is not a language we can pick up and put down at will (as, say, we can learn French, or German, and switch back and forth between them); rather, it is constitutive of our culture. To get outside it, or to work against it is a complex and difficult task that requires specific and, in some ways, peculiar strategies.

36. Derrida, "The Ends of Man," *Margins of Philosophy*, 135.

37. According to Moi, Shoshana Felman questions Irigaray's own position in relation to her work (Felman, "Women and Madness: The Critical Phallacy," *Diacritics* 5 [winter 1975]: 3; cited by Moi, 138). Is Irigaray speaking as a woman, for a woman, in the place of a woman, Felman asks? I would argue that Irigaray is, in some sense, speaking from all such loci and from none of them. Irigaray's analysis reveals that there is no "place" for "woman." The place assigned to the female by phallocentrism is either a cheap imitation of a man's place or no place at all. Irigaray herself assumes all these positions and more, thereby showing that they are not the final word on woman. Irigaray's strategic use of *mimetisme* overdoes this locating and shows that woman always exceeds these locatings / locations.

38. "The imaginary economy only has a meaning and we only have a relationship to it insofar as it is inscribed in a symbolic order which imposes a ternary relationship" (Lacan, "Le moi dans la théorie de Freud et dans la technique de la psychanalyse," in *Le séminaire II*, 1954–55 [Paris: Seuil, 1978], 296; translated and quoted by Rose in "Introduction II" in Mitchell and Rose, 36).

39. Moi, e.g., reads Irigaray as accepting and valorizing the place "outside" the symbolic that has been relegated to woman. Since there is nothing outside the symbolic but psychosis, she reads Irigaray as proposing that women *should*

babble incoherently and leave logic to the men (see Moi, 100). Nye makes the same criticism (see Nye, 152–53). Moi's misreading may stem in part from an overly strong separation of what one might call Irigaray's critical strategy (*mimetisme*) and her constructive strategy (*parler-femme* or *l'écriture feminine*). One cannot do the latter without doing the former; they are two sides of same coin or two styli of same pen. Moi, e.g., reads the essays on the philosophers in *Speculum* as of a piece and following a certain trajectory that enables them to feed off one another. However, she takes "La mysterique" as if its location within this trajectory were either immaterial or perplexing. Moi reads it as though it were coming from a completely different—and essentialist—agenda (see Moi, 136–43). I find Philippa Berry's reading much more compelling (see the section "Supplementation's First Fruits," above).

40. This quotation suggests a direction for reading Irigaray that refutes another of Moi's criticisms of her work. Building on Monique Plaza's original criticism of Irigaray, Moi argues that Irigaray fails to make her case that *mimetisme* is the appropriate strategy for overcoming women's oppression/repression. It is not enough to be a woman engaging in mimetic strategies for this other discursive economy to emerge. Depending upon her political stance, a woman can mime the masculine so well that she will sound like a man (e.g., Margaret Thatcher). Moi argues that Irigaray fails to recognize that point (139–43). I would argue instead that Irigaray provides the *explanation* for that very occurrence. Clearly, being a biological female would be no guarantee that one could break through to the other side of phallogocentrism. When one recalls that women can assume the subject position as well as men can (only they have to relinquish their sexuality to do so), it only makes sense that we would find someone like a Margaret Thatcher in politics or like Mary Daly's fembots in so many aspects of our everyday lives. Irigaray fails, however, to recognize that there are other positions from which one could challenge the economy of the same (e.g., from the position of a black man, or a gay man, etc.).

41. Moi seems to miss this "essential" plurality in her discussion of Irigaray's criticism of the desire at work in phallocentrism. Irigaray argues that this economy is structured by a desire for same; a *hom(m)osexualité* (a desire for same/male) in which woman serves as mirror of that sameness. Moi reads Irigaray as arguing that woman's *own* desire for same is repressed in this economy (135). It is clear that, whatever "woman's desire" would mean for Irigaray, it would not be a simple desire for same. That would be a reinstatement of phallocratism.

42. I am obviously reading this claim about woman as a normative one, in some sense; hence, I write "essence" and immediately call it into question. It is difficult to see how "never being simply one," being always elsewhere, etc., could describe an essence in its usual sense of permanently enduring features (in this case, of woman) regardless of location. A plural, always differing/deferring, decentering, moving essence, seems to me to be, if not an oxymoron, at least paradoxical. Naomi Schor also suggests this may be the best defense against essentialist readings of Irigaray ("The Essentialism Which Is Not One: Coming to Grips with Irigaray," *differences* 1 [summer 1989], 56).

43. I want to distinguish carefully my reading of the question of multiplicity both from that which Whitford criticizes and from that which she puts forward

(see *Luce Irigaray*, 84–90). Whitford is right to insist that jumping simply from unity to *sheer* multiplicity threatens to bypass sexual difference altogether. She also recognizes that multiplicity is very much a part of Irigaray's thinking about sexual difference. However, she fails to see the degree to which it problematizes any easy equation of woman with subjectivity or, to approach it from the opposite point, the degree to which the multiplicity on the side of woman challenges the economy of the Same.

44. See, e.g., the works by Hazel V. Carby, Paula Giddings, and bell hooks discussed throughout this project.

45. Resistance to this pedestal often defines the agenda of whitefeminism, as I argued in the first chapter, which renders it foreign to the experiences of black women. Delores Williams reports that the problem of a lack of self, a consequence of this consignment to passivity, struck absolutely no resonant chords with black churchwomen whom she was trying to interest in feminism (see "The Color of Feminism," 42–43). Spelman likewise notes, as does Patricia Hill Collins, that black women have had to contend against stereotypes of matriarch and whore rather than ornament (Spelman, 119–21; Collins, chap. 4). However, the Vanessa Williams/Miss America controversy suggests both ways in which this ideal may be expanding its territory and ways in which it remains stubbornly the same. Insofar as this pageant is indicative of where our society stands with regard to our ideal of womanhood, it would seem that Vanessa Williams's selection in September 1983 (as well as other women of color after her) suggests that our culture is more willing to see women of (at least a little) color in this role of cultural ideal. On the other hand, Williams's resignation nine months into her reign after publication of "provocative" photos in the magazine, *Penthouse*, provides a most fascinating illustration of the pageant's marking by what Irigaray describes as a further assignment of woman to a double movement of exhibition and chaste retreat. The pageant itself features this double movement. It encourages the contestants to exhibit their bodies, but from a distance, and only carefully veiled by clothing designed to frame the exhibit perfectly and demurely. When it turns out that the winner has violated this double movement by stripping herself for public view thereby ending the mystery and revealing "the horror of nothing to see," she must give up her crown for violating her role as "our Ideal."

46. See esp. Giddings, 314–24.

47. Gloria Naylor's novel, *Linden Hills* (New York: Ticknor & Fields, 1985; Penguin Books, 1986), offers an illustration of that very conflict, although its protagonists are not members of radical groups. The novel is set in a middle-class black neighborhood. One of the principal characters is a woman who leaves her professional career and independent lifestyle to become a submissive wife to a man. She takes his name and bears his children all in what she perceives to be the best interests of her race. She finds herself in an all too literal prison, her husband's basement.

48. One of the most blatant examples occured around Shahrazad Ali's highly controversial book, *The Blackman's Guide to Understanding the Blackwoman* (Philadelphia: Civilized Publications, 1990). According to the *Philadelphia Inquirer* (Amy S. Rosenberg, "Book Spawns Controversy among Blacks," 22 June 1990, 1-C and 4-C), Ali (a woman, amazingly enough) writes, "The Blackwoman is

out of control. . . . Rise Blackman, and take your rightful place as ruler of the universe and everything in it. Including the Blackwoman" (1-C). She describes black women as suffering from "self-inflicted nearly psychotic insecurity" as a result of slavery "when our men did not protect us" (1-C).

49. Most recently, see Robin Wiegman, *American Anatomies: Theorizing Race and Gender* (Durham, N.C.: Duke University Press, 1995), chap. 1.

50. For a recent philosophical account of the phenomenon of invisibility as described by Ralph Ellison, Franz Fanon, and others, see Lewis R. Gordon, "Existential Dynamics of Theorizing Black Invisibility" in Gordon, *Existence in Black*, 67–79. I heard an interview on National Public Radio in the spring of 1991 where the interviewee noted that Hollywood directors for years refused to film black actors on the incredible grounds that they would not show up on film. I also recall black students at my graduate school reporting being treated by white students as though they were invisible.

51. Cornel West, *Prophesy Deliverance: An African-American Revolutionary Christianity* (Philadelphia: Westminster Press, 1982), 48–64.

52. See Sander Gilman, "Black Bodies, White Bodies: Toward an Iconography of Female Sexuality in Late Nineteenth-Century Art, Medicine, and Literature," in *"Race," Writing, and Difference*, edited by Henry Louis Gates, Jr. (Chicago: University of Chicago Press, 1985), 223–61.

53. Patricia Huntington also sees this as the fundamental limit to Irigaray's usefulness in thinking race. "Nothing in Irigaray's privileging the feminine as the key to unlocking these ideologies encourages white feminist theorists to grapple with their racial locus" ("Fragmentation, Race, and Gender," 197).

54. *Sexes et parentés* (Paris: Éditions de Minuit, 1987) has been translated as *Sexes and Genealogies*, translated by Gillian Gill (New York: Columbia University Press, 1993). Hereafter *Sexes and Genealogies* will be referred to as *SG*. An earlier version of this portion of my argument appeared in my "Crossing the Boundaries" in Holland, *Feminist Interpretations of Jacques Derrida*.

55. The particularly relevant essays for my discussion here are "Sexual Difference," "The Envelope," "An Ethics of Sexual Difference," and "The Love of the Other." In this context, it is interesting to note that Irigaray reads the pronouncements of the death of God made by Nietzsche and Heidegger not as proclamations of the final disappearance of divinity altogether, but as holding out the possibility of the coming of new deities ("The Love of the Other" in *An Ethics of Sexual Difference*, 140).

56. Grosz argues that Irigaray's turn to discourse about the divine moves away from concerns about women's subjectivity. It seems clear to me that Irigaray thinks women's ability to enter into genuine exchanges with each other and with men rests upon being subjects in their own right (as defined by Irigaray). See especially "Divine Women" and "Belief Itself," but also "The Universal as Mediation" and "Each Sex Must Have Its Own Rights" in *SG*.

57. See esp. Grosz's "Irigaray and the Divine" in *Transfigurations*.

58. A full exploration and assessment of Irigaray's use of religious motifs lies outside the scope of this essay, but the fact that Irigaray's failure to maintain woman's differing in such a context signals the necessity for whitefeminist theology to take on her work. In another essay (where an earlier version of this reading of Irigaray on religion appears), I argue that reading Derrida on

religion as Irigaray's *supplément* undercuts some of these disturbing tendencies. See my "Crossing the Boundaries" in *Feminist Interpretations of Derrida*.

59. Irigaray asserts sexual difference's claim to priority in the opening sentence of "Sexual Difference," the first essay in *An Ethics of Sexual Difference*. Noting that Heidegger suggested that each era confronts a particular question, Irigaray identifies sexual difference as the question for our epoch. (In addition to the translation by Burke and Gill, "Sexual Difference" is also translated by Séan Hand in *French Feminist Thought: A Reader*, edited by Toril Moi [Oxford: Basil Blackwell, 1987]. Hand's translation is reprinted in *The Irigaray Reader*, edited and with an introduction by Margaret Whitford [Oxford: Basil Blackwell, 1991]). Chanter argues (rightly, I think) that this applies to feminism as much as it does to any aspect of culture. As I noted in the introduction, she reads Irigaray as offering a Heideggerian critique of feminism. Just as philosophy obscured and forgot the question of Being, according to Heidegger, so feminism has tended to obscure and forget the question of sexual difference. Chanter identifies feminism's dominance by a politics of equality and by the sex / gender distinction as symptoms of its forgetting of its own question (*Ethics of Eros*, 131, 230).

60. Irigaray's later work will extend this differential accounting to relationships between men and women. See, e.g., the closing pages of *L'oubli de l'air chez Martin Heidegger*.

Chapter 5

1. In addition to texts cited in chap.1 below, see, e.g., John D. Caputo, *Against Ethics: Contributions to a Poetics of Obligation with Constant Reference to Deconstruction* (Bloomington: Indiana University Press, 1993); Charles Scott, *On the Advantages and Disadvantages, Ethics and Politics* (Bloomington: Indiana University Press, 1996). I discuss work by Bernasconi and Criterlay below.

2. Tina Chanter builds her account of Irigaray's relationship to Derrida through this same intertextual network. It is an important nexus, since sexual (in)difference constitutes the terrain of their encounter. One of Derrida's readings of Levinas approaches him from the (non)place of the sexually differentiated other (see "At This Very Moment Here I Am," in Bernasconi and Critchley, 11–48). Some of Irigaray's work on Levinas also addresses Derrida (for Irigaray on Levinas, see "The Fecundity of the Caress" in *An Ethics of Sexual Difference*). For discussions of this nexus, see Chanter, 207–24 and 231–39 and Critchley, chap. 3.

3. Although I cannot develop this point here, Irigaray suggests problems with this approach, at least for feminism. She argues that to start with the ethical-in-general is to have always already bypassed sexual difference. If it arises at all, it will arise at a derivative level (at the ontic rather than ontological level, to use Heideggerian language). See Irigaray's *An Ethics of Sexual Difference*, especially the chapter, "An Ethics of Sexual Difference," 116–29. I would extend Irigaray's point to racial difference as well.

4. Robert Bernasconi, "Politics beyond Humanism: Mandela and the Struggle against Apartheid," in *Working through Derrida*, edited by Gary Madison (Evanston, Ill.: Northwestern University Press, 1993), 95–119.

5. Derrida, "The Ends of Man," in *Margins of Philosophy*, 109–36. For details

on the impact of the revisions, see Bernasconi, "Politics beyond Humanism," in Madison, 100–101.

6. A thorough discussion of feminists who raise such questions is found in chaps. 2 and 3 above.

7. Here Derrida has in mind especially Heidegger's "Letter on Humanism" (see *Martin Heidegger: Basic Writings*, edited by David Farrell Krell [New York: Harper & Row, 1977], 193–242), which traces the development of the concept of man from its early roots in Greek philosophy through Husserl. Derrida admires this analysis very much. Heidegger's success at exposing the roots of humanism makes it all the more remarkable that its project succeeds in marking his own work.

8. The logic here is, as Derrida notes, that of making the implicit explicit, i.e., of unveiling. In *Sein und Zeit*, Heidegger unveils *Dasein*'s most primordial structures that underlie *Dasein*'s everyday existence-as-human-being. The proximity (indeed inseparability) of the question of being and *Dasein* continues into Heidegger's later work. I would argue that the existential analytic of *Dasein* undergoes a *rélève* itself in the motif of the clearing where truth/Being gives itself for thinking. The importance of unveiling (and withdrawal) for Heidegger's rethinking of truth as *aletheia* and the *es gibt* of Being immediately comes to mind. That recollection also calls up Derrida's allusions to Heidegger and the *es gibt* in *Spurs* as well as the entirety of his discussion of unveiling and the *es gibt* in relation to woman-as-truth. All I can do here is to point to the resonance of this *solicitation* of Heidegger with the thematics of Derrida's *solicitation* of Nietzsche and recognize that moving to the problematics of subjectivity does not mean abandoning (or evading) the sites of the play of gender in previous chapters on Derrida. I will follow out other indications that the territory remains the same as the argument proceeds. To follow this one is beyond the scope of the present work.

9. John Llewelyn also reads "The Ends of Man" as developing a complex account of man's telos in several senses: "Ends" wants to think man as finite, man's telos as goal as infinite, and man as directed toward his telos in both senses (death and goal). Finitude also takes on particular meaning as abyssally located by *différance* in history in the question, Who are we? Stating a "we," defining a "we," implies a mastery that is not achievable. While Llewellyn notes that Derrida situates his essay in France in 1968, he has nothing to say about the specific role of politics in Derrida's thinking of man's telos (see Llewelyn, 37–40).

10. It is interesting to note that the United States is itself a product of this expansion. It carries out its inheritance with vigor both on its own shores (from its dealings with Native Americans, to its importation of Africans as slaves, to its immigration laws, which both limit legal immigration and allow—through leaks, to be sure—thousands of illegal immigrants to come in to serve as a source of cheap labor) and abroad. The days of overt colonialization are virtually over, but U.S. foreign policy seems designed to preserve its status as both a military and economic superpower that controls, to the degree that it can and by whatever means necessary (from diplomacy, to embargoes, to illegal arms deals, to outright violence to special deals for U.S.-based multinational corporations), the status of other nations' relationships to it. For example, the

United States consistently ignores human rights violations by countries it considers strategically important and friendly in order to ensure that its interests are protected and furthered. Surely this constitutes a place where the concept of *man* reaches its limit.

11. It is also interesting to look at the assassinations of King and Malcolm X from the perspective of their special status in relation to the white community. King's public reception by whites was that of the heroic spokesperson for the movement. In some white circles, he firmly occupied the place of man; indeed, for some he embodied its ideal. Perhaps that very status (and the visibility that it reflected) made him a particularly appealing target for the forces of assassination. Malcolm X, on the other hand, was viewed by the white community largely as an agitator for violence. That would both make him more obviously threatening *and* simultaneously relatively easy to dismiss as an extremist. Given this context, the timing of Malcolm X's assassination is noteworthy. It occurred while he was working for the more universal image of "brotherhood," which only appeared possible to him after his pilgrimage to Mecca where he saw true humanity exhibited by Muslims of all ethnic backgrounds. Thus, when Malcolm X comes to the point of envisioning the possibility of the universalization of man (at least for men across ethnic and national lines), he is eliminated. I am not proposing a Great White Conspiracy theory here (I am, e.g., aware that members of Elijah Muhammed's Nation of Islam were convicted of the murder, although some question the quality of justice they received). I am merely pointing out what one might call the discursive screen against which these events can be read.

12. The texts under discussion here are Jacques Derrida, "Racism's Last Word" (translated by Peggy Kamuf, *Critical Inquiry* 12 [autumn 1985]: 290–99; reprinted in Gates's *"Race," Writing, and Difference*, 329–38); Anne McClintock and Rob Nixon, "No Names Apart: The Separation of Word and History in Derrida's 'Le dernier mot du racisme' " (*Critical Inquiry* 13 [autumn 1986]: 140–54; reprinted in *"Race," Writing, and Difference*, 339–53); Jacques Derrida, "But beyond . . . (Open Letter to Anne McClintock and Rob Nixon)" (translated by Peggy Kamuf, *Critical Inquiry* 13 [autumn 1986]: 155–70; reprinted in *"Race," Writing, and Difference*, 354–69) and "The Laws of Reflection: For Nelson Mandela in Admiration" (translated by Mary Ann Caws and Isabelle Lorenz, in *For Nelson Mandela*, edited by Jacques Derrida and Mustapha Tlili [New York: Seaver Books, Henry Holt, 1987], 13–42). Subsequent references to these essays will be as "Last Word," "No Names," "Beyond," and "Laws of Reflection," respectively (pagination for "Last Word," "No Names," and "Beyond" refer to that found in the Gates volume).

13. By that, I mean that Britain helped itself to the homelands of indigenous people and redrew boundaries, established colonial governments with a western legal system, etc., all of which became South Africa. I do not mean that there was nothing in that place before South Africa came into existence; rather, colonialism overwrote/overrode what was there (people, communities, ways of living, etc.).

14. McClintock and Nixon identify this phrase as a symptom of either Derrida's willful ignorance of racism as a worldwide phenomenon or his naiveté with regard to apartheid's links to other racisms. Bernasconi argues that Der-

rida is drawing on Heidegger's thinking of "end" in the sense of completion ("Politics beyond Humanism," 104–6). I concur with both Bernasconi's point and with Derrida's defense of himself against McClintock and Nixon's charges. Derrida's invocation of apartheid as racism's last word accords with my use of the multivalency of "end" throughout this essay. To call apartheid the "last word" in racism is to link it with other racisms by identifying it with racism's telos; "apartness" constitutes the logic of racism from its inception. Its inception, as this analysis is showing, is hardly limited to the boundaries of South Africa. South Africa is racism's last word insofar as South Africa constitutes a place where that logic reaches its greatest fulfillment (in that it becomes the law of the land).

15. The complex series of laws that grew up in a very short time to provide the machinery of enforcement for apartheid daily reenacted the violence of South Africa's creation.

16. As McClintock and Nixon note, the ethnic groupings of the Bantustans were largely artificial divisions created or exaggerated by the apartheid government—a "divide and keep conquered" strategy with deep western roots ("No Names," 342–46).

17. The former South African government, ever on the alert for ways to clean up apartheid's image in order to maintain important economic and strategic alliances, compared its "homeland" system to the relationships between the European nation-states. Each European country represents a relatively homogeneous ethnic collectivity. The Bantustans, they argued, were similar collectivities. Thus, the problems faced by South Africa, its government argued, were like those faced by any confederation—even a loose one, like Europe–of different ethnicities/nationalities. Conflicting interests will always disrupt attempts at harmonious relations. Although the former government glossed over the substantial differences between Europe and South Africa, McClintock and Nixon argue that this linguistic disguise worked on European and U.S. governments.

18. I use this term "movements of resistance" in order to emphasize the discursive screen against which specific political movements (the African National Congress's work, organizations against apartheid in this country, etc.) appear. These movements enact not only political resistance, but also resist the discursive forces and structures that fund/found political oppression and repression. I describe Mandela as a figure of resistance because of the way I will argue that the figure of Mandela functions in Derrida's text.

19. Nelson Mandela, *The Struggle Is My Life* (London: International Defence and Aid for Southern Africa, 1978).

20. Derrida also notes that Christianity funds the energies of much of that resistance ("Last Word," 336). Thus, Christianity also stands within the site of contestation under discussion here.

21. For a complementary account of the figure of the law in Derrida's reading of Mandela and its relationship to Derrida on politics, see Leonard Lawlor, "From the Trace to the Law: Derridean Politics" in *Philosophy and Social Criticism* 15, no. 1 (1989): 1–15, esp. 7–12.

22. Mandela, 141; cited by Derrida (with emphasis added) in "Laws of Reflection," 24.

23. Robert Bernasconi points out ways that Derrida could have further sub-stantiated his point here. Bernasconi argues that Derrida ultimately reinscribes Mandela within western political and metaphysical discourse by pulling Man-dela too tightly into Rousseau's orbit. Derrida reduces Mandela's appeal to conscience to individualism and reads his appeal to a new South Africa in terms of social contract theory. Both readings, Bernasconi claims, miss ways that an African context resists these terms and takes them in other directions. See "Politics beyond Humanism," 108–15.

24. Derrida, *De l'espirit* (Paris, Galilée, 1987), 86–87; *Of Spirit: Heidegger and the Question,* translated by Geoffrey Bennington and Rachel Bowlby (Chicago: University of Chicago Press, 1989), 55. Quoted by Bernasconi in "Politics Be-yond Humanism," 117.

25. This assignation bears all too close a resemblance to strategies followed by both the Civil Rights movement and the black power movements, as ana-lyzed by Paula Giddings. Both of these movements were conflicted over the place of women's issues in relation to issues of racial justice. More often than not, women's issues took a back seat to issues deemed more universal. See pt. 3 of Giddings's book.

26. See discussion of Spelman in chap. 1 above.

27. In the late 1980s evidence came to light that also tainted one of Derrida's American followers, Paul de Man, with complicity with Nazism. For many, this conclusively consigned deconstruction to the no-man's-land of the antieth-ical. For different views on this controversy's effects, see Paul Morrison, *The Poetics of Fascism: Ezra Pound, T. S. Eliot, Paul de Man* (New York: Oxford Uni-versity Press, 1996), 109–45; and Critchley, 188–200.

28. "*Geschlecht II:* Heidegger's Hand," in *Deconstruction and Philosophy: The Texts of Jacques Derrida,* edited by John Sallis (Chicago: University of Chicago Press, 1987), 161–96. Subsequent references to this essay will occur as *Geschlecht II,* or *GII.*

29. It is, I would argue, yet another indication of the depth to which Heideg-ger's work is shaped by its German idiom. Although it is common to speak of Heidegger's supposed *Kehre* as a "turn to language," any careful reader of *Sein und Zeit* would realize that language was always already of vital concern to Heidegger even in his phenomenological "phase." The care with which he chooses words and exploits the flexibility inherent in the layers of their mean-ing is crucial to the success of the existential analytic of *Dasein.* In that respect, *Sein und Zeit* is very much a German work. The complexities of German gram-mar and the resonances between words are crucial to thinking what Heidegger wants to think. Much of this is lost in Macquarrie's translation (which, like the French translations to which Derrida refers in "The Ends of Man," leans too far toward existentialism). Joan Stambaugh's recently published translation sacrifices smoothness in English for a closer, if more awkward, translation of key terms in Heidegger's lexicon (see Martin Heidegger, *Being and Time: A Translation of Sein und Zeit,* translated by Joan Stambaugh [Albany: State Uni-versity of New York Press, 1996]). See also David Krell's discussion of the *Kehre* in his introductions to Heidegger's introduction to *Sein und Zeit* (translated by Joan Stambaugh, J. Glenn Gray, David Krell), "On the Essence of Truth," (translated by John Sallis), and "The End of Philosophy and the Task of Think-

ing," (translated by Joan Stambaugh) in *Martin Heidegger: Basic Writings*, 38–40, 114–16, 370–72, respectively.

30. See Derrida's analysis of Heidegger's rectorship address in *Of Spirit*, 31–46. Derrida notes an "inflammation" of another uniquely German term, *Geist* (which carries hefty German philosophical baggage of its own) in the address. Given by Heidegger on the occasion of his assumption of the rectorship of the University of Freiburg, the address lays out his vision of a German university and its place in the renewal of Germany. For the text of Heidegger's speech, see Martin Heidegger, "The Self-Assertion of the German University," in *Martin Heidegger and National Socialism: Questions and Answers*, edited by Günther Neske and Emil Kettering, translated by Lisa Harries (New York: Paragon House, 1990), 5–13.

31. Martin Heidegger, *What Is Called Thinking?* translated by Fred D. Wieck and J. Glenn Gray (New York: Harper & Row, 1968), 16; as quoted by Derrida in *GII*, 168.

32. Heidegger, ibid., 16; as quoted by Derrida in *GII*, 174.

33. Heidegger's polemic against technology rests on its obscuring of what man essentially is. Technology treats man like a being-present-to-hand (*Zuhandensein*), a mode of *Dasein*'s having-to-do-with, which is appropriate for *Dasein*'s dealings with tools, perhaps, but not for its dealings with other *Daseins* (whose essence it is to dwell with Being).

34. The implications I draw out in the following pages are my own. Donna Haraway attempts to establish the historical sweep of the affiliation between racism (and, interestingly, sexism) and the distinction between man and ape in her book, *Primate Visions: Gender, Race, and Nature in the World of Modern Science* (New York: Routledge, 1991). As I will note momentarily, some African American theorists draw similar connections. For an overview of the link between apes and racist ideology, see chap. 1 of George Mosse's *Toward the Final Solution: A History of European Racism* (New York: Howard Fertig, 1978).

35. The cover of the guide for the exhibition, "Degenerate Music" (Dusseldorf, 1938), provides a particularly potent and public example. The figure on the cover, a dark-skinned saxophone player with an apelike face, wears a large hoop earring in one ear and a Star of David on the lapel of his tuxedo. "Degenerate Music" traveled with the infamous exhibition entitled "Degenerate Art" to several cities. Through these exhibitions, the Nazis denounced and denigrated what had been avant garde culture in Germany (modernist art and music, including jazz). See Michael Meyer, "A Musical Façade for the Third Reich" in *"Degenerate Art": The Fate of the Avant-Garde in Nazi Germany*, edited by Stephanie Barron, 171–183; illus. 181 (New York: Harry N. Abrams; Los Angeles: Los Angeles County Museum of Art, 1991).

36. *"Geschlecht: Sexual Difference, Ontological Difference," Research in Phenomenology* 13 (1983): 65–83. Subsequent references to this piece will occur as *Geschlecht I*, or *GI*.

37. Tina Chanter's assessment is the most positive. She reads *Geschlecht I* as uncovering a sexual differentiating that is not reducible to a binary. She argues that retrieving such dispersibility would not have been possible without feminism. Derrida is somewhat amiss, in her view, for failing to acknowledge that debt sufficiently. See "On Not Reading Derrida's Text," in Feder et al., 97–99.

38. See Grosz's essay, "Ontology and Equivocation" in Holland's *Feminist Interpretations of Derrida*, 73–101. See Oliver, *Womanizing Nietzsche*, chap. 3. Oliver discusses *Geschlecht I* (specifically on 62–65). She argues that, in describing dispersibility as "dissemination," Derrida has enclosed *Dasein*'s sexual differing within a masculine figure. I do not see that this word exercises that kind of control over Derrida's text. On the other hand, as I will say below, thinking through dispersibility in ways that can be productive for feminism certainly requires thinking through specifically female/feminine figures—as well as through other sorts of figures.

39. On sexes and genders, see, e.g., Michel Foucault's *History of Sexuality*, vol. 1 (New York: Vintage, 1980); Thomas Laqueur's *Making Sex: Body and Gender from the Greeks to Freud* (Cambridge, Mass.: Harvard University Press, 1992); and Denise Riley's *"Am I That Name?"* For a critical philosophical account of the historical conditions that produced the (pseudo)concept of race as a biological artifact, see Naomi Zack, *Race and Mixed Race* (Philadelphia: Temple University Press, 1993). She summarizes this argument briefly in "Race, Life, Death, Identity, Tragedy, and Good Faith" in Gordon, 99–109.

40. Thus, Braidotti's and Cornell's misreadings of Derrida's resting place could be argued to parallel the anthropologistic readings of *Dasein*. The textual grounds for them lie in Derrida's text just as the textual grounds for the misreadings of *Dasein* lie in Heidegger's texts.

Chapter 6

1. Sarah Kofman, "Ça cloche," in *Les fins de l'homme: À partir de travail de Jacques Derrida* (Paris: Galilée, 1981): 89–116.

2. Certainly Ruth Frankenberg's book, *White Women, Race Matters: The Social Construction of Whiteness* (Minneapolis: University of Minnesota Press, 1993) constitutes one approach to this issue. Frankenburg uses social scientific methods to elicit information about how whiteness as a racial identity is currently experienced by white women. Robin Wiegman's *American Anatomies* provides yet another approach. Wiegman investigates the history that produced the paradigm of "blacks and women" that has so dominated and troubled identity politics.

3. Henry Louis Gates, Jr., *Figures in Black: Words, Signs, and the "Racial" Self* (New York: Oxford University Press, 1987), 14. Hereafter referred to as *Figures*.

4. Gates also recounts stories of grand experiments in Europe and the United States in which men of African descent were sent to universities to see whether or not they were capable of learning. He notes many successes among these experiments (including the famous abolitionist and author, Frederick Douglass). In Gates's words, these men were not "competing, as it were, with Newton; [but rather] distinguishing [themselves] from the apes" (*Figures*, 14).

5. Literacy could significantly alter a slave's status. Gates recalls the numerous stories of slaves like Job Ben Solomon who, by writing a letter to his father (in Arabic) which wound up in James Oglethorpe's possession, "literally wrote his way out of slavery" (*Figures*, 13). Oglethorpe, the founder of the colony of Georgia, was so impressed with Solomon's writing skills that he bought the slave's freedom.

6. Barbara Christian, *Black Women Novelists: The Development of a Tradition, 1892–1976* (Westport, Conn.: Greenwood Press, 1980).

7. Harriet Jacobs [Linda Brent], *Incidents in the Life of a Slave Girl, Written by Herself* (edited by Lydia Maria Child, 1861; reprint Cambridge, Mass.: Harvard University Press, 1987). Edited and with introduction by Jean Fagan Yellin.

8. Spillers, "Kinship and Resemblances" in *Feminist Studies* 11, no. 1 (spring 1985): 110–25.

9. Higginbotham's discussion is drawn from A. Leon Higginbotham Jr.'s article, "Race, Sex, Education and Missouri Jurisprudence: *Shelly v. Kraemer* in a Historical Perspective," *Washington University Law Quarterly* 67 [1989]: 684–85; see E. Higginbotham, 257–58.

10. See also Patricia Williams's meditation on property law as it applied to slave women (15–20, 156–65).

11. Gates proposes Signifyin(g) as a way of describing the relationship between African American literature and the figures and conventions of white literary forms. The term names a set of discursive practices indigenous to African American culture from its streets to its bookshelves. At the same time, the term itself "signifies" on the appropriation of deconstruction by literary critical theory by recalling the (so-called) explosion of the correspondence between signifier and signified by Derrida, which has yielded poststructuralism. Signifyin(g) is intertextual. The signifier takes material given to him or to her by the person about to be signified on and, through a strategic repetition of that text, tropes or reverses its meaning, often with the result of poking fun at the signified. See *Figures*, 236–76, and Gates's *The Signifying Monkey: A Theory of Afro-American Literary Criticism* (New York: Oxford University Press, 1988).

12. Valerie Smith, *Self-Discovery and Authority in Afro-American Narrative* (Cambridge, Mass.: Harvard University Press, 1987), 28–43.

13. Claudia Tate, "Allegories of Black Female Desire; or, Rereading Nineteenth-Century Sentimental Narratives of Black Female Authority," in *Changing Our Own Words: Essays on Criticism, Theory and Writing by Black Women*, edited by Cheryl Wall (New Brunswick, N.J.: Rutgers University Press, 1989): 98–126; esp. 109.

14. Minrose C. Gwin, "Green-Eyed Monsters of the Slavocracy: Jealous Mistresses in Two Slave Narratives," in *Conjuring: Black Women, Fiction, and Literary Tradition*, edited by Marjorie Pryse and Hortense J. Spillers (Bloomington: Indiana University Press, 1985), 39–52.

15. Jacobs's portrayal of Brent as mother similarly challenges race as the line of demarcation separating blackness from the figure of the true woman.

16. Frances Smith Foster, *Witnessing Slavery: The Development of Ante-bellum Slave Narratives* (Westport, Conn.: Greenwood Press, 1979), 131; cited by Carby, 32.

17. Claudia Tate, "Allegories of Black Female Desire," 98–126.

18. Glenda Gilmore, *Gender and Jim Crow: Women and the Politics of White Supremacy in North Carolina, 1896–1920* (Chapel Hill: University of North Carolina Press, 1996).

19. See Abel et al., *Female Subjects;* and Ann Pellegrini, *Performance Anxieties: Staging Psychoanalysis, Staging Race* (New York: Routledge, 1997).

20. Hortense Spillers, " 'The Permanent Obliquity of an In(pha)llibly

Straight': In the Time of the Daughters and the Fathers," in Wall, 127–49. Lewis R. Gordon argues that psychoanalysis cannot understand black men and women. As he puts it, their "alienation is not neurotic. It is the historical reality of a phobogenic complex" (Gordon, "Existential Dynamics of Theorizing Black Invisibility," 75).

21. Hortense Spillers, "Mama's Baby, Papa's Maybe: An American Grammar Book," *Diacritics* 17, no. 2 (1987); reprinted in *Within the Circle: An Anthology of African American Literary Criticism from the Harlem Renaissance to the Present*, edited by Angelyn Mitchell (Durham, N.C.: Duke University Press, 1994), 454–81. Hereafter referred to as "Mama's Baby."

22. Lewis R. Gordon also offers a highly complex analysis of the intersections of race, gender, and sexuality that the legacy of slavery has left behind. See his "Race, Sex, and Matrices of Desire in an Antiblack World: An Essay in Phenomenology and Social Role" in *Race/Sex: Their Sameness, Difference, and Interplay*, edited by Naomi Zack (New York: Routledge Press, 1997): 119–32.

23. Angela Davis, Patricia Hill Collins, and Patricia Williams also criticize this concept of African American families and mothers.

24. Naomi Zack offers a stinging indictment of the impact of slavery's legacy on current stereotypes of black vs. white mothers. "White women with more than two or three children are viewed as nurturing, self-sacrificing, . . . as well as not very smart. But, holding social class constant, black women who have more than two to three children are popularly stereotyped as irresponsible, selfish, over-sexed, and scheming" ("The American Sexualization of Race" in Zack, 145–56; quote on 151). She argues further that the children themselves are valued differently. "These days, what was once eagerly created, slaveowner's capital, i.e., black progeny, has been reconceptualized (recathected) as the unearned plunder that black women, out of lust and greed, extract from an otherwise financially solvent system" (151).

25. Several African American feminist theorists take critical note of the effects of this economy on African American women. In another essay, "Interstices: A Small Drama of Words" (in *Pleasure and Danger: Exploring Female Sexuality*, edited by Carole S. Vance [Boston: Routledge, 1984]: 73–100), Spillers argues that African American women's desire is silent and silenced. In "Black (W)holes," Evelynn Hammonds also identifies sexuality as an area of discussion that has been silenced.

26. See, esp., Gwin.

27. See also Spillers's reading of *Uncle Tom's Cabin*, which yields a complex account of race, sex, gender as imbricated in the novel's rendering of white women's desire. See Hortense Spillers, "Changing the Letter: The Yokes, the Jokes of Discourse, or, Mrs. Stowe, Mr. Reed," in *Slavery and the Literary Imagination*, edited by Deborah McDowell and Arnold Rampersad (Baltimore: Johns Hopkins University Press, 1989), 25–61.

28. Certainly, taking on these projects would draw on feminist and antiracist work on these scholars that already exists. Race figures into this context as well, especially in the figure of so-called primitive religion. This figure often occupied the lowest point in the teleological constructions of religious development that were common within the discipline of religious studies as it emerged in the modern period.

29. See, e.g., brief indications of Christianity's involvement in racism and antiracism (n. 21) in chapter 5 above.

30. See my "Divine Speculations in Derrida and Irigaray," presented to the annual meeting of the Society for Phenomenology and Existential Philosophy, Seattle, Wash., 1 October 1994.

31. See Jacques Derrida, "Khora," translated by Ian McLeod, in *On the Name*, Crossing Aesthetics (Stanford, Calif.: Stanford University Press, 1995), 89–127.

32. For Irigaray's reading of Nietzsche, see *Marine Lover of Friedrich Nietzsche*; for her reading of Heidegger, see *L'oubli de l'air*. For discussions of Irigaray on Nietzsche and Heidegger, see Ellen Mortenson, "'*Le féminin*' *and Nihilism: Reading Irigaray with Nietzsche and Heidegger* (Oslo: Scandinavia University Press, in press), and her essay, "Women's Untruth and 'Le féminin': Reading Luce Irigaray with Nietzsche and Heidegger" in Burke et al., 211–28. See also Tina Chanter, esp. chap. 4; Kelly Oliver, *Womanizing Nietzsche*, chap. 4; and my "Questions of Proximity."

33. I develop this argument in "Questions of Proximity." Here, I borrow the French *genres* to prevent assignations of man and woman to either side of the nature/culture divide. I also preserve these figures' connections to textuality, a point that has been central to my argument.

34. Jacques Derrida, *The Gift of Death*, translated by David Wills (Chicago: University of Chicago Press, 1995).

35. Derrida's interpreters would give mixed response to this question. John Caputo suggests that it might be considered the brother text to *Memoirs of the Blind: The Self Portrait and Other Ruins* (translated by Pascale-Anne Brault and Michael Naas [Chicago: University of Chicago Press, 1993]). See Caputo's *The Prayers and Tears of Jacques Derrida: Religion without Religion* [Bloomington: Indiana University Press, 1997], 310, insofar as *Memoirs* and "Circumfession" can be read as figuring masculine and feminine figures, respectively. Kelly Oliver notes approvingly that, in *The Gift of Death*, Derrida asks after the absence of women in the Abraham/Isaac story. However, she also argues that Derrida fails to take this inquiry as far as she would like. See Kelly Oliver, "Fatherhood and the Promise of Ethics," *Diacritics* 27, no. 1 (1997): 45–57.

36. When asked whether "the theoretical radicality of deconstruction [can] be translated into a radical political praxis," Derrida replies: "The available codes for taking such a political stance are not at all adequate to the radicality of deconstruction. . . . All of our political codes and terminologies still remain fundamentally metaphysical, regardless of whether they originate from the right or the left" ("Deconstruction and the Other," *Dialogues with Contemporary Continental Thinkers: The Phenomenological Heritage*, edited by Richard Kearney [Manchester: Manchester University Press, 1984], 119). Derrida insists that this does not mean deconstruction is necessarily noncommitted. "The difficulty is to gesture in opposite directions at the same time: on the one hand to preserve a distance and suspicion with regard to the official political codes governing reality; on the other, to intervene here and now in a practical and *engaged* manner whenever the necessity arises" (120).

Works Cited

Abel, Elizabeth, Barbara Christian, and Helene Moglen, eds. *Female Subjects in Black and White: Race, Psychoanalysis, Feminism*. Berkeley and Los Angeles: University of California Press, 1997.

Alcoff, Linda. "Cultural Feminism versus Post-Structuralism: The Identity Crisis in Feminist Theory." *Signs* 13, no. 3 (spring 1988): 405–36.

Ali, Shahrazad. *The Blackman's Guide to Understanding the Blackwoman*. Philadelphia: Civilized Publications, 1990.

Allen, Jeffner, and Iris Marion Young, eds. The *Thinking Muse: Feminism and Modern French Philosophy*. Bloomington: Indiana University Press, 1989.

Altizer, Thomas J. J., Max A. Myers, Carl A. Raschke, Robert P. Scharlemann, Mark C. Taylor, and Charles E. Winquist. *Deconstruction and Theology*. New York: Crossroads, 1982.

Armour, Ellen T. "Divine Speculations in Derrida and Irigaray." Paper presented at the annual meeting of the Society for Phenomenology and Existential Philosophy, Seattle, October 1994.

———. "The (Im)possible Possibility of Theology without God." Paper presented to the Theology and Religious Reflection Section at the American Academy of Religion, Philadelphia, November 1995.

———. "Questions of Proximity: 'Woman's Place' in Derrida and Irigaray." *Hypatia* 12, no. 1 (winter 1997): 63–78.

Benhabib, Seyla, and Drucilla Cornell, eds. *Feminism as Critique*. Minneapolis: University of Minnesota Press, 1987.

Bennington, Geoffrey. *Jacques Derrida*. Chicago: University of Chicago Press, 1993.

Bernasconi, Robert. "Politics beyond Humanism: Mandela and the Struggle against Apartheid." In *Working through Derrida*, edited by Gary Madison, 95–119. Evanston, Ill.: Northwestern University Press, 1993.

———. "Seeing Double: *Destruktion* and Deconstruction." In *Dialogue and Deconstruction: The Gadamer-Derrida Encounter*, edited by Diane P. Michelfelder and Richard E. Palmer, 233–50. Albany: State University of New York Press, 1989.

Bernasconi, Robert, and Simon Critchley, eds. *Re-Reading Levinas*. Bloomington: Indiana University Press, 1991.

Braidotti, Rosi. *The Nomadic Subject: Embodiment and Sexual Difference in Contemporary Feminist Theory*. New York: Columbia University Press, 1994.

———. *Patterns of Dissonance*. New York: Routledge, 1991.

Brennan, Teresa, ed. *Between Feminism and Psychoanalysis*. New York: Routledge, 1989.

Briggs, Sheila. "The Politics of Identity and the Politics of Interpretation." *Union Seminary Quarterly Review* 143 (1989): 163–80.

———. "What Feminist Theology Is Saying about Race and Class." Antoinette Brown Lecture. Vanderbilt Divinity School, 19 March 1990.

Burke, Carolyn, Naomi Schor, and Margaret Whitford, eds. *Engaging with Irigaray*. New York: Columbia University Press, 1994.

Butler, Judith. *Bodies that Matter: On the Discursive Limits of "Sex."* New York: Routledge, 1993.

———. "Burning Acts: Injurious Speech." In *Deconstruction Is/in America: A New Sense of the Political*, edited by Anselm Haverkamp, 149–80. New York: New York University Press, 1995.

———. *Excitable Speech: A Politics of the Performative*. New York: Routledge, 1997.

———. *Gender Trouble: Feminism and the Subversion of Identity*. New York: Routledge, 1990.

———. *Psychic Life of Power: Theories in Subjection*. Stanford, Calif.: Stanford University Press, 1997.

Butler, Judith, and Joan Scott. *Feminists Theorize the Political*. New York: Routledge, 1992.

Cannon, Katie G. *Black Womanist Ethics*. American Academy of Religion Academy Series, no. 60. Atlanta: Scholars Press, 1988.

Caputo, John. *The Prayers and Tears of Jacques Derrida: Religion without Religion*. Bloomington: Indiana University Press, 1997.

Carby, Hazel V. *Reconstructing Womanhood: The Emergence of the Afro-American Woman Novelist*. New York: Oxford University Press, 1987.

Chanter, Tina. *Ethics of Eros: Irigaray's Rewriting of the Philosophers*. New York: Routledge, 1995.

Chopp, Rebecca. *The Power to Speak: Feminism, Language, God*. New York: Crossroad, 1989.

Christensen, Kimberly. " 'With Whom Do You Believe Your Lot Is Cast?' " White Feminists and Racism." *Signs* 22, no. 3 (spring 1997): 617–48.

Christian, Barbara. *Black Women Novelists: The Development of a Tradition, 1892–1980*. Westport, Conn.: Greenwood Press, 1980.

———. "The Race for Theory." In *Within the Circle: An Anthology of African American Literary Criticism from the Harlem Renaissance to the Present*, edited by Angelyn Mitchell, 348–59. Durham, N.C.: Duke University Press, 1994.

Clément, Catherine. *The Lives and Legends of Jacques Lacan*, translated by Arthur Goldhammer. New York: Columbia University Press, 1983.

Clément, Catherine, and Hélène Cixous. *The Newly Born Woman*, translated by Betsy Wing, with an introduction by Sandra M. Gilbert. Theory and History of Literature, no. 24. Minneapolis: University of Minnesota Press, 1986.

Cobb, John. "Two Types of Postmodernism: Deconstruction and Process." *Theology Today* 47 (July 1990): 149–58.

Collins, Patricia Hill. *Black Feminist Thought: Knowledge, Consciousness, and the Politics of Empowerment*. London: Harper Collins Academic Press, 1990.

Cooey, Paula M. *Religious Imagination and the Body: A Feminist Analysis*. New York: Oxford University Press, 1994.

Cornell, Drucilla. *Beyond Accommodation: Ethical Feminism, Deconstruction and the Law.* New York: Routledge, 1991.

―――. *The Imaginary Domain: Abortion, Pornography, and Sexual Harassment.* New York: Routledge, 1995.

―――. *Transformations: Recollective Imagination and Sexual Difference.* London: Routledge, 1993.

Coward, Harold, and Toby Foshay, eds. *Derrida and Negative Theology.* Albany: State University of New York Press, 1992.

Cox, L. Hughes. "The Paradox of the Limit, the Parable of the Raft, and Perennial Philosophy." *Listening* 24 (winter 1989): 20–28.

Critchley, Simon. *The Ethics of Deconstruction: Derrida and Levinas.* Cambridge, Mass.: Blackwell, 1992.

Daly, Mary. *Beyond God the Father: Toward a Philosophy of Women's Liberation.* Boston: Beacon Press, 1973.

―――. *The Church and the Second Sex.* New York: Harper & Row, 1968.

―――. *Gyn/Ecology: The Metaethics of Radical Feminism.* Boston: Beacon Press, 1978.

―――. *Pure Lust: Elemental Feminist Philosophy.* Boston: Beacon Press, 1984.

Davaney, Sheila Greeve. "The Limits of the Appeal to Women's Experience." In *Shaping New Vision: Gender and Values in American Culture,* edited by Clarissa W. Atkinson, Constance H. Buchanan, and Margaret R. Miles, 31–49. Harvard Women's Studies in Religion Series, no. 5. Ann Arbor: UMI Research Press, 1987.

Davis, Angela Y. *Women, Race, and Class.* New York: Random House, 1981.

de Lauretis, Teresa. "The Essence of the Triangle or, Taking the Risk of Essentialism Seriously: Feminist Theory in Italy, the U.S., and Britain." *differences: A Journal of Feminist Cultural Studies* 1 (summer 1989): 3–37.

―――. *The Practice of Love: Lesbian Sexuality and Perverse Desire.* Bloomington: Indiana University Press, 1994.

Derrida, Jacques. "But beyond . . . (Open Letter to Anne McClintock and Rob Nixon)," translated by Peggy Kamuf. *Critical Inquiry* 13 (autumn 1986): 155–70. Reprinted in *"Race," Writings, and Difference,* edited by Henry Louis Gates, Jr., 354–69. Chicago: University of Chicago Press, 1986.

―――. "Choreographies." An interview with Christie V. McDonald. *Diacritics* 12 (summer 1982): 66–76.

―――. "Deconstruction and the Other." In *Dialogues with Contemporary Continental Thinkers: The Phenomenological Heritage,* edited by Richard Kearney, 106–33. Manchester: Manchester University Press, 1984.

―――. *Dissemination,* translated by Barbara Johnson. Chicago: University of Chicago Press, 1981.

―――. *Éperons: Les styles de Nietzsche/Spurs: Nietzsche's Styles,* translated by Barbara Harlow. Chicago: University of Chicago Press, 1978; French/English version, 1979.

―――. "*Geschlecht:* Sexual Difference, Ontological Difference." *Research in Phenomenology* 13 (1983): 65–83.

―――. "*Geschlecht II:* Heidegger's Hand." In *Deconstruction and Philosophy: The Texts of Jacques Derrida,* edited by John Sallis, 161–96. Chicago: University of Chicago Press, 1987.

————. *The Gift of Death,* translated by David Wills. Chicago: University of Chicago Press, 1995.

————. *Given Time: I. Counterfeit Money,* translated by Peggy Kamuf. Chicago: University of Chicago Press, 1992.

————. *Glas.* Paris: Galilée, 1974.

————. "How to Avoid Speaking: Denials," translated by Ken Frieden. In *Derrida and Negative Theology,* edited by Harold Coward and Toby Foshay, 73–142. Albany: State University of New York Press, 1992. Originally published as "Comment ne pas parler: Dénégations," in *Psyché: Inventions de l'autre.* Paris; Galilée, 1987.

————. "The Law of Genre," translated by Avital Ronell. *Glyph* 7 (1980): 202–32.

————. "The Laws of Reflection: For Nelson Mandela in Admiration," translated by Mary Ann Caws and Isabelle Lorenz. In *For Nelson Mandela,* edited by Jacques Derrida and Mustapha Tlili, 13–42. New York: Seaver Books, Henry Holt, 1987.

————. "Living On: Borderlines," translated by James Hulbert. In *Deconstruction and Criticism,* edited by Harold Bloom. New York: Seabury Press, 1979.

————. *Margins of Philosophy,* translated by Alan Bass. Chicago: University of Chicago Press, 1982.

————. *Memoirs of the Blind: The Self Portrait and Other Ruins,* translated by Pascale-Anne Brault and Michael Naas. Chicago: University of Chicago Press, 1993.

————. *Of Grammatology.* Translated by Gayatri Chakravorty Spivak. Baltimore: Johns Hopkins University Press, 1976.

————. *Of Spirit: Heidegger and the Question,* translated by Geoffrey Bennington and Rachel Bowlby. Chicago: University of Chicago Press, 1989.

————. *On the Name.* Crossing Aesthetics Series. Stanford, Calif.: Stanford University Press, 1995.

————. *Positions,* translated by Alan Bass. Chicago: University of Chicago Press, 1981.

————. *The Post Card: From Socrates to Freud and Beyond,* translated by Alan Bass. Chicago: University of Chicago Press, 1987.

————. "Racism's Last Word," translated by Peggy Kamuf. *Critical Inquiry* 12 (autumn 1985): 290–99. Reprinted in Gates, *"Race," Writing and Difference,* 329–38.

————. "Roundtable on Translation." In *The Ear of the Other: Otobiography, Transference, Translation,* edited by Christie McDonald, 92–161. Translated by Peggy Kamuf. Lincoln: University of Nebraska Press, 1985.

————. "Women in the Beehive: A Seminar with Jacques Derrida." In *Men in Feminism,* edited by Alice Jardine and Paul Smith, 189–200. New York: Routledge, 1987.

————. *Writing and Difference,* translated by Alan Bass. Chicago: University of Chicago Press, 1978.

Derrida, Jacques, and Gerald Graff. "Afterword: Toward an Ethic of Discussion." In *Limited, Inc.,* 111–60. Evanston: Northwestern University Press, 1988.

Duchen, Claire. *Feminism in France: From May '68 to Mitterand*. London: Routledge & Kegan Paul, 1986.

DuCille, Ann. "The Occult of True Black Womanhood: Critical Demeanor and Black Feminist Studies." *Signs* 19, no. 3 (spring 1994): 591–629; reprinted in Abel, 21–56.

Farley, Wendy. *Eros for the Other: Retaining Truth in a Pluralistic World*. University Park: Pennsylvania State University Press, 1996.

Feder, Ellen K., Mary C. Rawlinson, and Emily Zakin, eds. *Derrida and Feminism: Recasting the Question of Woman*. New York: Routledge, 1997.

Foucault, Michel. *The History of Sexuality*, vol. 1. New York: Vintage, 1980.

Frankenberg, Ruth. *White Women, Race Matters: The Social Construction of Whiteness*. Minneapolis: University of Minnesota Press, 1993.

Freud, Sigmund. *The Standard Edition of the Complete Psychological Works of Sigmund Freud*, 24 vols. Edited by James Strachey. London: Hogarth Press, 1953–74.

Fulkerson, Mary McClintock. *Changing the Subject: Women's Discourses and Feminist Theology*. Philadelphia: Fortress Press, 1994.

Fuss, Diana. *Essentially Speaking: Feminism, Nature, and Difference*. New York: Routledge, 1989.

Gall, Robert S. "Of/From Theology and Deconstruction." *Journal of the American Academy of Religion* 58 (fall 1990): 413–37.

Gasché, Rodolphe. *Inventions of Difference: On Jacques Derrida*. Cambridge, Mass.: Harvard University Press, 1994.

———. *The Tain of the Mirror: Derrida and the Philosophy of Reflection*. Cambridge, Mass.: Harvard University Press, 1986.

Gatens, Moira. "A Critique of the Sex/Gender Distinction." In *A Reader in Feminist Knowledge*, edited by Sneja Gunew. London: Routledge, 1991.

———. *Imaginary Bodies: Ethics, Power, and Corporeality*. London: Routledge, 1996.

Gates, Henry Louis, Jr. *Figures in Black: Words, Signs, and the "Racial" Self*. New York: Oxford University Press, 1987.

———, ed. *"Race," Writing, and Difference*. Chicago: University of Chicago Press, 1986.

———. *The Signifying Monkey: A Theory of Afro-American Literary Criticism*. New York: Oxford University Press, 1988.

Giddings, Paula. *When and Where I Enter: The Impact of Black Women on Race and Sex in America*. New York: William Morrow, 1984; reprint, New York: Bantam Books, 1985.

Gilmore, Glenda. *Gender and Jim Crow: Women and the Politics of White Supremacy in North Carolina, 1896–1920*. Chapel Hill: University of North Carolina Press, 1996.

Gordon, Lewis R., ed. *Existence in Black: An Anthology of Black Existential Philosophy*. New York: Routledge, 1997.

Grant, Jacquelyn. *White Women's Christ and Black Women's Jesus: Feminist Christology and Womanist Response*. American Academy of Religion Academy Series, no. 64. Atlanta: Scholars Press, 1989.

Grosz, Elizabeth. *Jacques Lacan: A Feminist Introduction*. New York: Routledge, 1990.

——. *Sexual Subversions: Three French Feminists.* Winchester, Mass.: Unwin Hyman, 1989.

——. *Volatile Bodies: Toward a Corporeal Feminism.* Bloomington: Indiana University Press, 1994.

Hammonds, Evelynn. "Black (W)holes and the Geometry of Black Female Sexuality." *differences: A Journal of Feminist Cultural Studies* 6, nos. 2–3 (1994): 126–45.

Haraway, Donna. *Primate Visions: Gender, Race, and Nature in the World of Modern Science.* New York: Routledge, 1991.

Hart, Kevin. *The Trespass of the Sign: Deconstruction, Theology, and Philosophy.* Cambridge, England: Cambridge University Press, 1989.

Harvey, Irene. *Derrida and the Economy of Différance.* Bloomington: Indiana University Press, 1986.

Hegel, G. W. F. *Science of Logic,* translated by A. V. Miller. New York: Humanities Press, 1969.

Heidegger, Martin. *Being and Time,* translated by John Macquarrie and Edward Robinson. New York: Harper & Row, 1962.

——. *Being and Time: A Translation of "Sein und Zeit,"* translated by Joan Stambaugh. Albany: State University of New York Press, 1996.

——. *Martin Heidegger: Basic Writings.* Edited and with an introduction by David Farrell Krell. New York: Harper & Row, 1977.

——. *What Is Called Thinking?* translated by Fred D. Wieck and J. Glenn Gray. New York: Harper & Row, 1968.

Higginbotham, Evelyn Brooks. "African-American Women's History and the Metalanguage of Race." *Signs* 17, no. 2 (winter 1992): 251–74.

Hirsch, Marianne, and Evelyn Fox Keller, eds. *Conflicts in Feminism.* New York: Routledge, 1990.

Hirsh, Elizabeth, and Gary A. Olson. " 'Je—Luce Irigaray': A Meeting with Luce Irigaray," translated by Elizabeth Hirsh and Gaeton Brulotte. *Hypatia* 10, no. 2 (spring 1995): 93–114.

Holland, Nancy, ed. *Feminist Interpretations of Jacques Derrida.* University Park: Pennsylvania State University Press, 1997.

——. *Is Women's Philosophy Possible?* Savage, Md.: Rowan & Littlefield, 1990.

——. "The Treble Clef / t: Jacques Derrida and the Female Voice." *Philosophy and Culture: Proceedings of the Seventeenth World Congress of Philosophy,* 2:654–58. Montreal: Editions Montmorency, 1988.

Hollywood, Amy. "Transcending Bodies?" *Religious Studies Review,* vol. 25, no. 1 (January 1999), in press.

hooks, bell. *Ain't I a Woman: Black Women and Feminism.* Boston: South End Press, 1981.

——. *Yearnings: Race, Gender and Cultural Politics.* Boston: South End Press, 1990.

Huntington, Patricia. "Fragmentation, Race, and Gender: Building Solidarity in the Postmodern Era." In *Existence in Black: An Anthology of Black Existential Philosophy,* edited by Lewis R. Gordon, 185–202. New York: Routledge, 1997.

Hurston, Zora Neale. *Their Eyes Were Watching God.* Philadelphia: Lippincott, 1937; reprint, Urbana: University of Illinois Press, 1981.

Irigaray, Luce. *An Ethics of Sexual Difference*, translated by Carolyn Burke and Gillian C. Gill. Ithaca, N.Y.: Cornell University Press, 1993.

———. *L'oubli de l'air chez Martin Heidegger*. Paris: Éditions Minuit, 1983.

———. *Marine Lover of Friedrich Nietzsche*, translated by Gillian C. Gill. New York: Columbia University Press, 1991.

———. *Parler n'est jamais neutre*. Paris: Éditions Minuit, 1985.

———. *Sexes and Genealogies*, translated by Gillian C. Gill. New York: Columbia University Press, 1993.

———. *Speculum of the Other Woman*, translated by Gillian C. Gill. Ithaca, N.Y.: Cornell University Press, 1985.

———. *This Sex Which Is Not One*, translated by Catherine Porter and Carolyn Burke. Ithaca, N.Y.: Cornell University Press, 1985.

Jacobs, Harriet [Linda Brent]. *Incidents in the Life of a Slave Girl, Written by Herself*, edited by Lydia Maria Child. N.p., 1861. Reprint, edited and with introduction by Jean Fagan Yellin, Cambridge, Mass.: Harvard University Press, 1987.

Jardine, Alice. *Gynesis*. Ithaca, N.Y.: Cornell University Press, 1985.

Jardine, Alice, and Paul Smith, eds. *Men in Feminism*. New York: Methuen, 1987.

Johnson, Elizabeth A. *She Who Is: The Mystery of God in Feminist Theological Discourse*. New York: Crossroad, 1992.

Joy, Morny. "Derrida and Ricoeur: A Case of Mistaken Identity (and Difference)." *Journal of Religion* 68 (October 1988): 508–26.

———. "Equality or Divinity: A False Dichotomy?" *Journal of Feminist Studies in Religion* 6 (spring 1990): 9–24.

Kamuf, Peggy, ed. *A Derrida Reader: Between the Blinds*. New York: Columbia University Press, 1991.

Kim, C. W. Maggie, Susan M. St. Ville, and Susan M. Simonaitis, eds. *Transfigurations: Feminist Theology and the French Feminists*. Philadelphia: Fortress Press, 1993.

Kintz, Linda. "In-Different Criticism: The Deconstructive 'Parole.'" In *The Thinking Muse*, edited by Jeffner Allen and Iris Marion Young, 113–35. Bloomington: Indiana University Press, 1989.

Kofman, Sarah. "Ça cloche." In *Les fins de l'homme: À partir de travail de Jacques Derrida*, 89–116. Paris: Galilée, 1981.

Laqueur, Thomas. *Making Sex: Body and Gender from the Greeks to Freud*. Cambridge, Mass.: Harvard University Press, 1992.

Lawlor, Leonard. "From the Trace to the Law: Derridean Politics." *Philosophy and Social Criticism* 15, no. 1 (1989): 1–15.

Llewelyn, John. *Derrida on the Threshold of Sense*. New York: St. Martin's Press, 1986.

Mackey, Louis. "Slouching toward Bethlehem: Deconstructive Strategies in Theology." *Anglican Theological Review* 65 (July 1983): 255–72.

Madison, Gary B. *Working through Derrida*. Evanston, Ill.: Northwestern University Press, 1993.

Magliola, Robert. *Derrida on the Mend*. West Lafayette, Ind.: Purdue University Press, 1984.

242   WORKS CITED

Mandela, Nelson. *The Struggle Is My Life*. London: International Defence and Aid for Southern Africa, 1978.

Marion, Jean-Luc. *God without Being*, translated by Thomas Carlson. Chicago: University of Chicago Press, 1991.

McClintock, Anne, and Rob Nixon. "No Names Apart: The Separation of Word and History in Derrida's 'Le dernier mot du racisme.' " *Critical Inquiry* 13 (autumn 1986): 140–54. Reprinted in Gates, *"Race," Writing and Difference*, 339–53.

McDowell, Deborah. *The Changing Same: Black Women's Literature, Criticism, and Theory*. Bloomington: Indiana University Press, 1995.

McFague, Sallie. *Metaphorical Theology: Models of God in Religious Language*. Philadelphia: Fortress Press, 1982.

———. *Models of God: Theology for an Ecological, Nuclear Age*. Philadelphia: Fortress Press, 1987.

Meyer, Michael. "A Musical Façade for the Third Reich." In *"Degenerate Art": The Fate of the Avant-Garde in Nazi Germany*, edited by Stephanie Barron, 171–183. New York: Harry N. Abrams; Los Angeles: Los Angeles County Museum of Art, 1991.

Milan Women's Bookstore Collective, The. *Sexual Difference: A Theory of Social-Symbolic Practice* (Non credere di avere dei diritte: La generazione della libertà femminile nell'idea e nelle vicende di un gruppo di donne), translated by Patricia Cicogna and Teresa de Lauretis. Theories of Representation and Difference Series, edited by Teresa de Lauretis. Bloomington: Indiana University Press, 1990.

Mitchell, Juliet, and Jacqueline Rose, eds. *Feminine Sexuality: Jacques Lacan and the école freudienne*, translated by Jacqueline Rose. New York: W.W. Norton, 1982.

Mohanty, Chandra Talpade. "Under Western Eyes: Feminist Scholarship and Colonial Discourses." *Boundary 2* 12, no. 3, and 13, no. 1 (spring/fall, 1984). Excerpted and reprinted in *The Post-Colonial Studies Reader*, edited by Bill Ashcroft, Gareth Griffiths, and Helen Tiffin, 259–63. New York: Routledge Press, 1995.

Moi, Toril. *Sexual/Textual Politics: Feminist Literary Theory*. London: Routledge, 1988.

Moraga, Cherrie, and Gloria Anzaldua, eds. *This Bridge Called My Back: Writings by Radical Women of Color*. New York: Kitchen Table Women of Color Press, 1983.

Morrison, Paul. *The Poetics of Fascism: Ezra Pound, T. S. Eliot, Paul de Man*. New York: Oxford University Press, 1996.

Mortenson, Ellen. *'Le féminin' and Nihilism: Reading Irigaray with Nietzsche and Heidegger*. Oslo: Scandinavia University Press, in press.

Mosse, George. *Toward the Final Solution: A History of European Racism*. New York: Howard Fertig, 1978.

Murray, Pauli. "Black Theology and Feminist Theology." *Black Theology: A Documentary History*, edited by Gayraud S. Wilmore and James H. Cone, 398–417. Maryknoll, N.Y.: Orbis Books, 1979.

Naylor, Gloria. *Linden Hills*. New York: Ticknor & Fields, 1985.

Nicholson, Linda, ed. *Feminism/Postmodernism*. New York: Routledge, 1989.

Norris, Christopher. *Derrida.* Cambridge, Mass.: Harvard University Press, 1987.

Nye, Andrea. *Feminist Theory and the Philosophies of Man.* London: Croom Helm, 1988.

Oduyoye, Amba (Mercy). "Reflections from a Third World Woman's Perspective: Women's Experience and Liberation Theology." In *Irruption of the Third World Challenge to Theology: Papers of the Fifth International Conference of the Ecumenical Association of Third World Theologians, August 17–29, 1981, New Delhi,* edited by Virginia Fabella and Sergio Torres. Maryknoll, N.Y.: Orbis Books, 1983.

O'Leary, Joseph. *Questioning Back: The Overcoming of Metaphysics in Christian Tradition.* New York: Winston Press, 1985.

Oliver, Kelly. "Fatherhood and the Promise of Ethics." *Diacritics* 27 (1997): 45–57.

———. *Reading Kristeva: Unravelling the Double Bind.* Bloomington: Indiana University Press, 1993.

———. *Womanizing Nietzsche: Philosophy's Relation to the "Feminine."* New York: Routledge, 1995.

Olthuis, James. "A Cold and Comfortless Hermeneutic or a Warm and Trembling Hermeneutic: A Conversation with John D. Caputo." *Christian Scholar's Review* 19 (1990): 345–62.

Pellegrini, Ann. *Performance Anxieties: Staging Psychoanalysis, Staging Race.* New York: Routledge, 1997.

Penn, Roslyn Terborg. *Afro-Americans in the Struggle for Woman Suffrage.* Ph.D. diss., Howard University, 1977. University Microfilms International, Ann Arbor, Mich.

Poovey, Mary. "Feminism and Deconstruction." *Feminist Studies* 14 (spring 1988): 51–65.

Rabine, Leslie Wahl. "Essentialism and Its Contexts: Saint-Simonian and Post-Structuralist Feminists." *differences: A Journal of Feminist Cultural Studies* 1 (summer 1989): 105–23.

———. "A Feminist Politics of Non-Identity." *Feminist Studies* 14 (spring 1989): 11–31.

Ragland-Sullivan, Ellie. *Jacques Lacan and the Philosophy of Psychoanalysis.* Chicago: University of Illinois Press, 1986.

Riley, Denise. *"Am I That Name?" Feminism and the Category of "Women" in History.* Minneapolis: University of Minnesota Press, 1990.

Rosenberg, Amy S. "Book Spawns Controversy among Blacks." *Philadelphia Inquirer,* 22 June 1990, sec. C, 1, 4.

Ruether, Rosemary Radford. *New Woman/New Earth: Sexist Ideologies and Human Liberation.* New York: Seabury Press, 1975.

———. *Sexism and God-Talk: Toward a Feminist Theology.* Boston: Beacon Press, 1983.

———. *Women-Church: Theology and Practice of Feminist Liturgical Communities.* San Francisco: Harper & Row, 1985.

Ruf, Henry, ed. *Religion, Ontotheology and Deconstruction.* New York: Paragon House, 1989.

Sanders, Cheryl J. "Womanist Theology/Feminist Theology: A Dialogue." *Daughters of Sarah* 15 (March–April 1989): 6–7.

Sanders, Cheryl J., Linda Mercadante, Marcia Riggs, Victoria Byerly, Renita J. Weems, Barbara H. Andolsen. "Roundtable Discussion: Racism in the Women's Movement." *Journal of Feminist Studies in Religion* 4, no. 1 (spring 1988): 93–114.

Sayers, Janet. *Biological Politics: Feminist and Anti-Feminist Perspectives.* New York: Tavistock, 1982.

Schmitz, Kenneth L. "From Anarchy to Principles: Deconstruction and the Resources of Christian Philosophy." *Communio: International Catholic Review* 16 (spring 1989): 69–88.

Schneider, Laurel. "From New Being to Meta-Being: A Critical Analysis of Paul Tillich's Influence on Mary Daly." *Soundings* 75, no. 2 (summer/fall 1992): 421–39.

Schor, Naomi. "The Essentialism Which Is Not One: Coming to Grips with Irigaray." *differences: A Journal of Feminist Cultural Studies* 1 (summer 1989): 38–58.

Scott, Charles. *The Language of Difference.* Atlantic Highlands, N.J.: Humanities Press International, 1987.

Smith, Barbara, ed. *Home Girls: A Black Feminist Anthology.* New York: Kitchen Table: Women of Color Press, 1983.

Smith, Valerie. *Self-Discovery and Authority in Afro-American Narrative.* Cambridge, Mass.: Harvard University Press, 1987.

Spelman, Elizabeth V. *Inessential Woman: Problems of Exclusion in Feminist Thought.* Boston: Beacon Press, 1988.

Spillers, Hortense. "Changing the Letter: The Yokes, the Jokes of Discourse, or, Mrs. Stowe, Mr. Reed." In *Slavery and the Literary Imagination,* edited by Deborah McDowell and Arnold Rampersad, 25–61. Baltimore: Johns Hopkins University Press, 1989.

———. "Interstices: A Small Drama of Words." In *Pleasure and Danger: Exploring Female Sexuality,* edited by Carole S. Vance, 73–100. Boston: Routledge, 1984.

———. "Kinship and Resemblances." *Feminist Studies* 11, no. 1 (spring 1985): 110–25.

———. "Mama's Baby, Papa's Maybe: An American Grammar Book." *Diacritics* 17, no. 2 (1987): 65–81. Reprinted in *Within the Circle: An Anthology of African American Literary Criticism from the Harlem Renaissance to the Present,* edited by Angelyn Mitchell, 454–81. Durham, N.C.: Duke University Press, 1994.

Spillers, Hortense, and Marjorie Pryse, eds. *Conjuring: Black Women, Fiction, and Literary Tradition.* Bloomington: Indiana University Press, 1985.

Spivak, Gayatri Chakravorty. "Displacement and the Discourse of Woman." In *Displacement: Derrida and After,* edited by Mark Krupnick, 169–95. Bloomington: Indiana University Press, 1983.

———. *In Other Worlds: Essays in Cultural Politics.* New York: Routledge Press, 1987.

———. "Love Me, Love My *Ombre, Elle.*" *Diacritics* (winter 1984): 19–36.

Spivak, Gayatri Chakravorty, with Rooney, Ellen. "In a Word: Interview." *differences: A Journal of Feminist Cultural Studies* 1 (summer 1989): 124–56.

Taylor, Mark C. *Altarity.* Chicago: University of Chicago Press, 1987.

————. *Erring: A Postmodern A/theology*. Chicago: University of Chicago Press, 1984.

————. *Nots*. Chicago: University of Chicago Press, 1993.

————, ed. *Deconstruction in Context: Literature and Philosophy*. Chicago: University of Chicago Press, 1986.

Thistlethwaite, Susan Brooks. *Sex, Race and God: Christian Feminism in Black and White*. New York: Crossroad, 1989.

Townes, Emilie M. "A Black Feminist Critique of Feminist Theology. In *Wesleyan Theology Today: A Bicentennial Theological Consultation*, edited by Theodore Runyon, 189–91. Nashville, Tenn.: Kingswood Books, 1985.

Wall, Cheryl, ed. *Changing Our Own Words: Essays on Criticism, Theory and Writing by Black Women*. New Brunswick, N.J.: Rutgers University Press, 1989.

Wall, John. "Deconstruction and the Universe of Theological Discourse, or Who Is Jacques Derrida and What Is He Saying about the Logos?" *Saint Luke's Journal of Theology* 28 (September 1985): 251–65.

Weedon, Chris. *Feminist Practice and Poststructuralist Theory*. London: Blackwell, 1987.

Welch, Sharon. *A Feminist Ethic of Risk*. Minneapolis: Fortress Press, 1990.

West, Cornel. *Prophesy Deliverance: An African-American Revolutionary Christianity*. Philadelphia: Westminster Press, 1982.

Whitford, Margaret, ed. *The Irigaray Reader*. Oxford: Basil Blackwell, 1991.

————. *Luce Irigaray: Philosophy in the Feminine*. London: Routledge, 1991.

Wiegman, Robin. *American Anatomies: Theorizing Race and Gender*. Durham, N.C.: Duke University Press, 1995.

Williams, Delores S. "The Color of Feminism." *Christianity and Crisis* 45 (29 April 1985): 164–65.

————. "The Color of Feminism: Or Speaking the Black Woman's Tongue." *Journal of Religious Thought* 42, no. 1 (spring/summer 1986): 42–58.

————. *Sisters in the Wilderness: The Challenge of Womanist God-Talk*. Maryknoll, N.Y.: Orbis Books, 1993.

Williams, Patricia. *The Alchemy of Race and Rights: Diary of a Law School Professor*. Cambridge, Mass: Harvard University Press, 1991.

Winquist, Charles. *Epiphanies of Darkness: Deconstruction in Theology*. Philadelphia: Fortress Press, 1986.

Wolofsky, Shira. "Derrida, Jabès, Levinas: Sign-Theory as Ethical Discourse." *Prooftexts: A Journal of Jewish Literary History* 2 (September 1982): 283–302.

Wyschogrod, Edith, Thomas J. J. Altizer, Alphonso Lingis, Joseph Prabhu, Mark C. Taylor. "On Deconstructing Theology: A Symposium on *Erring: A Postmodern A/Theology*." *Journal of the American Academy of Religion* 54 (fall 1986): 523–57.

Zack, Naomi, ed. *Race/Sex: Their Sameness, Difference and Interplay*. New York: Routledge, 1997.

Name Index

Subject Index

African American feminist theory
on African American women's literature, 169, 170–77
critiques of queer theory, 192n. 37
on race and gender, 168–69, 171–77,
179
as *supplément* to Derrida and Irigaray,
168, 173
in whitefeminist theory, 185nn. 2–3, 5
on woman, body of, and race, 171, 175,
177, 179
Aletheia (truth), 88, 209n. 35, 226n. 8
Alterity, 33, 103, 180
Derrida and, 51–52, 137, 181, 200n. 15,
201n. 25
divine, 180–81
and woman, 110, 155, 181, 212n. 46
Amnesty International, 147
Apartheid, 165, 227–28nn. 14–17
Christianity's role in, 146, 228n. 20
Derrida on, 138, 139, 144–55, 159, 227n.
12, 227–28n. 14, 228nn. 18, 20, 229n. 23
as specular reflection of European
ideals, 146, 150
Ape, figure of
and racism, 158, 230nn. 34–35, 231n. 4
and sexism, 230n. 34
Appropriation (*see* propriation, economy of)
Aufhebung (sublation, *relève*), 56, 57, 58,
141, 226n. 8

Begriff (concept), 56
Blackness, (in)visibility of, 130, 224n. 50
in whitefeminist theology, 28–30, 30–
31, 38–39
in whitefeminist theory, 19, 20, 38–40
Black power movement, 229n. 25

Capitalism, woman's place in, 119–20,
132

Castration
and truth, 86, 87, 88, 91
and woman, 87, 88, 91, 93, 96
Civil rights movement, 129, 143, 229n. 25
Cogito, 115
Colonialism, 226–27n. 10, 227n. 13
Coup (cut), 77, 89, 93
Cult of domesticity. *See* womanhood,
cult of true

Dasein, 229n. 29
as dispersible, 160–62, 163, 164, 166–67
and metaphysical humanism, 141–42,
230n. 33; and ethnocentrism / racism,
158–59, 163; and racial difference,
161–62, 163; and sexual difference,
159–62, 226n. 8, 231n. 40
Deconstruction, 201n. 26. *See also* Derrida, Jacques
African American feminists' views on,
40–41, 195–96n. 65
as "cure" for whitefeminism, 44, 182
and death: of the author, 195–96n. 65;
of God, 47, 62–63, 71, 154, 163; of
the subject, 138, 153
definition of, 3
Derrida's relationship to, 186n. 10
and *destruktion,* 3, 186n. 11
and ethics, 5, 135; negative assessments of, 48, 70, 156–57, 200n. 14,
213n. 51; positive assessments of,
137–38, 153–54, 201n. 22
and feminism, 45, 48, 71, 79–102, 122;
beyond the race / gender divide, 167,
182; feminist theorists' views on,
198–99nn. 11–12, 213nn. 51, 53
as a method, 42–43
and Nazism, 229n. 27
and nihilism, 3–4, 45–46, 51–52, 70,
197n. 4